QUICK ESCAPES™
DENVER

"A creative, entertaining and detailed guide to weekend jaunts from Denver. Tourists and residents alike will find it packed with useful ideas."

   —Bob Sheue, travel editor, *The Denver Post*

QUICK ESCAPES™
DENVER

25 WEEKEND GETAWAYS
FROM
THE MILE HIGH CITY

BY

SHERRY SPITSNAUGLE

The
Globe
Pequot
Press

OLD SAYBROOK, CONNECTICUT

Cover photo by J. Buehner/H. Armstrong Roberts
Cover design by Laura Augustine
Interior design by Nancy Freeborn
Maps by Maryann Dubé

Library of Congress Cataloging-in-Publication Data

Spitsnaugle, Sherry.
        Quick Escapes Denver : 25 weekend getaways from the mile high city /
    by Sherry Spitsnaugle. -- 1st ed. p. cm. -- (Quick escapes series) Includes index.
        ISBN 0-7627-0197-8
        1. Denver Region (Colo.)--Guidebooks. I. Title. II. Series.
    F784.D43S65 1998
    917.88'830433--dc21
                                                                                    97-47754
                                                                                    CIP

Manufactured in the United States of America
First Edition/First Printing

This book is for my mom, who taught me to always look at the scenery, and for Don.

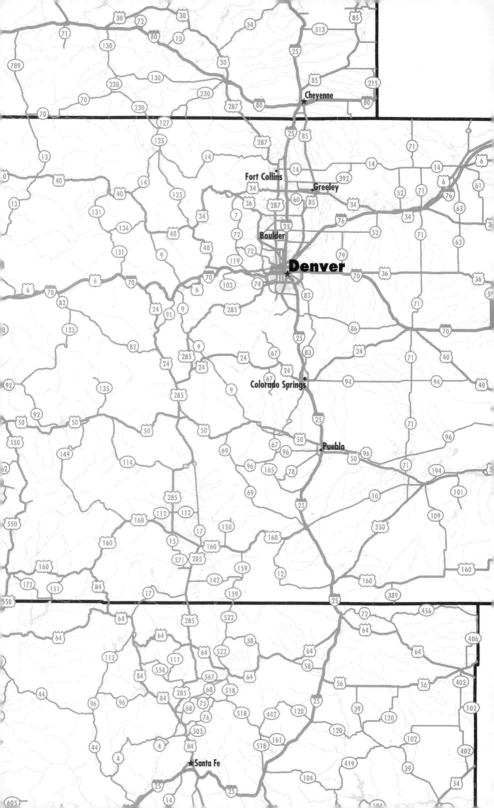

CONTENTS

SOUTHERN ESCAPES

Help Us Keep This Guide Up to Date

Every effort has been made by the author and editors to make this guide as accurate and useful as possible. However, many things can change after a guide is published—establishments close, phone numbers change, facilities come under new management, etc.

We would love to hear from you concerning your experiences with this guide and how you feel it could be made better and be kept up to date. While we may not be able to respond to all comments and suggestions, we'll take them to heart and we'll also make certain to share them with the author. Please send your comments and suggestions to the following address:

The Globe Pequot Press
Reader Response/Editorial Department
P.O. Box 833
Old Saybrook, CT 06475

Or you may e-mail us at:
editorial@globe-pequot.com

Thanks for your input, and happy travels!

INTRODUCTION

Colorado and its surrounding states are a traveler's nirvana. From statuesque mountains to wide-open prairies, opulent spas to rustic dude ranches, and rodeo to opera, it's all here. Described as "one big scenic drive," Colorado offers stunning landscape and compelling natural beauty. Take off in any direction and you'll discover peaks, grasslands, canyons, or deserts, waiting to provide unlimited adventure.

It's difficult to describe the Centennial State without giving in to well-worn clichés and a list of superlatives. Sights can be portrayed, photographed, and visualized, but you'll want to experience the grandeur of the area firsthand.

Traveling spontaneously can work well when luck is on your side, but for the most part a little advance planning will help make a successful trip. Whether you're a local, a tourist, or a new resident, this book will escort you to places you've heard about, such as Aspen, Vail, and Colorado Springs. Other towns, like Saratoga, Wyoming, and WaKeeney, Kansas, may be new to you. The ritzy resorts and cosmopolitan cities provide an exceptional choice of activities, but the small towns reveal a special charm and homespun hospitality.

Each chapter details an itinerary for a different city and area. You'll want to set your own pace and may not be able to see all the sights on one trip, but that provides a good reason to plan a return visit. At the end of the chapter, **There's More** points you in the right direction for additional sights and activities. **Special Events** lists festivals and annual happenings, and **Other Recommended Restaurants and Lodgings** gives you ideas for dining and accommodations in addition to those named in the itinerary. **For More Information** lets you know names, addresses, and phone numbers of the tourist office of the area you're visiting. Travel information can change at any time, and it's best, when planning, to write or call ahead for confirmation.

This guidebook will steer you to well-known tourist sites and obscure finds. You'll travel on scenic byways and visit breweries, hot springs, and dinosaur remains. Often the best way to see the countryside is to hike it, bike it, or raft it. And as for skiing, in these parts trying to name the best downhill ski area is asking for a debate. Aspen takes the prize for glitz, while Steamboat Springs revels in its reputation for bottomless powder.

The undisputed fact remains that sometimes you crave to escape routine for a few days. So put the office on auto pilot, pack your Stetson, and hit the road. After all, isn't that what weekends are all about?

The prices and rates listed in this guidebook were confirmed at press time. We recommend, however, that you call establishments before traveling to obtain current information. Maps provided at the beginning of each section are for reference only and should be used in conjunction with a road map. Distances suggested are approximate.

NORTHERN ESCAPES

NORTHERN

Boulder

BERKELEY IN THE ROCKIES

1 NIGHT

*Outdoor walking mall • 100 miles of hiking trails •
Tour of atmospheric research facility • University of
Colorado • Western art gallery • Brew pubs • Historic park •
Summer Shakespeare festival*

Only a New Age crystal's throw from the big city—make no mistake—
Boulder is a universe apart from Denver. Politically and environmentally cor-
rect, hip, progressive, diverse, offbeat, alternative, and most of all outdoorsy,
Boulder is where Birkenstocks, bicycles, and good vibes rule.

Boulder is, well, so very "Boulder-esque."

Spend some time strolling the wonderfully eclectic outdoor Pearl Street
Mall and you're likely to see a grunge-clad performer crooning a 1970s tune
or a psychedelically dressed juggler entertaining children.

Geographically, the striking red sandstone slabs that form the backdrop of
Boulder, along with the pine-covered foothills that surround this happening
town, make for a positively stunning setting.

With nearly 100 miles of hiking trails practically right in their backyard,
it's no wonder that Boulderites are smitten by the great outdoors. Biking is
big business in Boulder, and it's safe to say that the majority of residents own
at least one bicycle. Some locals possess an inventory of outdoor gear that
might include a pair of in-line skates, downhill and cross-country skis, rock-
climbing gear, a backpack or two, and perchance a kayak.

Home to the University of Colorado, Boulder has that academic and
youthful spirit unique to college towns.

Mo Siegel, founder of Celestial Seasonings, the nation's largest herb-tea
manufacturer, is known as the local youth-turned-millionaire. Located out-

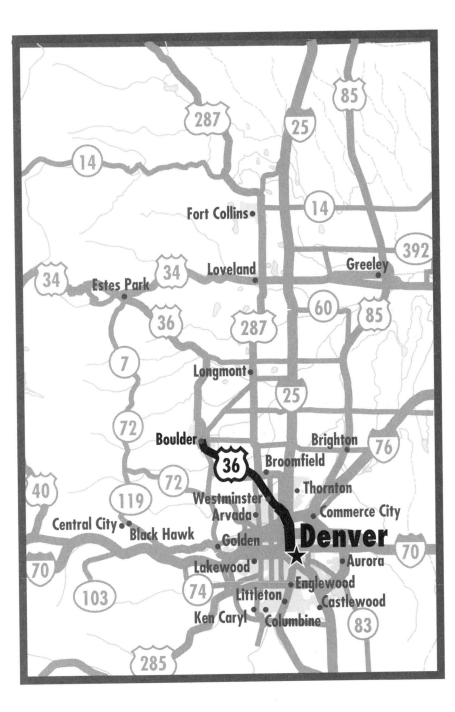

side Boulder on Sleepytime Drive, Celestial Seasonings offers tours of its facility.

Whether you spend your time people-watching on the mall, exploring UC's campus, shopping the boutiques, or hiking the trails of historic Chautauqua Park, you'll no doubt absorb the good karma of this wonderfully with-it city.

DAY 1

Morning

Connect with U.S. Highway 36 (also known as the Boulder Turnpike) off I–25 north for the 30-mile drive to Boulder.

BREAKFAST: You'll get an instant flavor of the city at **Dot's Diner** (799 Pearl Street; 303–449–1323). Here you'll find not only tofu, soy, and *huevos rancheros* but also "diner" food such as biscuits with ham and eggs covered with gravy. Open weekdays from 7:00 A.M. to 2:00 P.M. and weekends from 8:00 A.M. to 2:00 P.M.

Head to the lively **Pearl Street Mall** (on Pearl Street from Eleventh to Fifteenth Streets), which is the soul and true essence of Boulder. This outdoor, pedestrian-only walkway is lined with galleries, boutiques, sculptures, and flowers. Wooden benches and outdoor cafes provide the perfect opportunity to observe the characters and array of shoppers, strollers, and other people-watchers. January or July, noon or midnight, the mall entertains.

LUNCH: The outdoor cafes on Pearl Street Mall are packed on warm days. Snag a table on a patio, linger through a leisurely meal, and savor the mood.

Afternoon

Chautauqua Park (Ninth Street and Baseline Road; 303–442–3282) is a great place to explore year-round. Stop at the Park Ranger Cottage (first cottage to the right as you enter the park) and pick up a map of the trails. The Park Ranger Cottage is open from 8:30 A.M. to 4:00 P.M. Monday through Friday. For additional information call the Ranger Station at (303) 441–3408.

During summer the twenty-six-acre park hosts programs featuring dance, music, theater, and film. **Chautauqua Dining Hall** has a sprawling porch and good views. The historic restaurant is open Memorial Day through Labor Day. If you want to spend the night in the cottages located at the park, call (303) 442–3282 for information.

Nestled against the majestic Flatiron Mountains, Boulder is home to the University of Colorado.

(photo courtesy Boulder Convention and Visitors Bureau)

Take a tour of **Celestial Seasonings** (4600 Sleepytime Drive; 303–581–1202) and discover how the spices and herbs are squeezed into tea bags. Be prepared to wear a hairnet on part of the tour, for sanitary reasons; you'll look and feel a bit silly, but so does everyone else. Take a deep breath in the aromatic "Mint Room," and be sure to walk through the herb garden. The Tea Shop and Emporium is a good place to buy teas at a discount.

Celestial Cafe serves breakfast, lunch, and tea. Try one of more than forty choices as you enjoy the view of the Continental Divide and the Rocky Mountain Front Range from the patio. The cafe is open Monday through Friday for breakfast from 7:30 to 9:30 A.M. and for lunch from 11:00 A.M. to 2:30 P.M. Weekend hours vary; it's best to call ahead.

To get to Celestial Seasonings, take the Longmont Diagonal (Colorado 119) heading northeast. Turn east on Jay Road, go 1 mile to Spine Road, and turn north. Continue 0.5 mile to Sleepytime Drive and turn left into Celestial Seasonings. Tour times are Monday through Saturday from 10:00 A.M. through 3:00 P.M. on the hour and Sunday from 11:00 A.M. through 3:00 P.M. on the hour. Children under five years are not permitted on the factory portion of the tour.

DINNER: A legend for more than twenty-five years, **Flagstaff House** (1138 Flagstaff Road; 303–442–4640) is the crème de la crème of fine dining. The candlelit dining room, panoramic view, and intimate ambience set the scene for romance. Perched on the ledge of Flagstaff Mountain, the restaurant offers a dramatic evening view of the glimmering lights of Boulder. The restaurant has been owned by the Monette family for more than a quarter-century. Scott Monette manages the dining room with absolute competence, while chef Mark Monette holds reign over the kitchen. Mark Monette, who trained in Paris, Singapore, Tokyo, Thailand, and Hong Kong, creates superb cuisine and shows off his amazing talents in the dishes served to guests. The menu, which changes daily, offers appetizers such as spinach-wrapped poached oysters and pâté of duck, and entrees such as Atlantic salmon, venison filet, Black Angus New York strip, and Maine lobster. The wine steward advises as necessary while you study the 212-page list of vintages.

While you're splurging, go ahead and order dessert. Chocolate strudel and a crisp hot apple tart with homemade cinnamon ice cream and caramel sauce are among the selections. You may sit at a table next to a celebrity or dignitary. Robert Redford has dined here, and when the Emperor and Empress of Japan visited the United States in 1994, the members of the entourage chose to eat at Flagstaff House. If it's fit for royalty . . . well, you know the rest. To reach Flagstaff House, drive south from Broadway and Canyon Boulevard to Baseline Road and turn west. Baseline Road curves to the right and eventually becomes Flagstaff Road. Follow the signs to the restaurant.

LODGING: For an especially memorable evening, choose the **Hotel Boulderado** (2215 Thirteenth Street, Boulder; 303–442–4344 or 800–433–4344). Brimming with history and style, this splendid hotel, named after Boulder and Colorado, will impress from the moment you enter the lavishly decorated inn. The graceful, rich cherry-wood staircase and ornate stained-glass ceiling beautify the main lobby. Opening day for the hotel was New Year's Day 1909, and since then this luxury inn has counted among its guests Louis Armstrong, Helen Keller, and Robert Frost.

Rooms are decorated Victorian-style, with floral wallpaper, chenille bed-spreads, and period antiques. The **Corner Bar** at Hotel Boulderado is a cozy place for a nightcap. Prices begin at $146 for a standard room. A deluxe room is $166, and a suite is $216.

DAY 2

Morning

BREAKFAST: Q's Restaurant, Hotel Boulderado; (303) 442–4880. This restaurant with its vintage, stained-glass windows and postmodern art, is a charmer. Cuisine is contemporary American. Try the pecan waffle with pear purée. Open Monday through Friday from 6:30 A.M. to 2:00 P.M. and from 5:00 to 10:00 P.M. On weekends the restaurant opens at 7:00 A.M.

It's time for a bike ride. After all, this is Boulder. The 16-mile **Boulder Creek Path** is the main east-west "mixed-use" passage through town and links up with miles of other trails. Shared by bicyclists, in-line skaters, hikers, runners, and dog-walkers, the wide, concrete path is fairly flat to the east and gains more elevation as you head west. Best of all, you won't encounter car traffic. The path continues on to Boulder Canyon and Four Mile Canyon. If you're feeling frisky, keep right on going to **Gold Hill,** a small mining town that is a popular destination for bicyclists. You can maneuver the paths on a mountain bike or a road bike.

Stop at **The Bikesmith** (2432 Arapahoe Avenue; 303–443–1132) to pick up a free *Boulder Greenways Self-Guided Tour Map,* which will give you options for parking, start and stop points, and sights to see on the way. The shop rents bikes and in-line skates and offers a full-service repair depart-ment. The Bikesmith is open May 1 through September 30 from 9:00 A.M. to 6:00 P.M. and during the off-season on an appointment basis. Interestingly enough, during winter you'll find a ski-rental shop at this location.

Rental bikes are also available at **University Bicycles** (839 Pearl Street; 303–444–4196). It's open year-round weekdays from 10:00 A.M. to 7:00 P.M., Saturdays from 9:00 A.M. to 7:00 P.M., and Sundays from 10:00 A.M. to 5:00 P.M.

LUNCH: You've earned that beer, so turn in the bikes and head for **Walnut Brewery** (1123 Walnut Street; 303–447–1345), one of Boulder's most popu-lar hangouts. Try the Buffalo Gold or Indian Peaks Pale Ale as you watch the brew brewing, and feast on a brewburger. For dessert, how about Raspberry

Passion, a brownie served with ice cream and a raspberry glaze? Catch live music Friday and Saturday nights at this Boulder favorite. Open daily from 11:00 to 2:00 A.M. except Sunday, when it closes at midnight.

Another option is **La Estrellita** (1718 Broadway; 303–939–8822). This restaurant serves delicious homemade green chile and fajitas, along with other Mexican favorites, and is located near Central Park, not far from the Boulder Creek Path. Sit outside on the huge patio, which seats up to 200, and soak up some rays as you replenish.

Afternoon

On your way back to Denver, stop in Louisville. Follow Highway 36 southeast out of Boulder for about 12 miles and take the Lousville exit. This former coal-mining town has a wonderful homespun appeal.

Visit the **Louisville Historical Museum** (1001 Main Street; 303–665–9048) for some local lore. The museum is small and the hours limited (1:00 to 3:00 P.M. Thursdays), but you can call to schedule an appointment. Admission is free.

Karen's in the Country (1900 Plaza Drive; 303–666–8503) is a long-time favorite in this area. Cozy, historic, and inviting, the restaurant serves Belgian waffles, thick-sliced bacon, charbroiled sausage, a Burrito de la Casa, and huge omelets. Lunch and dinner are also served. Karen's is open Monday through Friday from 8:00 A.M. to 8:00 P.M.; Saturday from 7:30 A.M. to 8:00 P.M., and Sunday from 9:30 A.M. to 1:00 P.M. (breakfast only on Sundays).

THERE'S MORE

Eldora Mountain Resort (P.O. Box 1697, Nederland, CO 80466; 303–440–8700) is just 21 miles from Boulder. Take Canyon Road to Nederland, turn south on Colorado 119, and follow the signs to the ski area. This friendly resort, with its forty-three downhill ski runs and nine lifts, offers what the big boys may not: no waiting in lift lines. The Nordic Center has 45 kilometers of cross-country trails.

National Center for Atmospheric Research, 1850 Table Mesa Drive, Boulder; (303) 497–1174. Take Table Mesa Road west from Broadway and follow the signs to NCAR (pronounced N-Car). Admission is free, and you can take a self-guided or a guided tour. Check out the mammoth computer system, the robots, and the weather station where scientists contemplate and study such occurrences as wind shear and the ozone.

Fiske Planetarium. Located on the University of Colorado campus, on Regent Drive. For some real celestial viewing, join university astronomers on Friday evenings for stargazing, a star talk, and glimpses through the observatory's 16- and 24-inch telescopes.

Boulder's Leanin' Tree Museum of Western Art, 6055 Longbow Drive, Boulder; (303) 530–1442. The museum has an extensive collection of western art and sculpture, as well as a gift shop that sells greeting cards produced at Leanin' Tree. Take the Diagonal Highway (Colorado Highway 119) north to Sixty-third Street; turn right and proceed to Longbow Drive. Admission is free, and the museum is open Monday through Friday from 8:00 A.M. to 4:30 P.M. and Saturday from 10:00 A.M. to 4:00 P.M.

Boulder Museum of Contemporary Art, 1750 Thirteenth Street; (303) 443–2122. This nonprofit facility offers works by local and national artists. Open Tuesday through Friday from 11:00 A.M. to 5:00 P.M., Saturday from 9:00 A.M. to 5:00 P.M., and Sunday from noon to 5:00 P.M.

Rockies Brewery, 2880 Wilderness Place, Boulder; (303) 444–8448. To get to the brewery, take Valmont to Wilderness Place. Tour the brewery Monday through Saturday at 2:00 P.M. and sample one of the fine ales brewed on-site. Try the brewery's best-seller and Gold Medal Winner at the World Beer Championships in 1996, the Extra Pale Ale. You can also sample the popular Boulder Igloo Ale or a Bolder Stout. Pub patrons can watch the brewhouse workings from the bar.

SPECIAL EVENTS

January. Polar Bear Club Ice Plunge at Boulder Reservoir; (303) 441–3461. Held New Year's Day. It will cost you $15, but you can dip into the icy lake, let out a shriek, then cavort onshore until you warm up. Spectators watch the fun for free.

May. Kinetic Conveyance Challenge, Boulder Reservoir; (303) 440–5600. Usually held the first Saturday in May. Watch as locals and college kids use their resources and wits to race across land and water on anything from beds to human-powered contraptions. It's silly and tons of fun for spectators and competitors alike.

Bolder Boulder 10K Race. Held Memorial Day Weekend. Walk, run, or just watch this fun event, but if you're in town don't miss it. The aura is vibrant and partylike, and the race takes place in pleasant surroundings. In

addition to a workout, you'll get a cool T-shirt and lunch. Join other runners after the race to watch the elite runners cross the finish line.

June–August. Chautauqua Auditorium hosts international musicians and
guest artists performing in a festival that is a Boulder summertime
favorite. Picnic on the vast lawn before the concert.

Colorado Shakespeare Festival. The performances take place at the outdoor
theater on the CU campus. Call (303) 492–0554.

OTHER RECOMMENDED RESTAURANTS AND LODGINGS

Boulder

The Harvest Restaurant and Bakery, 1738 Pearl Street; (303) 449–6223.
From the moment you walk in and smell the cinnamon-spice tea brewing, you'll know you're going to be treated to something good and
healthy at this natural foods restaurant. Try the smoked salmon salad,
wok-fried vegetables, or Harvest veggie burger. The bakery produces
awesome pastries, such as lemon poppyseed scones and giant gingersnaps.
Desserts include bread pudding and peach crepes. Dining alone? Join
other solo guests at the community table, where you can chat with your
neighbor or bury your nose in a book. This twenty-year Boulder tradition is an all-time favorite among locals and visitors. Open 7:00 A.M. to
10:00 P.M. daily.

Briar Rose, 2151 Arapahoe Avenue; (303) 442–3007. As Boulder's first
B&B, this graceful inn offers such niceties as featherbed comforters (during cold weather), afternoon tea and shortbread cookies, and a pleasant
courtyard. The B&B is conveniently located about a mile from the Pearl
Street Mall. Breakfast of fresh-squeezed orange juice, homemade granola,
and croissants can be delivered to your room, or you can enjoy breakfast
on a lace tablecloth in the dining room.

FOR MORE INFORMATION

Boulder Convention and Visitors Bureau, 2440 Pearl Street, Boulder, CO
80302; (303) 442–2911.

Louisville Chamber of Commerce, 901 Main Street, Louisville, CO 80027;
(303) 666–5747.

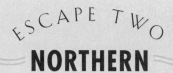

NORTHERN

Estes Park and Rocky Mountain National Park

THE GREAT OUTDOORS

1 NIGHT

Trail Ridge Road • Aerial tramway • Shopping • Dramatic views • Historic landmark hotel • Fishing, hiking, golf

Estes Park is so accessible from Denver that you can leave the city Friday afternoon and in an hour and a half be sipping a glass of cabernet by the fireplace in the elegant lobby of the historic Stanley Hotel.

The village of Estes Park sits at 7,522 feet above sea level and is surrounded by towering mountains. Picturesque and tourist-friendly, Estes Park swells with travelers during summer, but spring, fall, and winter are also great times to visit.

Rocky Mountain National Park, which is the main show in the neighborhood, borders the town of Estes Park. The park traces its history to after the turn of the century, when a hardworking, devoted group of naturalists fought for the area to be granted national park status. The region officially became Rocky Mountain National Park in 1915.

The park flaunts its rugged beauty with columbine-covered meadows, shimmering turquoise lakes, inviting streams, and awesome views of craggy, snowcapped peaks. During the fall elk mating season at Rocky Mountain National Park fascinates visitors. At dusk bulls bugle and battle as they compete for rank. Observers may also see mule deer or the occasional bear.

Summer in the park brings out alpine wildflowers, campers, backpackers, and outdoor enthusiasts in general. Serious climbers may want to attempt Longs Peak, the highest mountain within the boundaries of Rocky Mountain

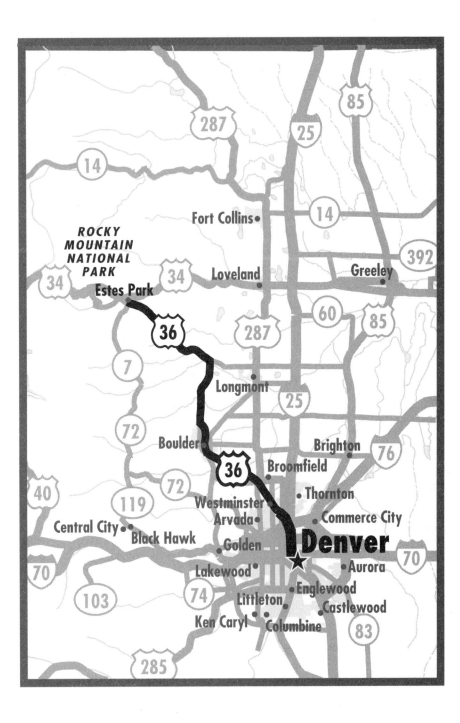

National Park. At 14,255 feet, Longs Peak is one of Colorado's more difficult "fourteeners" to scale.

Ponderosa pines, grand peaks, majestic elk, and emerald terrain create a wondrous place. Meander down a quiet trail, loaf beside a clear mountain lake, or get a workout by gaining elevation on one of the climbs. With more than 350 miles of hiking trails, you could spend a lifetime exploring the park's paths and woods.

DAY 1

Afternoon

From Denver travel north on I–25 and connect with U.S. Highway 36 through Boulder, then continue on to Estes Park. The driving is effortless and you don't have to cross any mountain passes.

Explore some of the 300 shops and galleries of Estes Park on **Elkhorn Avenue.** You'll discover everything from fine crystal to Old West–style clothing. Several of the shops have been owned and operated for generations by the same family. **Craftsmen in Leather** (135 West Elkhorn; 970–586–2400) is a great place to try on hats. **Rocky Mountain Connection** (141 East Elkhorn; 970–586–3361) has a good selection of outdoor gear.

DINNER: Estes Park Brewery (470 Prospect Village Drive; 970–586–5421) uses water from the nearby Big Thompson River to brew its beer. Taste a couple of the complimentary samples, such as Longs Peak Raspberry Wheat or Estes Park Pale Ale. As the town's only brewery, this restaurant-bar is a popular spot for locals and visitors. Freshly brewed root beer is on the menu, as are appetizers such as Jalapeño Poppers and entrees that include thick-crust pizza, burgers, and the Beer Brat Sandwich, made with the brewery's porter beer. Guests share the upstairs dining room with patrons playing pool and video games. If weather cooperates, sit outside at a picnic table on the upstairs deck, which is quieter than the restaurant and has mountain views. Estes Park Brewery is open daily from 11:00 A.M. until late evening.

LODGING: The Stanley Hotel, 333 Wonderview, P.O. Box 1767, Estes Park, CO 80517; (970) 586–3371 or (800) 976–1377. Remember the hair-raising movie *The Shining,* in which Jack Nicholson spooked theatergoers everywhere? Contrary to what you may have heard, the movie was not filmed here, but the hotel did inspire Stephen King to draft the novel on

The historic Stanley Hotel *overlooks the town of Estes Park.*
(photo by Sherry Spitsnaugle).

which the film was based. The television miniseries, which aired in 1996, was shot at The Stanley; King was executive producer. Not only can you overnight in this grand old hotel as a guest, but you can tour the history-filled site.

This regal old inn, with its attractive white clapboard exterior, overlooks the town of Estes Park and was known as one of the most glamorous hotels of its day when it first opened in 1909. In those days The Stanley offered its boarders luxuries such as billiards and stables. Today guests delight in the elegant lobby and comfortable rooms. Rates range from $90 to $199.

DAY 2

Morning

BREAKFAST: You'll feel oh-so-elegant as you sip coffee on the expansive veranda of **The Stanley Hotel** and admire glorious views of Longs Peak. Then put on comfortable shoes, pack a picnic lunch, fill your water bottle, and prepare for a day in the great outdoors.

Head straight to **Rocky Mountain National Park**. From Estes Park take U.S. 34 or U.S. 36. The entrance fee is $10 per car and is valid for a week.

There are lots of activities for kids, and park rangers go out of their way to educate youngsters in an informative and entertaining way. The staff at **Park Headquarters** (970–586–1206), at the south entrance on the eastern side of the park, can recommend a hiking trail and provide other information. Summer hours are 8:00 A.M. to 9:00 P.M.

The **Kawuneeche Visitor Center** (970–627–3471), on the west side of the Continental Divide, has some nice displays on the history of the park. Summer hours are 8:00 A.M. to 7:00 P.M. Winter hours for both Kawuneeche and Park Headquarters are 8:00 A.M. to 4:30 P.M.

LUNCH: Enjoy a picnic at one of the outdoor tables, or spread a blanket on the ground and take in the views.

Afternoon

Hiking opportunities abound in the park, and you can essentially name your distance, difficulty level, and terrain preference. Easy walks include those around **Sprague Lake** and **Bear Lake,** both of which are wheelchair accessible. For both walks, take the Beaver Meadows (south) entrance (U.S. 36) and follow the signs to Bear Lake.

If fishing is on your agenda, check with rangers for a copy of the park rules. The staff at **Scot's Sporting Goods,** 1.5 miles west of Estes Park on U.S. 36 (870 Moraine Avenue, Estes Park), can set you up with gear and a guided trip. They'll tell you where the fish are biting too.

Colorado Bicycling Adventures (184 East Elkhorn Avenue, Estes Park; 970–586–4241) rents bikes, helmets, and other gear for any biking adventure you have in mind. Ask the staff for information about guided mountain-bike tours. You can rent other equipment at **Colorado Wilderness Sports** (358 East Elkhorn Avenue, Estes Park, CO 80517; 970–586–6548).

During summer, drive to Grand Lake via **Trail Ridge Road** (Highway 34), which climbs over the Continental Divide in Rocky Mountain National Park. To get to Trail Ridge Road, enter the park at either Beaver Meadows or Fall River. This route, which is usually open from Memorial Day until late fall, is the highest continuous paved highway in the country. The road stretches between Estes Park and Grand Lake and climbs to 12,183 feet in elevation. Trail Ridge Road was an immediate tourist-pleaser when it opened in 1932.

The best way to appreciate the incredible views is to stop at one of the scenic overlooks, get out of your car, take a deep breath, and admire the lofty peaks of the Continental Divide. For a short, but strenuous hike, follow the 1-mile, round-trip path to **Toll Memorial.** Rock Cut Trailhead, where the path begins, is located about 6 miles east of the Alpine Visitor Center. For additional information call the visitor center at (970) 586–1206.

THERE'S MORE

Estes Park Aerial Tramway, 420 East Riverside Drive, Estes Park; (970) 586–3675. Admission is $8.00 for adults; $4.00 for children under twelve. You'll see extensive views of the Continental Divide, Rocky Mountain National Park, Longs Peak, and the village of Estes Park. At the top you can hike, picnic, or browse the gift shop and snack bar.

Estes Park Golf Course, 1080 South Saint Vrain; (970) 586–8146. This 18-hole course stretches through the woodland and is wonderfully scenic. The course is one of the oldest in Colorado.

Enos Mills Cabin and Gallery. Located 8 miles south of Estes Park on Colorado Highway 7; (970) 586–4706. Enos Mills, photographer, naturalist, and author of many books describing his escapades and adventures in the region, first visited this area in 1884 as a young boy. Mills resided and worked in a one-room log cabin for many summers during his life. Today you can visit the home of this man who was devoted to writing about the wonders of the Rockies. The Enos Mills Cabin and Gallery is open from Memorial Day to Labor Day from 10:00 A.M. to 5:00 P.M. and during the winter by appointment only. Donations requested.

Climbing. For information about technical climbing or hiking, call the Colorado Mountain School (Estes Park; 970–586–5758).

Estes Park Area Historical Museum, 200 Fourth Street at U.S. Highway 36; (970) 586–6256. This small but well-appointed museum caters to kids. Children will get to experience hands-on activities while parents browse the gallery. Admission is $2.50 for adults; $1.00 for children under twelve. Open May through October, Monday through Saturday from 10:00 A.M. to 5:00 P.M. and Sunday from 1:00 to 5:00 P.M.; November through April, Friday and Saturday from 10:00 A.M. to 5:00 P.M. and Sunday from 1:00 to 5:00 P.M.

SPECIAL EVENTS

June. Wool Market is a two-day event that includes demonstrations, seminars, spinning and weaving contests, and the display and sale of wool-related items. This is the largest llama and alpaca show in the country. The event takes place at Stanley Park Fairgrounds on U.S. Highway 36. For information call (970) 586–6104.

June–mid August. SummerFest Concert Series, sponsored by the YMCA of the Rockies, features everything from jazz to classical. Call (970) 586–3341.

July–early August. Estes Park Music Festival presents the Colorado Music Festival Orchestra in a series of six concerts on Monday evenings. For details call the Cultural Arts Council of Estes Park at (970) 586–9203.

September. Longs Peak Scottish Irish Festival. Held the weekend after Labor Day. The festival features a parade and contests such as the hammer throw and tin whistle and fiddle competition. You'll hear bagpipes a-playin' during this three-day Celtic event that attracts about 40,000 visitors and is one of the town's favorite celebrations.

OTHER RECOMMENDED RESTAURANTS AND LODGINGS

Estes Park

Wapiti Bar & Grill, 247 West Elkhorn; (970) 586–5056. Locals recommend the fajitas at this cozy cafe. The menu also offers buffalo stew, halibut steak, and burger baskets.

Estes Park Center YMCA of the Rockies; (970) 586–3341. This self-contained facility sits on 1,400 acres neighboring Rocky Mountain National Park. The Estes Park Center offers a choice of lodge-style accommodations or cabins, and you can stay here for a fraction of the price it would cost to stay in resorts around the state. The cabins, some of which have a fireplace, offer either two or four bedrooms and come with an equipped kitchen. This is an ideal family location, and the entire brood can choose from cross-country skiing, horseback riding, swimming, tennis, hiking, snowshoeing, or exploring the backcountry. Take U.S. Highway 36 west to Colorado 66 south to the camp. To book accommodations, write YMCA of the Rockies, Estes Park, CO 80511. Reservations are recommended.

Romantic Riversong Bed and Breakfast Inn, P.O. Box 1910, Estes
   Park, CO 80517; (970) 586–4666. You'll mellow out almost instantly after
   you arrive at this B&B tucked away in the backwoods near the Big
   Thompson River. Relax, kick back, and appreciate your homey bedroom
   and roaring fire. For directions and reservations contact the inn directly.

FOR MORE INFORMATION

Estes Park Chamber Resort Association, 500 Big Thompson Avenue, Estes
   Park, CO 80517; (970) 586–4431 or (800) 443–7837.
Rocky Mountain National Park; (970) 586–1206.

Grand Lake

SPORTS PARADISE

1 NIGHT

Dogsledding, snowbiking, snowmobiling, ice fishing • Mountain biking, golf • Colorado's largest natural lake • Fishing, boating, waterskiing on Grand Lake • Dude ranches • Shadow Mountain Reservoir • Summer retreat • Arapaho National Forest

This charming town sits essentially at the "end of the road," at least during winter, which is one of the many reasons Grand Lake is so inviting and laid-back. From its wooden boardwalks to the hitching post in front of the Lariat Saloon, Grand Lake overflows with rustic charm. Here you can two-step the night away to a western band or curl up in the comfort of your cabin.

From approximately 400 full-time residents during winter, Grand Lake expands to several thousand visitors during the height of the summer travel season. Situated a little more than a mile from the western entrance of Rocky Mountain National Park, this is a choice location to set up base camp. You can drive from Grand Lake on Trail Ridge Road from May through late fall. The narrow, curving 50-mile route crosses the Continental Divide and provides spectacular views of snowcapped peaks.

At an elevation of 8,369 feet, Grand Lake has pure mountain air, exceptional outdoor recreation, and Colorado's largest natural lake. Surrounded by forested shoreline in a splendid alpine setting, the town's namesake lake offers endless year-round activities.

The entire area is a sportsman's paradise, boasting hunting, hiking, skiing, and most watersports. Late autumn brings a quiet existence to the village, when many businesses shut their doors. Trail Ridge Road closes, which cuts off traffic through Rocky Mountain National Park, leaving only one entrance into town.

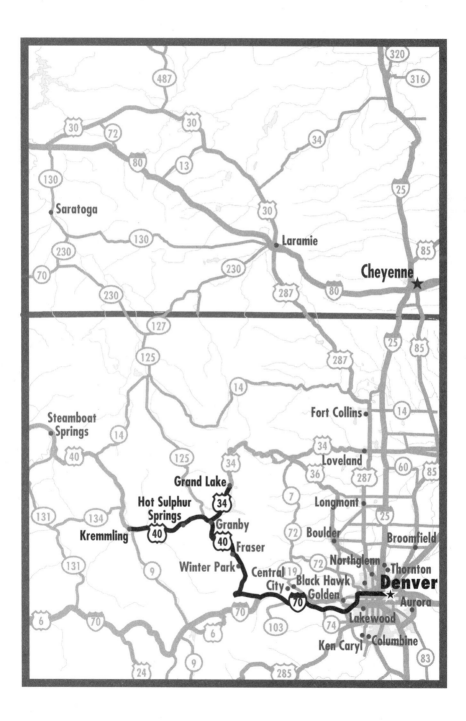

When winter arrives, the area becomes a glorious snow-covered mecca for sports enthusiasts. Locals snowmobile or cross-country ski down Grand Avenue. You've just got to love a town with that kind of gusto.

DAY 1

Morning

Grand Lake is approximately 100 miles northwest of Denver. Travel via I–70 west to U.S. Highway 40 and turn north. Follow Highway 40 over Berthoud Pass through the towns of Winter Park, Fraser, and Granby.

BREAKFAST: Bertie's (52 Fourth Street, Granby; 970–887–3632) cuts its own meat and is known for excellent steaks. For a stick-to-your-ribs breakfast, try the six-ounce steak served with eggs, or opt for biscuits and sausage gravy. Lunch favorites include chicken-fried steak and fresh trout. Bertie's is open daily from 6:00 A.M. to 9:00 P.M. (Sunday hours are 6:00 A.M. to 2:00 P.M.). To get to the restaurant, go a block north on Fourth Street off Highway 40.

After you leave Granby, travel north on U.S. 34 to Grand Lake. Park on Grand Avenue and spend time browsing the shops. You'll notice the western atmosphere immediately as you stroll along the wooden boardwalk of this down-home mountain town.

The Grand Lake area was once home to the Native American Ute and Arapaho tribes. Judge Joseph Wescott settled in 1867 and trapped and fished the bounteous wilderness. Prospectors arrived in 1879 after gold was discovered, and by the end of the year the town had its first hotel, general store, and residential area. Today you'll find shops, cafes, galleries, and the occasional saloon along Grand Avenue.

LUNCH: Grand Pizza (717 Grand Avenue, Grand Lake; 970–627–8390) serves awesome pizza. Try the Greek pizza, topped with feta cheese, tomatoes, and artichoke hearts, or the Mexican or Cajun pizza. The restaurant is open daily from 11:00 A.M. to 9:00 P.M. Winter hours and days vary.

Afternoon

Grand Lake offers an unusually nice variety of shops. Stop at **Grand Lake Art Gallery** (1117 Grand Avenue; 970–627–3104) and browse the selection of paintings, sculpture, pottery, stained glass, wood products, jewelry, and textiles, all crafted by Colorado artists. The gallery is open May through October daily from 10:00 A.M. to 5:00 P.M., and during winter on weekends only, from 10:00 A.M. to 5:00 P.M.

The **Kauffman House** (407 Pitkin; 970–627–3372) is a restored log house that was built by Ezra Kauffman in 1892 and was operated as a hotel until the early 1920s. You'll get a feel for life as it was in the late 1800s and early 1900s in this pioneer museum. Admission is free, and the house is open for tours during summer from 1:00 to 5:00 P.M.

Boaters Choice (1246 Lake Avenue; 970–627–9273) offers boat tours of Grand Lake that last from forty-five minutes to an hour. The cost is $9.00 for adults and $5.00 for children ten and older; kids under ten tour free. Dinner cruises are also available.

DINNER: **E.G.'s Garden Grill** (1000 Grand Avenue, Grand Lake; 970–627–8404) is a charmingly rustic cafe owned and run by two brothers. E.G. is the creative chef, and Stanton manages the dining room just as well as his brother runs the kitchen. For starters try the Steamed New Zealand Greenlip Mussels. Entrees include E.G.'s Cowboy Steak, a twenty-two-ounce, bone-in rib eye steak served with red chile onion rings, and Seafood Tortilla-Crusted Salmon, as well as other choices. Dessert selections include key lime pie and brownie a la mode.

The restaurant is open daily from 11:00 A.M. to 9:00 P.M.; the hours extend to 10:00 P.M. June through September. Winter hours vary. During summer catch live music in the beer garden from noon to 4:00 P.M. weekends. Reservations are recommended for parties of eight or more and on weekends.

LODGING: **Lemmon Lodge,** P.O. Box 514, Grand Lake, CO 80447; (970) 627–3314 (summer) or (970) 725–3511 (winter). To get to the lodge, go to the east end of Grand Avenue and follow the sign that says LEMMON LODGE BEACH CABINS. You will be a five-minute walk from downtown Grand Lake and will still have plenty of peace and quiet.

This lodge offers seclusion, a sand beach, mountain and lake views, and a private dock. Choose from one of twenty-three cabins, which vary in size from a basic cabin to one with full kitchen. The lodge is open from the middle of May through the end of September. Rates during high season (third week of June through Labor Day) range from $80 to $260. Book as early as possible. The lodge is a favorite for return visitors and is often reserved a year in advance.

DAY 2

Morning

BREAKFAST: The Chuck Hole (1119 Grand Avenue, Grand Lake; 970–627–3509) offers robust servings of bacon and eggs, pancakes, and omelets. Hours are 6:30 A.M. to 3:00 P.M. daily, year-round.

To see the mountains in all their splendor, drive the **Colorado River Headwaters Scenic and Historic Byway,** which starts at the Kawuneeche Visitor Center in Rocky Mountain National Park. The route follows U.S. Highway 34 through Grand Lake to Granby, then turns west along U.S. Highway 40 to Hot Sulphur Springs and Kremmling. The route is marked by signs with Colorado's state flower, the blue columbine.

Tour **Grand County Historical Museum,** located at the east end of Hot Sulphur Springs on U.S. Highway 40 (970–725–3939). This is an unusually fine museum for such a small community. Housed in a 1924 schoolhouse, the museum reflects Grand County life in the early days, including displays and photographs on skiing. The museum also has a good selection of regional books for sale. Admission is $3.00 for adults, $2.00 for seniors, and $1.00 for children. The museum is open during summer from 10:00 A.M. to 5:00 P.M. daily and in winter from 10:00 A.M. to 5:00 P.M. Wednesday through Friday.

Visit the newly renovated **Hot Sulphur Springs Resort and Spa** (800–510–6235), located at the west end of Hot Sulphur Springs. Follow the signs off Highway 40 to reach the resort. Soak in one of five outdoor pools; treat yourself to a massage, facial, or body wrap; or relax in the solarium. The resort is open from 7:30 A.M. to 10:00 P.M. daily, and prices range from $8.50 to $10.00 for pools and baths.

LUNCH: The Lone Moose (Highway 40 at the west end of Kremmling; 970–724–9987) is nothing fancy but does serve great meat-and-potatoes-style meals and good burgers. Breakfast is served all day. The restaurant is open from 6:00 A.M. to 8:30 P.M. year-round and is closed Tuesdays.

THERE'S MORE

Snowmobiling. The Grand Lake area, with more than 150 miles of groomed trails, is known as the Snowmobile Capital of Colorado. Rev up your machine, take off into the backcountry, and glide along the trails in the woods of Arapaho National Forest. Spirit Lake Rentals, Inc. (970–627–9288) rents equipment. Full-day rates (eight hours) are $160.00/double (two persons on a machine) and $140.00/single (one person on a machine). A four-hour rental will cost $100.00/double and $85.00/single; a two-hour rental, $70.00/double and $55.00/single. Helmet, trail map, and gas are included in the rates, and you can rent an insulated suit, boots, and gloves for $5.00 a day. You'll be glad to know that the snowmobiles have heated hand-warmer grips.

Silver Creek Resort proudly claims to be Colorado's smallest ski resort. This is an advantage for visitors, because you'll get plenty of attention here. Try snowbiking, the latest craze at Silver Creek. Lessons are encouraged, but you'll get the hang of this sport in no time. A snowbike looks like a bicycle, but with skis instead of wheels. The price for a bike rental, a full-day lift ticket, and a lesson is $50. Another adrenaline rush is snowboarding, for those thrill-seekers who wish to shred the slopes. A package including a snowboard rental, a lift ticket, and a lesson at Silver Creek Resort is $65. To get to Silver Creek from Grand Lake (18 miles), take U.S. 34 south to Highway 40. Contact Silver Creek Resort, P.O. Box 1110, 1000 Village Road, Silver Creek, CO 80446; (800) 754–7458.

Grand Lake. Spirit Lake Rentals, Inc. (970–627–9288) rents not only snowmobiles but also personal watercraft. Rates are $200.00 for eight hours, $135.00 for four hours, and $45.00 for one hour. Transportation to the lake, instruction, a life vest, and gas are included. Wet suits are available for $5.00 a day.

Grand Lake Golf Course. This challenging 18-hole course has views of the Continental Divide, and at 8,420 feet your ball is sure to travel farther. Follow Highway 34 from Grand Lake north for 0.25 mile, turn left onto County Road 48 for 1 mile, and follow the signs to the course. For information call (970) 627–8008.

Fishing. Grand Lake, Shadow Mountain Reservoir, and Lake Granby offer cutthroat, brown, and rainbow trout, as well as spectacular scenery. Try ice fishing in the winter. Check with Boaters Choice, 1246 Lake Avenue, Grand Lake; (970) 627–9273 (summer) or (970) 627–8918 (winter).

SPECIAL EVENTS

March. High Altitude Sled Dog Championships. This event attracts more than a hundred teams from Canada and the United States as they compete in the final event of Grand County's Triple Crown of sled-dog racing. The mushing commences midmorning, and the races are exciting to watch. Wander the grounds and visit with owners of the Alaskan huskies, Siberian huskies, and Samoyeds. For dates call the Grand Lake Chamber of Commerce at (970) 627–3402.

July 4. Independence Day brings spectacular fireworks over Grand Lake and a rollicking good time in the county. For specifics call the Greater Granby Area Chamber of Commerce at (800) 325–1661.

August. Grand Lake Regatta and Lipton Cup Races. This is a lively spectator sport, and you'll enjoy cheering on members of the Grand Lake Yacht Club as they vie for the distinguished solid sterling silver cup, donated by English tea baron Sir Thomas Lipton. The Grand Lake Yacht Club's claim to fame is holding the title as highest yacht club in the world.

October. Kremmling hosts its annual Roadkill Supper during hunting season. A fundraiser for the local chamber of commerce (970–724–3472), this dinner attracts mainly hunters and locals, and it features a selection of wild game that may include venison, elk, moose, or antelope. Buy a roadkill T-shirt with the menu printed on the back. Bundle up—the unique feast is served outside in the town square, 213 Park Center Avenue.

OTHER RECOMMENDED RESTAURANTS AND LODGINGS

Grand Lake

Grand Lake Lodge Restaurant (north of Grand Lake on U.S. 34; (970–627–3967) has a selection of entrees that include buffalo burger, grilled rainbow trout, and Norwegian salmon. The restaurant follows the lodge's schedule and is open June through mid-September. The restaurant serves champagne brunch Sundays from 9:30 A.M. to 1:30 P.M.

Lariat Saloon on Grand Avenue (970–627–9965) doesn't have a street number, but you can't miss it—look for the hitching post out front. The Lariat serves hamburgers, chicken teriyaki, and Polish sausage in an honest-to-goodness western bar. Open 11:00 A.M. to 2:00 A.M. seven days a week, year-round. Catch live music on weekends.

Grand Lake Lodge, north of Grand Lake on U.S. 34, is a historic lodge with character and charm. Built in 1925, the lodge offers striking views of Shadow Mountain Reservoir and Grand Lake. Take a break on the inn's porch or relax by the pool. Contact Grand Lake Lodge, P.O. Box

569, Grand Lake, CO 80447 (970–627–3967), for a reservation. The lodge is open from the first weekend in June through mid-September.

Kremmling

Latigo Ranch, P.O. Box 237, Kremmling, CO 80459; (800) 227–9655. Secluded, authentic, and cozy, this dude ranch offers incredible views of the Indian Peaks. The ranch cuisine is marvelous. You're sure to enjoy your stay, whether you join a cattle roundup or settle in with a favorite book.

Silver Creek

The Inn at Silver Creek, P.O. Box 4222, Granby, CO 80446; (800) 526–0590. This resort has suites (some with fireplaces), studios, and standard rooms. You can catch the complimentary shuttle to Silver Creek Ski Resort, located 2 miles from the lodge. Facilities include a hot tub, an exercise room, a sauna, an indoor/outdoor pool, racquetball courts, and a restaurant.

Granby

C Lazy U Ranch, P.O. Box 379, Granby, CO 80446; (970) 887–3344. This ranch manages to pull off being luxurious and western at the same time. You'll get personal pampering if you so desire (the staff-to-guest ratio is almost one to one), and you'll dine on superb meals. Horseback riding, tennis, racquetball, fishing, and cross-country skiing are available, and if you still have energy, there's an exercise room. Book well in advance.

FOR MORE INFORMATION

Grand County Colorado Tourism Board, P.O. Box 208, Winter Park, CO 80482; (800) 729–5821.

Grand Lake Area Chamber of Commerce, P.O. Box 57, Grand Lake, CO 80447; (800) 531–1019 or (970) 627–3402.

For information about wilderness regulations, call the Sulphur Ranger District of the U.S. Forest Service, (970) 887–3331.

Greater Granby Area Chamber of Commerce, P.O. Box 35, Granby, CO 80446; (800) 325–1661.

Kremmling Area Chamber of Commerce, P.O. Box 471, Kremmling, CO 80459; (970) 724–3472.

Colorado Dude and Guest Ranch Association, P.O. Box 300, Tabernash, CO 80478; (970) 887–3128.

Central City
and Black Hawk

OPERA IN A MOUNTAIN SETTING

1 NIGHT

*Opera • Casino gambling • Historic mining town • Museums •
Gold mine •Jazz festival • Victorian B&B*

Whether you're into casino gambling, opera, or history, Central City has the
ticket.

With nearly thirty casinos in Central City and nearby Black Hawk, this
area has returned to the lively atmosphere that existed in the 1860s when
Central City thrived as a booming mining town. In 1859 John Gregory discovered gold here. The site is marked by the Gregory Monument, near the
city limits. Shortly after his strike, several thousand people, hoping to unearth
riches, moved into the area known as Gregory Gulch.

Completed in 1878, the gorgeous Central City Opera House opened its
ornate doors for the first time with a gala event that attracted dignitaries,
theater lovers, and members of society.

Both Central City and Black Hawk became nearly deserted as a result of
the dwindling gold production at the beginning of the twentieth century.
The beautiful opera house was boarded up until 1932, when the Central
City Opera Association restored the building to its former glory.

The Central City Opera House, one of the West's most distinguished,
reigns as the area's majestic prize. The lovingly restored structure is a beautiful example of early architecture. Appreciate a true opera with its silvery
sounds and incredible costumes in this 1878 setting. Performances, which are
sung in English, will delight the most discriminating fan and may even occa-
sionally convert the nonenthusiast into an opera lover.

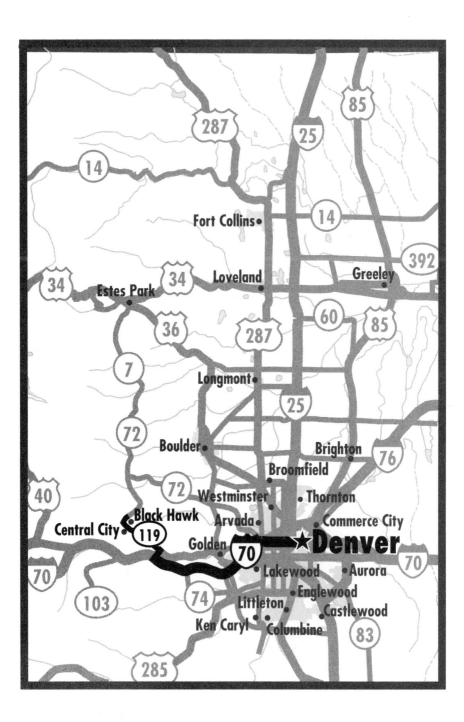

DAY 1

Morning

Take I–70 west out of Denver and continue past the Evergreen/El Rancho exit about 8 miles. Take the Golden/Central City exit (number 244). Turn right on Highway 6 and follow the signs for Central City. Travel about 3 miles to the intersection with CO 119; turn left and follow the signs for Central City and Black Hawk. Driving time from central Denver is approximately an hour.

LUNCH: Madeline's Restaurant, at the Teller House Casino (120 Eureka Street, Central City; 303–582–3200), serves salads, sandwiches, a great buffalo burger, fish-and-chips, and steak, as well as other selections. The restaurant is open daily from 9:00 A.M. to midnight.

Afternoon

Depending on your interests, you can begin rolling the dice or choose other activities. Even if gambling isn't your thing, you'll want to at least peek into the casinos, some of which have been built in mansions. One is in a former jail. Slot machines are generally the favorite, but gambling enthusiasts can try their luck at blackjack or poker. The age limit of twenty-one is strictly enforced at all casinos for gambling.

To learn some interesting tidbits about the area, take a self-guided **Historic Walking Tour** of Central City. Thanks to the Central City Opera House Association, the State Historical Fund, and the Gilpin County Historical Society, you can read about the history of the area. Ask at the offices of the Gilpin County Chamber of Commerce, 281 Church Street, Blackhawk, for details and a map.

The **Teller House Museum** (120 Eureka Street, Central City; 303–582–3200) was once one of the classiest hotels in the area. Completed in 1872, the hotel was said to be the most elegant building in Colorado. Rooms rented for $2.00 a night and a suite was $3.00, excessive amounts for the times. Visitors flocked to the lavish hotel to enjoy running water, fine furnishings, and excellent cuisine. The Teller House was the gathering place for Central City society. Today you can glance in the guest room where President Grant stayed. On the first floor in what is now the Face Bar, inspect the famous *Face on the Barroom Floor,* painted by a Denver journalist in 1936. The price for the Teller House tour is $3.00 per person. Although the Teller House has undergone a $15 million restoration, overnight accommodations are not available. The opera crowd still gathers at the Face Bar for cocktails before the performance.

DINNER: Black Forest Inn, 260 Gregory Street, Black Hawk; (303) 279–2333. A cheerful restaurant with a menu featuring German/American fare and wild game, Black Forest Inn is a favorite for locals and out-of-towners. Feast on elk steak, a bottle of wine from the extensive selection, and exquisite pastries.

Evening

Central City Opera (200 Eureka Street, Central City) is the best attraction in town. The opera runs from mid-July through mid-August. Call the box office at (303) 292–6700 or (800) 851–8175 for tickets. Prices range from $24 to $52, depending on the day you attend and where you wish to sit in the opera house. Ask about bus transportation from Denver to Central City on the Express Charter Opera Bus. Parking in Central City can be a challenge, and the bus offers a relaxing ride, classical music, and convenience.

The Central City Opera House shines as the jewel of the area. Patrons are treated to an elegant matinee or evening in this magnificent setting. Restored to reflect its original grandeur, the opera house today seats 756 patrons. Productions include such classics as *Madame Butterfly, The Merry Widow,* and the opera's signature presentation, *The Ballad of Baby Doe.* Enjoy the flawless acoustics, ornate ceiling, opulent ambience, and splendid performance. During intermission check the back of your chair for the name, carved in the wood, of a Colorado citizen, performer, or pioneer. Opera supporters and other special persons have been honored by this tradition since the early days. If you wish to introduce yourself to one of the singers or get an autograph after the performance, linger on the patio just outside the opera house, where the performers exit. They are generally pleased to oblige.

When you call for reservations, inquire about special events such as salon recitals, presented Saturday and Sunday at 11:45 A.M. Artists perform a thirty-minute solo as guests dine on a gourmet lunch in the Victorian beauty of the Teller House. Reservations are essential. There is also a thirty-minute cabaret opera, *The Face on the Barroom Floor,* that details the tale of the face painted on the floor of the Teller House. The short production takes place across the street from the Teller House in the historic Williams Stables on Saturdays and Sundays at 1:15 P.M.

Tours of the opera house are available year-round for $3.00 unless a practice or performance is taking place. Call the Teller House at (303) 582–3200.

The Central City Opera House *first opened its doors in 1878.*

(photo by Mark Kiryluk).

LODGING: Chateau L'Acadienne (325 Spring Street, Central City, CO 80427; 303–582–5209 or 800–834–5209) is a lovely, restored nineteenth-century home located within walking distance of the opera and casinos. The name *Chateau L'Acadienne* translates to "big house of the Cajun," and the entire house is decked in Victorian and Louisiana French decor. Built in the 1870s during the gold-mining boom, the house features grand bay windows, 10-foot-high ceilings, antique crystal chandeliers, and three well-appointed guest rooms.

The Victorian Room is decorated with period furniture, an antique crystal chandelier, and a large bay window that overlooks Central City. This room offers a king bed and a daybed and accommodates up to four persons.

The Emerald Room offers a queen canopy bed and an antique dresser and was named for its view of Central City. The New Orleans Room features French decor and a marble-top dresser. Room rates are $75 to $125, and reservations are recommended. The guest parking is especially convenient.

DAY 2

Morning

BREAKFAST: Chateau L'Acadienne. You'll eat family-style on weekends (continental breakfast is served Monday through Friday) as owners James and Shirley Voorhies share stories of Central City and the history of their home. Ask about Gwendolyn, the friendly resident ghost; the stories flourish come Halloween. Full breakfast served on weekends may include Grand Marnier French Toast, Crispy Potato Quiche, or Baked Eggs L'Acadienne—Shirley's own slightly spicy creation, which includes eggs, cayenne, and oregano.

Drive through Central City on Eureka Street about 2 miles west (the road becomes dirt) to the **century-old cemeteries** that stretch over the horizon. Wander the area and spend time reading the aged tombstones. The grounds are unkempt but interesting, and you'll no doubt avoid crowds.

Kids love to tour **Lost Gold Mine** (231 Eureka Street; 303–642–7533), which, according to guides, still has gold deposits. Bring a jacket, since the inside temperature hovers at forty-eight degrees year-round. Open from 9:00 A.M. to 7:00 P.M. in summer and from 10:00 A.M. to 6:00 P.M. in winter. Prices are $4.00 for adults and $2.00 for children ages five to eleven.

LUNCH: The **Ponderosa Restaurant,** located upstairs in the Famous Bonanza Casino (107 Main Street, Central City; 303–526–7568), may require a wait, but the Philly Cheesesteak is worth it. The menu includes aged and slow-cooked prime rib, burgers, sandwiches, and made-from-scratch red chile, green chile, guacamole, and other Mexican food selections. The restaurant is open from 11:00 A.M. to 9:00 P.M. Sunday through Thursday and from 11:00 A.M. to midnight Friday and Saturday.

THERE'S MORE

Gilpin County Historical Museum (228 East High Street, Central City; 303–582–5283) is located in a restored 1870 schoolhouse. The museum chronicles the area's rich history, and you'll get a sense for what life was like in the late 1800s by browsing through the chambers, which include mining memorabilia and an antique doll collection. Open daily from 10:00 A.M. to 4:00 P.M. Memorial Day through Labor Day. Admission is $3.00. The **Operatique,** across Eureka Street from the Opera House (both

303–582–5202), has a nice selection of special books about the Central City Opera House, along with T-shirts and other merchandise.

SPECIAL EVENTS

June. Madam Lou Bunch Days, Central City. Held the third weekend in June. Ladies dress in "Sporting House Girl" and "Madam" costumes (the Madam outfits are the more conservative) and gentlemen wear western attire for the Parade of Madams and Dandy Dans. The weekend includes bed races down Main Street and the traditional Madams and Miners Ball.

August. Central City Music Fest. Jazz and contemporary musicians from around the country perform during the third weekend in August. Main Street closes, and the town parties with street dancing and celebrating.

OTHER RECOMMENDED RESTAURANTS AND LODGINGS

Central City

Full Moon Saloon, in the Coyote Creek Casino (98 Lawrence; 303–582–1990), is known for its barbecued ribs and homemade corn-bread; the restaurant also has a great jalapeño cheeseburger. It's open from 10:00 A.M. to 9:00 P.M. weekdays and from 10:00 A.M. to 10:00 P.M. weekends.

Harveys Wagon Wheel Casino and Hotel, 321 Gregory Street, Central City; 800–HARVEYS or (800) 427–8397. With 118 rooms this hotel is the largest in the area, and it is conveniently located near the opera house. Suites and nonsmoking rooms are available. The price during mid-week for a standard room is $75; for a deluxe room, $95; and for a suite, $130 to $165. Weekend prices are $110 for a standard room and $125 for a deluxe room; the suite price remains the same.

Primrose Inn (310 East First High, Central City; 303–582–5808) is a restored Victorian home built in the 1860s and has three double rooms available.

FOR MORE INFORMATION

Central City Opera House Association, 621 Seventeenth Street, Suite 1601, Denver, CO 80293; (303) 292–6500.

Gilpin County Chamber of Commerce, Box 343, Black Hawk, CO 80422; (303) 582–5077.

Central City Information, (800) 542–2999 or (303) 582–5251.

NORTHERN

Fort Collins

BREWING UP A GOOD TIME

1 NIGHT

*Historic Old Town Square • Colorado State University •
Brewery tours • Horsetooth Reservoir • Cache la Poudre River
• Flower farm*

Home to college kids, business executives, and escapees of the big city, Fort
Collins is a relaxed town located in a picturesque setting between the Colorado Rockies and the eastern plains. Even with its population of more than
100,000, Fort Collins retains that small-town feeling. Residents here indulge
in the good life with magnificent outdoor recreation and enough restaurants, galleries, and microbreweries to enjoy a night on the town.

Established in 1864 as a post to protect settlers and travelers along the
Overland Trail, the city was once an active military fort. Today the mixture
of lifestyles—students, farmers, ranchers, professors, and retirees—helps create
the community's charm.

As the home of Colorado State University, Fort Collins has the attractions
that every good college town should: excellent bookstores, outdoor cafes,
unique shops, and that youthful intellectual edge found in a university setting.

DAY 1

Morning

From Denver take I–25 north for 60 miles to Fort Collins.

BREAKFAST: Silver Grill Cafe (218 Walnut Street; 970–484–4656) has a history that traces back to 1912. Today this restaurant is a favorite among locals,

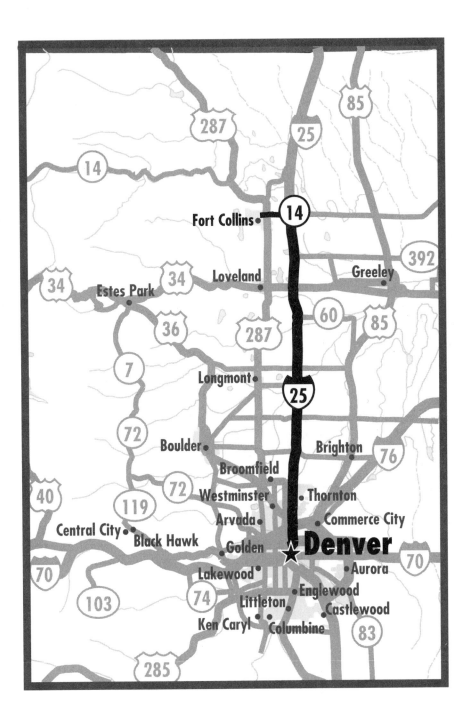

and you'll find marvelous baked goods and menu items such as homemade sausage gravy served over fresh biscuits.

Whether you want to tool around town or head into the wilderness, Fort Collins and the surrounding area offer both. Stroll College Avenue and the renovated **Historic Old Town Square,** which extends in a triangle from the intersection of College Avenue and Mountain Avenue. Many of the shops and restaurants are frequented by students, which makes exploring all that much more interesting. Be sure to visit **Stone Lion Bookstore** (107 North College; 970–493–0030); the tidy, well-stocked shelves and helpful staff at this inviting store make for a pleasant browsing or buying experience.

For a unique selection of western-style furniture and accessories, visit **Rocky Mountain Home Collection** (128 South College Avenue; 970–482–8608). You'll find hand-carved wooden coffee tables and fishing-motif decor for sale here. The birdbaths, fountains, and books at **The Perennial Gardener** (154 North College Avenue; 970–224–3987) are interesting for nongardeners as well as those with a green thumb. **The Cupboard** (152 South College Avenue; 970–493–8585) is another wonderful store, and as its name implies, this shop is filled with kitchen accessories, pots and pans, cookbooks, and specialty foods.

When you need a break, stop at **Starry Night Coffee Company** (112 South College; 970–493–3039) for an espresso drink and a slice of coffee cake as you linger over the local newspaper.

LUNCH: Austin's American Grill (100 West Mountain Avenue, Fort Collins; 970–224–9691) is a contemporary restaurant that's a newcomer to town but has already attracted a local following. Big-band swing music plays in the background as you look over the menu with choices such as baby back ribs, served with the house barbecue sauce, ranch beans, and garlicky mashed potatoes. The restaurant has a full-service bar and a relaxing outdoor dining area. The chef will prepare any of the meals "to go" if you prefer to picnic in one of the local parks. Austin's is open daily for lunch and dinner from 11:00 A.M. to 10:00 P.M.; hours are extended to 11:00 P.M. Thursday through Saturday.

Afternoon

Referred to as the Napa Valley of Breweries, Fort Collins is a great place to spend the afternoon brewery-hopping.

You don't need to be a beer lover to enjoy a tour of **Anheuser-Busch Brewery.** Located at 2351 Busch Drive, (970–490–4691), Anheuser-Busch

The Cache la Poudre River *near Fort Collins*
(photo courtesy Fort Collins Convention and Visitors Bureau)

offers a free tour, which lasts an hour and twenty minutes. You'll hear the Budweiser theme song, smell hops, and see the high-speed packaging lines that fill thousands of cans and bottles every minute, as you are guided through this immense facility. You can sample the beer in the hospitality room, but the real highlight is a visit to the eye-catching barn to see the world-famous Clydesdales.

To get to Anheuser-Busch Brewery, take I–25 to Mountain Vista Drive and turn right onto Busch Drive. Tours are available from 10:00 A.M. to 4:00 P.M. Thursday through Monday, November through May; from 9:30 A.M. to 5:00 P.M. daily, June through August; and from 10:00 A.M. to 4:00 P.M. daily, September through October. There is a special Budweiser Clydesdale Camera Day the first Saturday of each month, year-round.

Next, stop at the more down-home **Odell Brewing Company** (800 East Lincoln; 970–498–9070), a much smaller operation than Anheuser-Busch. At Odell's your guide may be one of the owners of the company. Sample the popular 90 Shilling or Cutthroat Porter Ale. Free tours are available weekdays at 3:00 P.M. and Saturdays from noon to 3:00 P.M. on the hour. The retail store and tasting room are open from 9:00 A.M. to 6:00 P.M. weekdays and from 10:00 A.M. to 6:00 P.M. Saturdays.

To see where Fat Tire Ale is brewed, visit **New Belgium Brewing Company** (500 Linden Street; 970–221–0524). In keeping with the "fat tire" theme, the tasting room has one original 1950s bike and one replica. You can take a self-guided tour from 10:00 A.M. to 5:30 P.M. Monday through Saturday. Guided tours are available at 2:00 P.M. weekdays and from 11:00 A.M. to 4:00 P.M. Saturdays on the hour.

DINNER: For first-class tableside service in a cozy cellar restaurant, dine at **Nico's Catacombs** (115 South College Avenue; 970–482–6426). The restaurant features an excellent continental menu. Steak tartare is a great appetizer, and the house special of Chateaubriand for two is delicious. You may prefer the Dover sole or fresh salmon. For a flaming dessert splurge on strawberries Romanoff. Nico's Catacombs is open for dinner only and begins serving at 6:00 P.M.

LODGING: The Edwards House (402 West Mountain Avenue, Fort Collins, CO 80521; 970–493–9191 or 800–281–9190) may be the most upscale lodging in Fort Collins and is the best located. This Victorian-era B&B, conveniently situated within minutes of Historic Old Town District, is the kind of tastefully decorated house where every nook and cranny holds discoveries.

You'll find an antique typewriter in the well-stocked, inviting library and a yellow rubber ducky near the tub in your room. Each of the six rooms has every amenity you'll need for a comfortable stay, including cable television with VCR, telephone, bathrobes, and a shower or clawfoot tub. Guests gather in the afternoon for a glass of wine and conversation in the elegant parlor.

The Montezuma Fuller Suite is the room requested most often by honeymoon couples. This spacious, third-floor bedroom has a gorgeous mahogany sleigh bed, a separate sitting room, a fireplace, and a Jacuzzi tub. The Avery Suite, named for its view of the historic Avery House across the street, is decorated with floral wallpaper, lace curtains, a pine armoire, a queen-size canopy bed, and a clawfoot slipper tub. Rates at The Edwards House range from $79 to $139.

DAY 2

Morning

BREAKFAST: You'll dine in the formal dining room of The Edwards House at an oval antique table once owned by actor Adolphe Menjou. Breakfast includes fresh fruit, home-baked scones, and an entree such as crepes, quiche, or eggs florentine. Order an espresso or cappuccino to complete your meal.

It would be a shame not to take advantage of the beauty and adventure of the great outdoor attractions that lie just beyond the city. Located fifteen minutes west of Fort Collins, **Horsetooth Reservoir** is a 6.5-mile-long body of water named for the nearby rock that resembles a horse's tooth. Popular with anglers, boaters, swimmers, campers, and picnickers, this lake attracts crowds during summer months for good reason: The scenic setting remains unspoiled and beautiful.

Nearby **Horsetooth Mountain Park** offers acres of public land available to hikers, mountain bikers, and horseback riders. To get to Horsetooth Reservoir and Horsetooth Mountain Park, take Taft Hill Road south; 0.5 mile south of Horsetooth, turn right on County Road 38E. That road takes you directly to the southern end of Horsetooth Reservoir; if you continue past the reservoir, you will arrive at the parking lot for Horsetooth Mountain Park. For more information contact Larimer County Parks Department at (970) 226–4517.

LUNCH: Picnic at one of the many sites at **Lory State Park,** which borders Horsetooth Reservoir. This park is another fantastic area for exploration.

Watch for deer and the occasional rattlesnake. During winter, cross-country skiers will find a network of relatively undisturbed trails. For information on horseback riding, contact **Double Diamond Stables** (710 Lodgepole Drive, Bellvue, CO 80512; 970–224–4200). For additional information contact Lory State Park (708 Lodgepole Drive, Bellvue, CO 80512; 970–493–1623).

River-rafting enthusiasts will want to float the **Cache la Poudre River,** which, according to legend, got its name, meaning "hide the powder," when early French traders stashed their gunpowder barrels next to the river. Today rafters, kayakers, and canoeists maneuver the significant whitewater of this twisting, scenic river that eventually flows into the South Platte. To arrange a guided raft trip, contact **Rocky Mountain Adventures** (1117 North Highway 287, Fort Collins, CO 80524; 970–493–4005 or 800–858–6808) or **Wanderlust Adventure** (3500 Bingham Hill Road, Fort Collins, CO 80521; 800–745–7238). For kayak instruction call **Poudre River Kayaks** at (970) 484–8480. To get to Poudre Canyon, take College Avenue (Highway 287) north out of Fort Collins and turn left on Highway 14, the entrance to Poudre Canyon.

THERE'S MORE

Avery House, (328 West Mountain Avenue, Fort Collins, CO 80521; 970-221-0533) is a historic house museum that was home to Franklin Avery, who founded First National Bank and was instrumental in developing water projects in northern Colorado. Today the Victorian house, gazebo, fountain, and carriage house are listed on the National Register of Historic Places. Tours of Avery House are available from 1:00 to 3:00 P.M. Sundays and Wednesdays.

Swetsville Zoo (4801 East Harmony Road, Fort Collins, CO 80525; 970–484–9509) doesn't boast a single live animal, but you'll still want to visit this sculpture park to see more than 150 animals and flowers constructed from scrap metal and old car parts. Swetsville Zoo is located 0.5 mile east of I–25 on Harmony. Admission is free, but donations are accepted. The zoo is open daily from dawn to dusk.

Buckhorn Llama Company (7220 North County Road 27, Loveland, CO 80538; 970–667–7411) offers guided pack trips, ranch tours, and various llama-related services, such as boarding and training. Visitors are welcome to view the llamas. The gift shop stocks clothing made from llama fiber. Be sure to visit Masonville Mercantile, located at the intersection of Country Road 38 and Country Road 27. It sells everything from snacks to wedding dresses.

Discovery Center Science Museum (703 East Prospect Road, Fort Collins, CO 80525; 970–493–2182) is a nonprofit institution devoted to science and technology. Kids love the hands-on exhibits, which include the opportunity to make arcs and sparks in the Electricity Room. StarLab Planetarium is another favorite. The museum is open Tuesday through Saturday from 10:00 A.M. to 5:00 P.M. and Sunday from noon to 5:00 P.M. Admission is $3.00 per person; children four and under are admitted free.

The Fort Collins Museum (200 Mathews Street, Fort Collins, CO 80524; 970–221–6738) emphasizes the local history of the area and its natural environment. The biggest attractions at the museum are the three historic cabins located in the courtyard. One of these, Auntie Stone's Cabin, is the only remaining building from the time when the fort was in operation. Admission is free. The museum is open Tuesday through Saturday from 10:00 A.M. to 5:00 P.M. and Sunday from noon to 5:00 P.M.; the facility is closed Monday.

The Farm Heritage Museum and the Farm at Lee Martinez Park (600 North Sherwood Street; 970–221–6665) offer visitors the chance to view farm animals in a rural setting. You'll see antique farm machinery, a barbed-wire collection, and a large horseshoe used by one of the Anheuser-Busch Clydesdale horses. Admission is free. The farm is open from 10:00 A.M. to 5:30 P.M. Wednesday through Saturday and from noon to 5:30 P.M. Sunday.

Windswept Farms (5537 North County Road 9, Fort Collins, CO 80524; 970–484–1124) is a family-owned flower farm that you can tour Monday through Friday, June through September. Stroll through the herb garden or watch the staff create dried floral arrangements.

SPECIAL EVENTS

July. Rendezvous and Skookum Day. The history of Fort Collins is re-enacted with demonstrations of blacksmithing, milking, quilting, branding, trapping, weaving, and more.

August. New West Fest celebrates the city's birthday in a long-weekend event with music, food booths, and arts and crafts for sale.

September. Fort Collins Annual Historic Homes Tour is a self-guided tour of several of the town's landmark homes. Proceeds benefit the Avery House Historic District and the 1882 Fort Collins Water Works.

OTHER RECOMMENDED RESTAURANTS AND LODGINGS

Fort Collins

Jay's American Bistro (151 South College Avenue; 970–482–1876) serves Italian-style pastas and a variety of seafood, wild game, and pizzas.

Mariposa on Spring Creek Bed and Breakfast (706 East Stuart Street, Fort Collins, CO 80525; 970–495–9604 or 800–495–9604) offers a full-service day spa in addition to comfortable accommodations. Make an appointment for a European facial, a mud wrap, or a full-body massage. A gourmet breakfast is included in the rate, which ranges from $85 to $95.

FOR MORE INFORMATION

Fort Collins Convention and Visitors Bureau, 420 South Howes, Suite 101, P.O. Box 1998, Fort Collins, CO 80522; (800) 274–3678.

Saratoga, Wyoming

WILD, WILD WEST

2 NIGHTS

Blue-ribbon trout fishing • Golf, tennis, horseback riding • Western lodge • Scenic highways • Wide-open spaces

The long, magical days of a Wyoming summer cast their spell. Rugged, vast, and beautiful, the Cowboy State evokes images of western novels and an untamed landscape.

Wyoming doesn't aspire to glitz and glamour. Here jeans and cowboy boots are appropriate attire anytime, anywhere. Saddle up and ride off into the lush canyons of the Yampa Valley or snag a trophy-size trout from the crystal-clear Upper North Platte River. Waterfalls, streams, and lakes are abundant with fish. Golf the spectacular 9-hole course at Saratoga Inn Resort and Hot Springs, or set off on a mountain bike to explore this uncrowded haven.

Surrounded by sprawling ranches, acres of national forest, and the Sierra Madre and Snowy Range Mountains, the town of Saratoga (population 1,950) offers a permanence and personality that fast-paced resorts may be missing. Unaffected western hospitality will greet you at every turn. This rural area has what many people want in a weekend retreat: peace and quiet, pristine wilderness, pleasant accommodations, excellent food, and a long list of outdoor activities. Saratoga possesses an indelible charm that you will find difficult to leave.

DAY 1

Morning

Saratoga is located just over the border from Colorado. Take I–25 north to Cheyenne, and stop for a midmorning breakfast and some sightseeing.

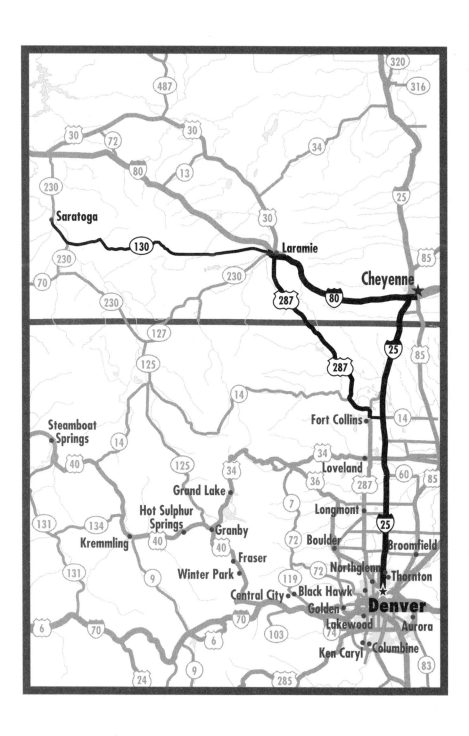

BREAKFAST: Located in the oldest brick home in Cheyenne, **Lexie's** (216 East Seventeenth Street; 307–638–8712) specializes in omelets. Eggs Benedict is another good choice, and if you're here at lunchtime, don't miss the restaurant's award-winning burger. Lexie's is open Monday from 8:00 A.M. to 3:00 P.M., Tuesday through Thursday from 8:00 A.M. to 8:00 P.M., and Friday and Saturday from 8:00 A.M. to 9:00 P.M.; closed Sunday.

For a history of Cheyenne Frontier Days and the West, visit **Cheyenne's Old West Museum** (4501 North Carey Avenue, Cheyenne, WY 82001; 800–778–7290), which also has one of the nation's largest carriage collections. The museum is open Monday through Friday from 9:00 A.M. to 5:00 P.M. and weekends from 10:00 A.M. to 5:00 P.M. Admission is $3.00 for adults; children twelve and under are admitted free.

The **Historic Governor's Mansion** (300 East Twenty-first Street, Cheyenne; 307–777–7878), built in 1904, is open year-round to visitors. Take a self-guided tour of this lovely 2½-story house. Admission is free, and the mansion is open Tuesday through Saturday from 9:00 A.M. to 5:00 P.M.

From Cheyenne continue west on I–80. At Laramie follow Highway 130 on the Scenic Byway through the Snowy Range Mountains, and continue north on Highway 230 to Saratoga. The stretch of highway between Laramie and the turnoff onto Highway 230 is one of the most spectacular drives in the country. The route winds across the grand Medicine Bow Mountains and past several crystalline lakes, including picture-perfect Lake Marie. During winter, when the Scenic Byway is closed, take Highway 230 west from Laramie.

LUNCH: When you arrive in Saratoga, slow down the pace from the outset at **Mom's Kitchen** (402 South First Street; 307–326–5842), a ma-and-pa place that serves simple food in a down-home atmosphere. Choose from catfish, liver and onions, or chicken-fried steak smothered with Mom's cream gravy, among other selections. The homemade cinnamon rolls are not to be missed. Mom's is open Tuesday through Saturday from 6:00 A.M. to 8:00 P.M., Sunday from 6:00 A.M. to 7:00 P.M., and Monday from 6:00 A.M. to 1:30 P.M.

Afternoon

The individualistic, frontier spirit that ruled the West of the 1800s still thrives in Saratoga. Folks and storekeepers will welcome you as you stroll through downtown. Shop for a new pair of waders and get the latest scoop on where the fish are biting at **Fishpaw Trading Company** (120 East Bridge Street; 307–326–5000). The store also sells antiques, art, and western collectibles.

Medicine Bow Drifters (307–326–8002), at the same location, can arrange a personally guided fly-fishing trip.

Get a trim, play a game of checkers, and catch up on the news at **Valley Tobacco Barber Shop** (122 East Bridge Street; 307–326–9990), a one-chair operation. You'll also find a nice selection of fresh cigars. The sign out front lists business hours as 9:00 A.M. to 5:00 P.M. Tuesday through Friday; Monday is "optional."

If you need a denim shirt or a cowboy hat, stop at **Whitney's Mercantile** (107 West Bridge Street; 307–326–5935). This stylish store carries the latest in contemporary and western fashion, and the Patsy Cline tunes playing in the background will get you in a western mood.

Join other guests in the **Trophy Room at Saratoga Inn Resort and Hot Springs** (601 East Pick Pike Road) for social hour, from 4:00 to 5:00 P.M. daily, and sample the inn's beer. The Rodeo Pale Ale and the Winkin' Willy's Wild Wheat are especially good. Or sip a glass of wine and nibble cheese and crackers as you admire the western wild mounts in the Trophy Room. Stroll outside to the terrace, which has an oversize hand-carved chess set. One set of pieces represents the Native Americans; the other, the Cavalry. Guests are welcome to play a game.

DINNER: Silver Saddle BBQ & Brewery, Saratoga Inn Resort and Hot Springs (307–326–5261), is the more casual of the inn's two restaurants, but the menus are quite similar. European-trained chef Roger Scheel presides over both restaurants with outstanding culinary know-how. Begin with the Grilled Game Sausage Medley for an appetizer, a combination of deer, pheasant, and buffalo, served with red chile and cilantro mustards. Entrees include blackened prime rib, grilled salmon filet, and sautéed jumbo trout, or you may prefer the barbecued chicken, spareribs, or pork chops hot off the smoker.

Evening

After dinner visit the Silver Saddle Bar, located next to the restaurant, where you can smoke a cigar, shoot some pool, or relax in the deep leather couches. No ordinary tavern, this bar is decorated with Navajo rugs, cowhide chairs, and a king's table with 6-foot-tall high-backed seats. Enjoy one of the inn's award-winning handcrafted beers from the on-site Sierra Madre Brewing Company.

LODGING: Saratoga Inn Resort and Hot Springs (601 East Pick Pike Road, P.O. Box 869, Saratoga, WY 82331; 307–326–5261) is a rare find.

This classic western lodge has recently undergone a multimillion-dollar renovation. Each of the fifty-six guest rooms and suites has a featherbed, a Pendleton blanket, western art, and custom-made lamps with cowhide shades. Warm chocolate chip cookies are delivered to your doorstep nightly, and you can choose from more than 400 movies to watch in the privacy of your room. Relax on the porch next to the outdoor fireplace, or lounge in the lobby with its soft leather couches, bull-hide rugs, and grandfather clock.

Rates begin at $119 per person and include three meals a day. The sports package, includes unlimited golf, trophy fishing, and horseback riding.

DAY 2

Morning

BREAKFAST: A huge buffet with made-to-order omelets, fresh fruit, cereals, and waffles is included with your stay at Saratoga Inn Resort and Hot Springs. You'll dine at Baron's Mesquite Grille, decorated with black tablecloths, red napkins, antiques, and original western art.

Plan ahead and order a picnic lunch from the inn—a couple of choices are the vegetarian pita and the chilled meatloaf sandwich—before you strike off on an outdoor adventure.

Fish for five, six, or even nine-pound rainbow trout in the majestic setting of **Sierra Madre Guest Ranch,** located about 20 miles from Saratoga Inn Resort and Hot Springs. A shuttle van will take you to the private property at 8:00 A.M. or 12:30 P.M. for a half-day of fishing. If you wish, the front desk will arrange for a guide, a boat, and equipment. Or simply step out the back door of Saratoga Inn and drop a line in the Upper North Platte River that runs through the resort.

Horseback riding is also available at Sierra Madre Guest Ranch. Head wrangler Steve Johnson will set you up with a horse to fit your riding ability, whether you want to gallop over the huge expanse of the ranch on your own or saunter along with a group, admiring the views that stretch as far as 300 miles. You'll have more than 50,000 acres to explore.

Afternoon

With three "over-the-river" shots and a cliff tee-off, the scenic **9-hole course** at Saratoga Inn Resort and Hot Springs is a golfer's dream. Clubs are available for rent at the pro shop. There's also mountain biking, tennis, or a dip in the inn's natural mineral hot spring 92-degree swimming pool.

After your active day soak in the other **natural hot spring pool,** located across the street from the inn. Once referred to by Native Americans as the Place of Magic Waters, this spring's temperature is a soothing 104 to 110 degrees.

DINNER: Baron's Mesquite Grille, Saratoga Inn Resort and Hot Springs, is decorated with elkhorn chandeliers, original western art, and barn-wood walls. An exquisite baby grand piano completes the setting. The menu includes grilled veal rib chop, a twelve-ounce New York strip, and iron skillet cornbread.

LODGING: Saratoga Inn Resort and Hot Springs.

DAY 3

Morning

BREAKFAST: Saratoga Inn Resort and Hot Springs.

Return to Denver via Highway 287 from Laramie. Connect with I–25 south at Fort Collins.

To tour one of the most significant military outposts on the Oregon Trail, stop at **Fort Laramie National Historic Site,** situated on the North Platte River, Laramie, Wyoming. Established as a fur trading post in 1834, Fort Laramie later became a major link for the Pony Express. Franklin Roosevelt designated the fort a National Historic Site in 1938. Today you can get a close-up look at the cavalry barracks where soldiers slept, the guardhouse that lodged prisoners, and the post's headquarters. Stop at the visitor center and pick up a map for the self-guided tour. The center is open daily from 8:00 A.M. to 7:00 P.M. mid-May to mid-September and from 8:00 A.M. to 4:30 P.M. the remainder of the year. For more information contact Fort Laramie National Historic Site, P.O. Box 218, Laramie, WY 82212; (307) 837–2221.

LUNCH: Coal Creek Coffee Company (110 Grand Avenue, Laramie, Wyoming; 307–745–7737) has coffee drinks and a "Light Food" menu that includes an Italian garden pita sandwich and a bagel melt.

THERE'S MORE

River rafting. The Class III and IV rapids of the North Gate Canyon on the North Platte will get your heart pounding. Half-day, full-day, and overnight whitewater trips are available through **Platte Valley Outfitters** (P.O. Box 900, Saratoga, WY 82331; 307–326–5750). You'll see petroglyphs and may catch a glimpse of a bald eagle or some mountain sheep as you float down the river.

Saratoga Museum (104 Constitution Avenue, Saratoga, WY 82331; 307–326–5511), located across from the airport on the town's south side, chronicles the story of Saratoga's pioneer ranchers, loggers, and merchants. Housed in the old Union Pacific Railroad Depot, the museum has an interesting photo gallery, with portraits of Platte Valley pioneers. The museum is open daily from 1:00 to 5:00 P.M. Memorial Day through Labor Day; call for an appointment the remainder of the year.

Hobo Pool (East Walnut Street, Saratoga, WY; 307–326–8855) is an outdoor pool fed by the warm mineral waters of Saratoga Hot Springs and is open twenty-four hours a day should you need a midnight soak. There is no charge for the mineral baths.

SPECIAL EVENTS

July. Cheyenne Frontier Days, Cheyenne, Wyoming, is a ten-day event with rodeos, parades, stage shows, square dancing, a world-class western art show, and some of Nashville's big-name entertainers. Attend a free pancake breakfast, watch bronco busting and steer wrestling, and see a melodrama, all in the same day. For ticket information contact Cheyenne Frontier Days, P.O. Box 2477, Cheyenne, WY 82003; (307) 778–7222 or (800) 227–6336.

August. Saratoga is home to Wyoming's Official State Microbrewery Competition, the "Steinley Cup," and is limited to Wyoming brewers. A $10.00 fee will buy a souvenir glass, unlimited sampling, and the chance to decide for yourself who has the best brew in the state. For further information call Saratoga/Platte Valley Chamber of Commerce at (307) 326–8855.

OTHER RECOMMENDED RESTAURANTS AND LODGINGS

Saratoga

Lollypops (107 East Bridge Street; 307–326–5020) has an old-fashioned soda fountain and serves sandwiches, soup, and pasta. Lollypops specializes in coffee drinks and ice cream. Order a hot fudge malt for something different.

Hotel Wolf (101 East Bridge Street, Saratoga, WY 82331; 307–326–5525) is 2½ stories high and is still the tallest building in Saratoga. Renovated in 1977, the Wolf offers rooms that are clean and quiet. The **Wolf Hotel Restaurant** has a reputation for excellent food. The menu includes prime rib, the Wolf Burger, and a soup-and-salad bar.

Cheyenne

Nagle Warren Mansion Bed and Breakfast (222 East Seventeenth Street, Cheyenne, WY 82001; 307–637–3333 or 800–811–2610) is a magnificent, 9,300-square-foot Victorian home with eleven antique-filled rooms. Ornate fireplaces, parquet floors, and stained glass windows grace this lovely B&B, which is listed on the National Register of Historic Places. Innkeepers Jim and Jacquie Osterfoss have endeavored to restore the mansion to its original elegance of the late 1800s. Afternoon tea and pastries are served daily, and breakfast may include eggs Benedict, quiche, or raspberry-chocolate-chip pancakes. Rates range from $65 to $125 per night.

FOR MORE INFORMATION

Wyoming Division of Tourism, I–25 at College Drive, Cheyenne, WY 82002; (307) 777–7777.

Cheyenne Convention and Visitors Bureau, P.O. Box 765, Cheyenne, WY 82003; (800) 426–5009.

Saratoga/Platte Valley Chamber of Commerce, P.O. Box 1095, Saratoga, WY; (307) 326–8855.

NORTHERN

Steamboat Springs

TAKE A SOAK

2 NIGHTS

Mountain biking, golf, hiking • Strawberry Park Hot Springs • Wacky winter festival • Champagne powder

Summer in Steamboat Springs is bliss. When all that snow melts, delicate wildflowers emerge in lush valleys and the landscape flourishes. Here you can soar in a hot-air balloon, climb steep rockfaces, or trek backcountry trails by llama. Anglers rave about fishing for rainbow trout in the more than eighty lakes and streams in the area. Take in the rodeo, dancing, or golf, or kick back and soak in the Rocky Mountain views and mellow atmosphere.

During winter, Steamboat Springs will win you over—even if you're not a skier. And if you are a downhill enthusiast, this schussing paradise will delight to no end. Not into tackling those moguls? Check this out: You can slip and slide through "ice driving" school, tour the hot springs, or cozy up under a wool blanket on an evening sleigh ride.

Steamboat labels itself Ski Town, USA, and the title fits. We're talking mega-snow: 400-plus inches of fluffy white stuff. According to locals, the expression *champagne powder* was born on these mountains. The area also prides itself on its western lifestyle. Remember Billy Kidd, the cowboy-hat-clad 1972 Olympic Silver Medalist ski racer? Steamboat was his stomping grounds and training site as he prepared for competition.

Kidd continues to reside in Steamboat and directs the Billy Kidd Center of Performance Skiing, a facility that provides training for promising young skiers. Steamboat Springs has produced more Olympians (forty-seven winter and four summer) than any other town in the country.

Steamboat Springs traces its history to the Native American Utes and later to the grizzled fur trappers who arrived in the early 1800s and found

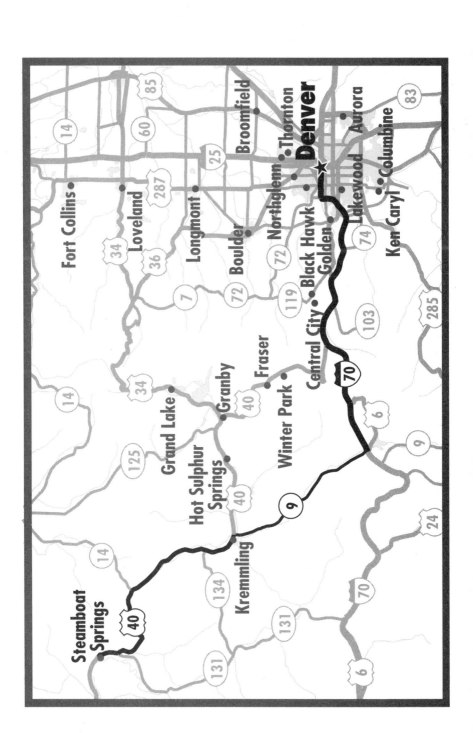

the area perfect for hunting and fishing. Legend has it that Carl Howelsen, who was nicknamed "the Flying Norseman," introduced skiing to the local townspeople in 1913, by flinging himself off a homemade ski jump. Howelsen originated the town's first Winter Carnival in 1914.

Steamboat still holds the annual week-long festival, which includes ski-jump competitions, ski races, shovel races, and merrymaking in general. The best event of all occurs when the local high school marching band takes to the streets on skis.

DAY 1

Morning

Steamboat Springs is located 160 miles northwest of Denver. To get to Steamboat, take I–70 west through the Eisenhower Tunnel to the Silverthorne exit. Continue north on Colorado Highway 9 to Kremmling, then west on U.S. 40 to Steamboat Springs.

BREAKFAST: Sunshine Cafe (240 Summit Place Shopping Center, Silverthorne, CO 80498; 970–468–6663) is as light and cheerful as its name suggests. The extensive breakfast menu offers originals such as the Alferd Packer Gourmet Three-Egg Omelet, with sautéed mushrooms, avocado, and alfalfa sprouts, and the Dillon Dam, an English muffin topped with ham, two eggs, cheese sauce, and avocado. To get to the restaurant, take the Silverthorne exit off I–70, turn left, and continue about 0.5 mile to the Summit Place Shopping Center. Sunshine Cafe is open from 7:00 A.M. to 3:00 P.M. and from 5:00 to 9:00 P.M. daily.

Return to Highway 9 headed north to Kremmling, and then go west on U.S. 40 to Steamboat Springs.

Begin with a 2-hour, two-mile **walking tour of the springs** of Steamboat. Considered sacred by the Native Americans, who soaked in the springs after battles to rejuvenate their strength, the hot springs remain effervescent and even somewhat mysterious yet today. Many regard the springs to have therapeutic and healing qualities. Pick up a map at the **Steamboat Springs Chamber Information Center** (1255 South Lincoln Avenue), and follow directions for a self-guided tour of seven springs.

LUNCH: You may have to wait in line along with locals at **The Shack Cafe** (740 Lincoln Avenue; 970–879–9975), but that's a good endorsement for any

The countryside near Steamboat Springs *offers mountain vistas and acres of beautiful hills to explore.* *(photo by Karen Schulenburg).*

restaurant. The "Shack" has an Old West, log-cabin decor. Take note of the colorful mural depicting life in the early days of the town and also the photo of the Steamboat Springs band skiing down the street. Shack favorites include fish-and-chips and a fresh-ground chuck burger smothered in homemade chili and beans. The Shack Cafe is open from 6:30 A.M. to 2:00 P.M. weekends and from 6:00 A.M. to 2:00 P.M. weekdays.

Afternoon

After seeing the thirty-seven road signs advertising everything from cowboy boots to overalls along the highway between Kremmling and Steamboat Springs, you'll be curious about the western store **F. M. Light & Sons**

(830 Lincoln Avenue, Steamboat Springs, CO 80487; 970–879–1822 or 800–530–8908). Frank Light moved to Steamboat Springs in the early 1900s with his wife and seven children and opened the store in 1905, selling merchandise brought in by freight wagon. Over the years this classic store has expanded, succeeded, and become a legend in the area. In 1928 more than 250 signs were erected within a 150-mile radius of Steamboat Springs.

Today many of the 1905 fixtures remain in this historic store. You'll also find stuffed jackalopes, old wagon wheels, bearskin rugs, and a life-size John Wayne cardboard cutout. Shop for the latest in cowboy boots, spurs, cowboy hats, jeans, and dusters. F. M. Light & Sons has an excellent reputation for quality merchandise and friendly service. Kids like to have their photo taken sitting on Lightning, the life-size horse in front of the store. F. M. Light & Sons is open from 8:30 A.M. to 10:00 P.M. Monday through Saturday and from 9:00 A.M. to 9:30 P.M. Sunday.

Located upstairs from Soda Creek Mercantile at Third and Lincoln, **Cookie Lockhart's Cowboy Collectables & Antiques** (970–879–2580) is packed with authentic western treasures. Here you can purchase a horsehair bridle, chaps, or a saddle. The store also has furniture, fine glassware, and western art. Don't miss **Into the West Furniture & Art Gallery** (807 Lincoln Avenue; 970–879–8377), a well-designed store that sells elk-antler chandeliers, leather furniture, and fine art.

DINNER: Steamboat Yacht Club (811 Yampa Avenue, Steamboat Springs, CO 80477; 970–879–4774) is the ideal place to park yourself on the patio about five in the afternoon, order a cocktail, and watch people float by on inner tubes down the Yampa River. In the winter, sit by the roaring fireplace in the dining room. Order the goat cheese and roasted garlic or duck quesadilla for an appetizer. Entrees include dishes such as mango salmon, orange pecan trout, elk, and Colorado lamb. The Yacht Club also serves salads, sandwiches, and soup.

LODGING: Sky Valley Lodge (31490 East Highway 40, P.O. Box 773132, Steamboat Springs, CO 80477; 970–879–7749 or 800–538–7519) is located on the edge of Rabbit Ears Pass, about seven minutes outside of Steamboat Springs, and offers seclusion in a serene country setting. The lodge nestles into the mountains and affords a stunning view of the valley. Relax in the outdoor hot tub and gaze out onto the picturesque backdrop, as you soothe your muscles after a day of skiing or hiking.

DAY 2

Morning

BREAKFAST: Sky Valley Lodge offers complimentary continental breakfast in the light-filled dining room or the pleasant outdoor patio.

Winter visitors will want to hit the slopes early, and summer visitors can pack a picnic lunch and head to **Fish Creek Falls** for a spectacular hike. Fish Creek Falls is 4 miles from Steamboat Springs. Take Third Street north to Fish Creek Falls Road, turn right, and follow the signs. There is an admission fee of $2.00 per car. You'll get a workout as you climb the short but steep trail to the awesome 280-foot waterfall. Continue up the trail to a second set of falls. This is a popular hike and you won't be alone, but the crowds thin out the farther you go. You'll eventually reach **Long Lake,** about 5 miles from the lower falls.

LUNCH: There are numerous places along the trail to eat your picnic lunch as you gaze at the majestic setting.

Afternoon

Opened in 1997, **Haymaker Golf Course,** located in the heart of the lush Yampa Valley, is a challenging 18-hole course designed after the Scottish-style links. *A warning:* Stay on the fairway or your ball will end up in the native grasses of this spectacular 233-acre course. Haymaker Golf Course is located at the corner of Highway 131 and U.S. 40. Call Steamboat Central Reservations (800–922–2722) for information. Another option is **Sheraton Steamboat Golf Club** (970–879–2220), an 18-hole mountain course that offers challenge as well as views of the Yampa Valley and Mount Werner.

During winter, steer your way through **The Bridgestone Winter Driving School.** Professional instructors teach the safest way to navigate difficult driving conditions on an ice- and snow-covered private circuit. Choose a half-day, full-day, or two-day program. Contact The Bridgestone Winter Driving School, P.O. Box 774167, 1850 Ski Time Square Drive, Steamboat Springs, CO 80477; (970) 879–6104.

DINNER: As Steamboat's first and largest brewery, **Heavenly Daze Brewery Grill** (at Ski Time Square; 970–879–8080), features award-winning beers made on the premises. Try the Dog's Breath Brown Ale along with an old-fashioned cheeseburger and fries. The bar on the first floor is a great place to have dinner, socialize, watch sports on television, or play a game of checkers. You can also dine on the second floor or the patio. The menu offers choices such as fettuccine primavera, rib eye steak, and shepherd's pie. Heavenly Daze has pool tables and Foosball tables on the second floor and live music at the **Avalanche Niteclub** on the third floor. Brewery tours are available. Heavenly Daze is open from 11:00 to 2:00 A.M. daily; food is served until 10:00 P.M.

LODGING: Sky Valley Lodge.

DAY 3

Morning

BREAKFAST: Sky Valley Lodge.

The **Tread of Pioneers Museum** (800 Oak Street, Steamboat Springs; 970–879–2214) features a firearm collection that includes weapons owned by Steamboat Springs' founding family, the Crawfords. You'll also see a collection of chairs crafted from bighorn sheep, moose, and elk antlers. The museum is open daily from 11:00 A.M. to 5:00 P.M. Admission is $2.50 for adults, $2.00 for seniors, and $1.00 for children; kids six and under get in free. During summer, the museum offers a walking tour of town on Wednesdays. Meet at 9:30 A.M. on the front porch of the museum for this hour-long, guided tour.

LUNCH: Steamboat Brewery & Tavern (Fifth Street and Lincoln Avenue; 970–879–2233) offers specials such as barbecued brisket of beef, with roasted garlic mashed potatoes and chili gravy, and grilled marlin, with *Pico de Gallo* sauce and a Caesar salad. Weather permitting, enjoy lunch on the patio.

Afternoon

In the earlier days visitors skied into **Strawberry Park Hot Springs,** but today you can reach the springs via auto. Located 7 miles north of Steamboat on County Road 36 (Strawberry Park Road), Strawberry Park Hot Springs is a natural rock-lined spring fed by source water and creek water to create the perfect-for-soaking, 102-degree temperature. Tentsites and four cabins are available for overnight accommodations. For additional information contact Strawberry Park Hot Springs, P.O. Box 773332, Steamboat Springs, CO 80477; (970) 879–0342.

Return to Denver via U.S. 40 to Kremmling, Highway 9 south, I–70 east.

THERE'S MORE

Sleigh rides. Bar Lazy L Ranch (26480 RCR 52 E, Steamboat Springs, CO 80487; 970–879–0095) offers an evening dinner ride. Draft horses pull your sleigh over the countryside as you snuggle under a blanket. You'll dine western-style after arrival at this family-owned ranch. In summer, activities include horseback rides, private fishing along the Elk River, and chuck wagon dinners. Reservations are necessary.

Mountain biking. State-of-the-art mountain bikes, maps, and helmets are available for rent at the ski base area. Mountain bikers riding on Steamboat Ski Resort trails are required to wear helmets. There are 40 miles of mountain-bike trails to accommodate beginners and more advanced riders. Call the Summer Activity Center at the base of the Silver Bullet gondola in Gondola Square (970–879–6111) for information.

Hot-air ballooning. Pegasus Balloon Tours (P.O. Box 773462, Steamboat Springs, CO 80477; 970–879–9191 or 800–748–2487) offers early-morning rides in summer and morning or afternoon rides during colder months. Drift in a balloon over the Yampa Valley for a bird's-eye view of Steamboat Springs and the Flat Tops Wilderness Area.

Llama trekking. Pyramid Llama Ranch (P.O. Box 839, Hayden, CO 81639; 970–276–3348) offers day hikes and overnight camping trips. Llamas carry the gear as you enjoy the scenery.

Gondola. Ride on Steamboat's Silver Bullet eight-passenger gondola to get a grand view of the area. At the top you'll find mountain dining, a souvenir shop, and a fabulous panorama.

SPECIAL EVENTS

February. Winter Carnival. Steamboat throws an awesome party in the doldrums of winter. Inaugurated in 1914, this festival is billed as the oldest continuing winter festival west of the Mississippi.

June. Yampa River Festival. Celebrate spring runoff in a grand style with amateur and advanced competition and a "whitewater" rodeo.

Mid-June–mid-August. Steamboat Springs PRCA ProRodeo Series. On weekends professional cowboys show their stuff as they compete in bull riding, steer wrestling, and barrel racing. Begin the evening with a plateful of barbecue served at the booth near the stands and then settle in for a night of real rodeo entertainment.

July. Steamboat Cowboy Roundup Days. Held July 4. An authentic western celebration, with parades, fireworks, rodeos, and partying.

Rainbow Weekend. The Annual Hot Air Balloon Rodeo is a marvelous gala, featuring more than fifty brilliantly colored hot-air balloons. Request a wake-up call for 6:00 A.M., because you'll want to be in the middle of the action as crews inflate the balloons. Buy a cup of coffee from a vendor, sit back on your blanket, and watch as the balloons launch. One event calls for the pilot to maneuver close enough to pop a helium-filled weather balloon tethered above the ground. Admission is free.

July–early August. Strings in the Mountains features renowned musicians performing classical music, chamber music, jazz, country, or rhythm and blues in the Performing Arts Tent at Torian Plum, located near the base of the ski area. You'll be protected from the weather but feel as if you're in the great outdoors as you sip a glass of wine and listen to the performance. For more information on Strings in the Mountains, call (970) 879–5056.

Labor Day Weekend. Annual Vintage Auto Race. Vintage cars race on the difficult mountain streets of Steamboat Springs. Classic sports cars are displayed on the courthouse lawn in downtown Steamboat Springs.

September. Steamboat's Fall Foliage Festival and Mountain Brewfest. Polka bands, autumn hues, and beer highlight this fun-filled weekend.

OTHER RECOMMENDED RESTAURANTS AND LODGINGS

Steamboat Springs

Off the Beaten Path (56 Seventh Street; 970–879–6830) serves lunch and is a great bookstore as well. Choose quiche, soup, salad, or a sandwich. The bookstore-coffeehouse is open 7:00 A.M. to 9:00 P.M. daily.

Torian Plum (1855 Ski Time Square Drive, Steamboat Springs; 970–879–8811) is a luxury ski-in/ski-out property that offers convenience, hospitality, and European ambience. For reservations, call Steamboat Premier Properties, Ltd. (800) 228–2458.

Vista Verde Guest & Ski Touring Ranch (P.O. Box 465, Steamboat Springs, CO 80477; 800–526–7433 or 970–879–3858) is located 25 miles north of Steamboat Springs and offers gourmet meals, a secluded environment, and personalized service.

FOR MORE INFORMATION

Steamboat Ski and Resort Corporations, 2305 Mount Werner Circle, Steamboat Springs, CO 80487; (970) 879–6111.

Steamboat Springs Chamber Resort Association, P.O. Box 774408, Steamboat Springs, CO 80477; (970) 879–0880.

Steamboat Central Lodging Reservations; (800) 922–2722.

Colorado Dude and Guest Ranch Association, P.O. Box 300, Tabernash, CO 80478; (970) 887–3128.

DENVER AND POINTS EAST

DENVER AND POINTS EAST

Denver

CULTURE AND MORE

1 NIGHT

Art museum • Fine dining • Live theater • First-class shopping • Butterfly Pavilion and Insect Center • Denver Zoo

Sometimes the most fun is in your own backyard. Denver is perfect for an in-town getaway.

If you're a local, try being a tourist for a couple of days and take in the sights you've been meaning to visit for years. Tour the U. S. Mint, the Botanic Gardens, and the Colorado State Capitol. If you're an out-of-towner, check out places locals frequent. Spend an afternoon lounging in an overstuffed chair at the Tattered Cover Book Store or cheering the Colorado Rockies from a bargain seat in the "Rockpile" at Coors Field.

Located 5,280 feet above sea level, the Mile High City offers not only views of the towering Rocky Mountains but also professional sports, performing arts, extraordinary museums, and great shopping. With the opening of the $4.3 billion Denver International Airport in 1995, Denver attracted worldwide attention.

Still, as far as cities go, Denver is laid-back. Even with the sophisticated likes of Cherry Creek Shopping Center and the upscale restaurants, boutiques, and galleries of Lower Downtown (LoDo), Denver retains an unmistakably western flair. That's not to say that everyone rides a horse or that the only cultural event is rodeo.

Since the 1850s, when Denver was home to a dozen or so theaters, the city has had a love affair with the arts. Today the Mile High City boasts the Denver Performing Arts Complex, a 4-square-block network that is home to several performing arts organizations.

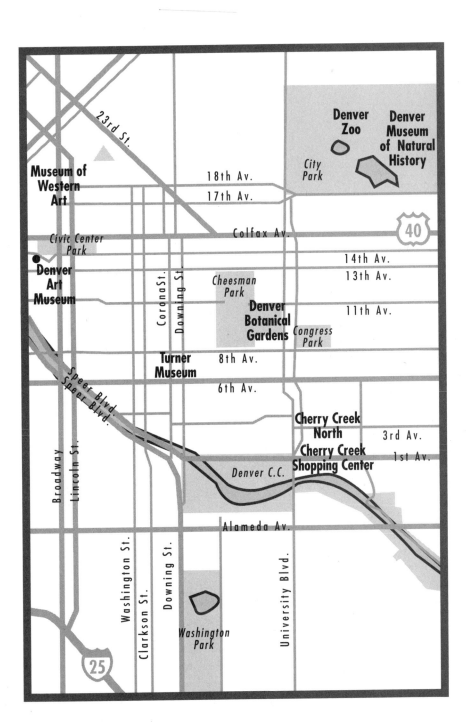

The following three Denver-getaway chapters focus on culture, history, and sports. Don't worry about finding things to do in Denver; rather, concern yourself with how you'll have time to do them all.

DAY 1

Morning

BREAKFAST: Many locals wouldn't dream of beginning their day without a cup of strong coffee and a pastry at **Starbucks** (303–388–7565), located at the corner of Second Avenue and Fillmore. Sitting in the heart of the action of Cherry Creek North Shopping District, this particular Starbucks is an ideal location for people-watching. Join other java lovers outside on the pleasant patio.

You could spend days or weeks exploring the boutiques and unique shops in **Cherry Creek North.** The streets of this trendy neighborhood are lined with fashionable restaurants and snazzy stores. Begin at the coolest of the cool, **The Wizard's Chest** (230 Fillmore; 303–321–4304), less than ½ block north of Starbucks. This one-of-a-kind toy store sells more than toys. You'll find computerized chess games, the latest in new and trendy playthings as well as old standbys like marbles and jacks, and an entire floor of costumes, masks, and makeup for children and adults. You won't find video games. The facade of the store looks like a castle.

For a truly unforgettable shopping experience at one of the best bookstores in the country, visit the **Tattered Cover Book Store** (2955 East First Avenue; 303–322–7727 or 800–833–9327). As Denver's premier bookstore, the Tattered Cover is famous for its superb service and extensive selection. Browsing and reading are encouraged, so sink into one of the comfy couches and curl up with a stack of books or magazines. The Tattered Cover is open daily from 9:00 A.M. to 11:00 P.M. and on Sundays from 10:00 A.M. to 6:00 P.M. **Fourth Story Restaurant and Bar** (303–322–1824), located on the fourth floor at the Tattered Cover, is a great spot for budding writers and authors to meet for lunch or dinner.

LUNCH: Bistro Adde Brewster (250 Steele, Denver; 303–388–1900) is a cozy cafe that exudes sophistication. The menu includes entrees such as Herbed Grilled Salmon with Basil Oil, served with Asparagus Risotto, and Lamb Chops with Braised Spinach and Artichokes. There's always the signature Bistro Burger to fall back on. Owner Adde Björklund knows how to work the room, moving from table to table and personally clearing plates and checking drinks. The restaurant is open for lunch from 11:30 A.M. to 5:00 P.M. and for dinner from 5:00 to 10:00 P.M. (the hours extend to 11:00 P.M. Friday and Saturday); closed Sunday.

Afternoon

With world-class shopping, stores such as Neiman Marcus, Lord & Taylor, and Saks Fifth Avenue, and more than one hundred shops and restaurants, it's no surprise that **Cherry Creek Shopping Center** (3000 East First Avenue) ranks among Denver's top tourist destinations, attracting about sixteen million visitors a year.

Featuring a large collection of Native American, western, and American art, the **Denver Art Museum** (100 West Fourteenth Avenue Parkway, Denver; 303–640–4433) is a must-see. Displays of Asian, pre-Columbian, and Spanish Colonial artwork have been recently upgraded. The Denver Art Museum is open Tuesday through Saturday from 10:00 A.M. to 5:00 P.M. and Sunday from noon to 5:00 P.M.; the museum is closed Monday. Admission is $4.50 for adults and $2.50 for seniors and students; children five and under are admitted free.

See where "money is made," at the **U.S. Mint** (320 West Colfax Avenue; 303–405–4761). The mint stamps forty million coins a day, adding up to eight billion coins a year. Free thirty-minute tours are available Monday through Friday from 8:00 A.M. to 2:45 P.M. (tours begin at 9:00 A.M. the last Wednesday of each month). The mint is closed on legal holidays.

DINNER: Tommy Tsunami's (1432 Market Street; 303–534–5050) attracts a crowd that is as polished as the decor of this hip restaurant. Surfboards hang from the ceiling; a motorcycle sits behind the bar; and a red neon sign flashes SAKE TO ME. The menu features sushi, hot or cold noodle bowls, and teriyaki, as well as entrees such as Asian bone-in rib eye pepper steak and macadamia-nut-crested Chilean sea bass.

Evening

To see an unparalleled blend of performing artists in a multifaceted facility, attend a production at the **Denver Performing Arts Complex,** a 4-block network that is located in the heart of downtown Denver and houses the Denver Center for the Performing Arts, the Colorado Symphony Orchestra, the Colorado Ballet, and Opera Colorado.

Boettcher Concert Hall, where the Colorado Symphony Orchestra and Opera Colorado perform, seats 2,634 and is the nation's first concert-hall-in-the-round. The **Temple Hoyne Buell Theatre,** which opened in 1991, is the newest theater in the complex. The **Helen G. Bonfils Theatre Complex** encompasses four smaller theaters, including the Stage, the Space, the Source, and the Ricketson. The **Garner Galleria Theatre** produces cabaret-style theater. For additional information on the Denver Center for the Performing Arts, call (303) 893–4000. For ticket information call (303) 893–4100. The Center Box Office is located at Fourteenth and Curtis.

To see premieres of New York Broadway and off-Broadway productions on a regional scale, attend a performance at **Theatre on Broadway** (13 South Broadway) or the **Phoenix Theatre** (1124 Santa Fe Drive). The Theatre Group (303–860–9360), which runs both, has brought new energy into the Denver theater scene. Productions run the gamut from cutting edge and sometimes scandalous to heartwarming and hilarious. The Theatre Group has received accolades and awards for its designers, directors, actors, and actresses. The 120-seat theaters sell out often, so call in advance for tickets.

LODGING: Loews Giorgio (4150 East Mississippi Avenue, Denver, CO 80222; 303–782–9300) is located in a contemporary black-glass structure. The hotel offers European charm and 183 guest rooms that are spacious and inviting. The lobby features original art, a hand-sculpted fireplace, and fresh-cut flowers. In the afternoon you'll find a tray of Italian cookies and wine available to guests in the Library Room next to the lobby.

DAY 2

Morning

BREAKFAST: For a hearty meal at an affordable price, begin your day at **Zaidy's Deli of Cherry Creek** (121 Adams, Denver; 303–333–5336). Black-and-white photographs on the wall of this light-filled cafe show Denver in the early 1900s. This family-owned, neighborhood deli serves fresh corned-beef hash, steak and eggs, and a Reuben omelet, along with plenty of other selections. Zaidy's is open Monday and Tuesday from 7:00 A.M. to 3:00 P.M., Wednesday through Friday from 7:00 A.M. to 8:00 P.M., and Saturday and Sunday from 8:00 A.M. to 7:00 P.M.

The **Denver Zoo,** located in Denver's City Park (East Twenty-third Street between York Street and Colorado Boulevard; 303–331–4100), is home to more than 2,500 animals. **Tropical Discovery,** a state-of-the-art rainforest housed in two glass pyramids, takes you down a winding pathway past waterfalls and along a tropical riverbank to a muggy marsh and a cypress swamp. The hot, humid climate and the sight of vampire bats or a Siamese crocodile make you feel as though you're exploring an equatorial jungle. **Primate Panorama** extends over seven acres and is home to howler monkeys, gorillas, and a six-ounce pygmy marmoset. With thick vegetation, thatched-roof huts, and waterfalls, the zoo offers an extensive and beautiful habitat for its more than 600 species.

LUNCH: Hungry Elephant, located near the Denver Zoo entrance, serves hamburgers, hot dogs, corn dogs, and tacos.

The Denver Zoo is open 365 days a year. From April 1 through September 30, hours are 9:00 A.M. to 6:00 P.M.; from October 1 through March 31, hours change to 10:00 A.M. to 5:00 P.M. Admission for persons ages thirteen and over is $6.00, children four to twelve are admitted for $3.00, and children three and under are admitted free.

Afternoon

To see what's blooming, visit the **Denver Botanic Gardens** (1005 York Street, Denver; 303–331–4000). No matter what time of year it is, you'll find this outdoor garden and tropical conservatory a serene spot. The Japanese Garden is particularly peaceful and is an excellent location for photographs. The Botanic Gardens are open daily from 9:00 A.M. to 5:00 P.M.; from May 1 through the end of September, hours extend to 8:00 P.M. Saturday through Tuesday. Admission is $4.00 for adults and $2.00 for seniors; children six and under are admitted free. During the Christmas season the Botanic Gardens feature **Blossoms of Lights,** a spectacular display of colorful lights in the shape of flowers.

THERE'S MORE

Park Meadows opened to rave reviews in 1996. Billed as a "retail resort," this dynamic center, with its Colorado mountain lodge atmosphere, will thrill shopping connoisseurs. Stone fireplaces, natural wood-beam ceilings, and more than $2 million in artwork create the total shopping experience. You'll find Denver's only Dillard's and the area's largest Foley's, as well as more than one hundred specialty shops and restaurants. Park Meadows is located at the intersection of I–25 and C–470.

Hudson Gardens (6303 South Santa Fe Drive, Littleton, CO 80120; 303–797–8565) is a superb, thirty-acre display garden located along the South Platte River in Littleton. Here you'll see rock gardens, colorful wildflowers, native shrubs, roses, waterfalls, and cacti in a setting so tranquil that you'll forget you're in the city. Don't miss the Secret Garden, located off the main pathway. Hudson Gardens is open Thursday, Saturday, and Sunday from 10:00 A.M. to 5:00 P.M. and Wednesday and Friday from 10:00 A.M. to 7:00 P.M.; the gardens are closed Monday and Tuesday. Admission is $4.00 for adults, $3.00 for seniors, and $2.00 for children ages six to twelve.

Butterfly Pavilion and Insect Center (6252 West Tenth Avenue, Westminster, CO 80020; 303–469–5441) is just fifteen minutes from downtown Denver. This incredible sanctuary is home to more than fifty species of butterflies. You'll feel as though you're exploring a rainforest bursting with brilliantly colored butterflies in the tropical temperature and lush foliage of the pavilion. The Insect Center provides a close-up look at tarantulas, cockroaches, mealworms, and other creepy-crawly things. The Butterfly Pavilion is open year-round Tuesday through Sunday from 9:00 A.M. to 5:00 P.M.

SPECIAL EVENTS

First Friday of every month. Sponsored by the Lower Downtown Arts District, this event is held the first Friday of each month throughout the year. Take a self-guided walking tour of the art galleries in Lower Downtown (LoDo), roughly defined as the northwestern edge of downtown.

July. Cherry Creek Arts Festival held Fourth of July weekend. This successful outdoor event is becoming one of the finest shows of its kind in the nation. Nearly 200 artists, who are chosen from 2,000-plus applicants, sell paintings, sculpture, photography, jewelry, and crafts. The arts festival takes place on the closed streets north of Cherry Creek Shopping Center and draws huge crowds, so be prepared to share the viewing venue with other festival-goers.

October. Denver International Film Festival, 1430 Larimer Square, attracts film lovers, actors, directors, and critics. This is an extremely popular event for locals, so call well in advance for a schedule and tickets. For information call the Denver Film Society at (303) 321–3456.

OTHER RECOMMENDED RESTAURANTS AND LODGINGS

Denver

The Tuscany Room, Loews Giorgio (4150 East Mississippi; 303–782–9300), features an excellent northern Italian menu in a romantic setting. The luxury decor, elaborate floral displays, crisp white linen tablecloths, and fine china and stemware of this candlelit room are matched by superb service and outstanding cuisine. Begin with an appetizer such as Calamari Fritti or Focaccia, followed by Caesar Salad or Tuscan White Bean Soup. Entrees include Spicy Chicken Linguine, Grilled Fillet of Salmon, and Spicy Orange Marinated Duck Breast, in addition to other selections. The Tuscany Room is open for breakfast, lunch, and dinner seven days a week. Brunch is served Sundays.

Denver Buffalo Company (1109 Lincoln Street, Denver, CO 80203; 303–832–0880) specializes in buffalo meat, considered to be low in fat and cholesterol, high in protein, and remarkably full of flavor. The restaurant has its own 14,000-acre ranch on the plains of eastern Colorado, where the bison graze. You can also order chicken, seafood, or pasta. Western artifacts fill the dining room, bar, and gift shop.

Cherry Cricket (2641 East Second Avenue, Cherry Creek North; 303–322–7666) is a lively local bar, with nineteen beers, including Guinness, on tap. The Cricket Burger and the chicken wings are all-time favorites, or you can order a No-Tofu sandwich or grilled meatloaf sandwich.

The Westin Hotel (1672 Lawrence Street, Denver, CO 80202; 303–572–9100 or 800–228–3000) deserves special mention. This fine hotel is beautifully decorated, is conveniently located in the heart of Denver, and offers theater and opera packages. The **Augusta Restaurant at the Westin** offers a spectacular view of the city, as well as an excellent breakfast and a superb Sunday brunch. The Augusta is open from 6:00 to 10:00 A.M. daily; brunch is served Sunday from 10:00 A.M. to 2:00 P.M.

Castle Marne (1572 Race Street, Denver CO 80206; 303–331–0621) describes itself as a luxury urban inn. As one of Denver's most imposing mansions, this B&B is furnished in authentic period antiques, yet it also offers modern amenities for business or pleasure travelers.

FOR MORE INFORMATION

Denver Metro Convention and Visitors Bureau, 1555 California Street, Denver CO 80202; (303) 892–1112 or (800) 645–3446.

ESCAPE TWO

DENVER AND POINTS EAST

Downtown Denver

A CAPITAL EXCURSION

1 NIGHT

*State-of-the-art library • Museums • Brown Palace Hotel
• Historic Larimer Square • State capitol*

For history buffs Denver is the ideal place to delve into the western past. The city is full of local lore and excellent museums. Denver's Museum of Natural History ranks as the fifth largest of its kind in the country. Specialized museums include the Denver Firefighters Museum and the Molly Brown House Museum.

In addition, visitors will find historic homes in residential neighborhoods, lovely old B&B inns brimming with tales of the past, and the grande dame of them all: the elegant, more-than-a-century-old Brown Palace Hotel. Royalty, celebrities, and politicians have spent the night at the Brown, but you don't need to be famous to be treated regally at this renowned hotel. From the magnificent lobby, with its shining marble floors and fresh flowers, to the genteel cigar room, with its leather chairs and rich atmosphere, the Brown Palace is gracious by any account.

Prices for lodging downtown may be a little higher than in the suburbs, but you'll observe much of what makes Denver unique by spending time in the downtown area.

DAY 1

Morning

BREAKFAST: If you go during the week, you'll get seated right away, but if you're there on Saturday or Sunday, the line may be out the door. **Dozens**

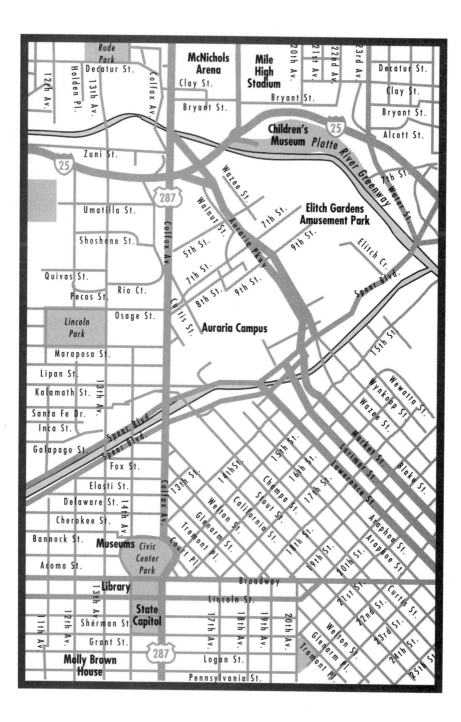

(236 West Thirteenth Avenue; 303–572–0066) packs them in for breakfast. Rock-bottom prices, a creative menu, and the casual atmosphere of this earthy restaurant appeal to the masses. Popular items include the Here's Your Aspen Omelet, served with avocado, tomato, and goat cheese, and Eggs Arnold, Dozens' version of eggs Benedict. Dozens is open from 6:30 A.M. to 2:00 P.M. daily.

An extravaganza of architecture, the $64 million **Denver Public Library** (Thirteenth Avenue and Broadway, Denver; 303–640–6200) opened in 1995 to excellent reviews. With its towers and turrets, the structure is one of the most distinctive and dramatic buildings in the city. Add to that the extraordinary collection of more than five million items and the result is a superior facility. The library is open Monday through Wednesday from 10:00 A.M. to 9:00 P.M., Thursday through Saturday from 10:00 A.M. to 5:30 P.M., and Sunday from 1:00 to 5:00 P.M.

Restored by the Colorado Historical Society, the **Byers-Evans House** (1310 Bannock Street; 303–620–4933) was formerly occupied by two prominent Denver families. William N. Byers, who founded the *Rocky Mountain News,* built the home in 1883. Six years later William Gray Evans, the son of Colorado's second territorial governor, John Evans, bought the home. The Evans family owned the home for ninety-five years before donating it to the Colorado Historical Society. Today you can tour the 2-story house, which exhibits furniture from the period 1912–1924. The Byers-Evans House is open Tuesday through Sunday from 11:00 A.M. to 3:00 P.M. and is closed Monday. Admission is $3.00 for adults, $2.50 for seniors, and $1.50 for persons ages six to sixteen.

Located in the carriage house of the Byers-Evans House is the **Denver History Museum** (303–620–4795), which details the city's colorful past, including Denver's gold-rush days. Laserdiscs allow visitors to electronically step back in time. Admission to the Byers-Evans House includes a visit to the Denver History Museum.

Colorado History Museum (1300 Broadway; 303–866–3682) tracks the past of fur trappers, miners, and pioneers of Colorado. Western photographs, dioramas, and old mining equipment are among the displays. The museum is open Monday through Saturday from 10:00 A.M. to 4:30 P.M. and Sunday from noon to 4:30 P.M.

LUNCH: "Take tea" at Denver's exquisite **Brown Palace Hotel** (321 Seventeenth Street, Denver; 303–297–3111). Afternoon tea takes place in the atrium lobby, where the entire scene brims with grace, charm, and the nostalgia of

Denver's skyline *sparkles in the early evening.*

(photo by Sherry Spitsnaugle).

yesterday. Sip properly steeped Earl Grey in a bone china teacup; nibble on dainty sandwiches, pastries, and scones with Devonshire cream; and listen to the soft tones of live harp and piano music. Afternoon Tea is served daily from 2:00 to 4:00 P.M. Reservations are a must, especially during the holidays. A Luncheon Tea, which includes a choice of entree salads, is also available daily, from noon to 2:00 P.M.

Afternoon

When it was completed in 1908, the **Colorado State Capitol** (200 East Colfax Avenue, Denver, CO 80203; 303–866–2604) was arguably the most impressive building downtown. Today, the Capitol with its gold-plated dome, remains a striking sight, especially as the light reflects off its 200 ounces of pure gold in the afternoon sun. The building's interior is a work of art, with rose onyx, brass banisters, stained glass, and a spiral staircase. People from around the world come to see the Women's Gold Tapestry, honoring women in Colorado history. Free tours of the capitol are available every thirty minutes weekdays from 9:30 A.M. to 3:30 P.M. and during the summer Monday through Saturday from 9:30 A.M. to 2:30 P.M. Don't miss the step located outside the building that marks the mile-high point, although the exact measurement continues to be a debate.

Train buffs and history enthusiasts will want to visit Denver's **Union Station** (1701 Wynkoop Street), a historic landmark that still functions with daily Amtrak service and has several shops and restaurants.

DINNER: If pizza is your idea of comfort food, you'll love **Josephina's Ristorante** (1433 Larimer Square; 303–623–0166). The National Champion Pizza, with spicy pepperoni, sausage, sweet red peppers, roasted garlic, fresh basil, red onion, and mozzarella, took first place in a national contest in Chicago in 1991. Or create your own pizza with items such as artichoke hearts, avocados, caramelized onions, and asparagus. The menu also features Italian favorites such as grilled eggplant marinara. For dessert, try tiramisù, espresso-soaked ladyfingers garnished with chocolate sauce and strawberries. Josephina's serves lunch and dinner daily Monday through Friday from 11:00 A.M. to 11:00 P.M. and on weekends from noon to midnight. The bar stays open later and features live music seven nights a week.

Evening

Before turning in, retreat to **The Churchill Bar,** located just off the atrium lobby of the Brown Palace Hotel (321 Seventeeth Street), for an after-dinner cocktail. Designed primarily as a cigar bar, this intimate room has enough atmosphere, appeal, and efficient ventilation that even nonsmokers will enjoy its rich ambience. Dark red leather wingback furniture, walls lined with books, soft lighting, and fine art create a library setting that's perfect for quiet conversation.

LODGING: The **Brown Palace Hotel,** 321 Seventeeth Street, Denver, CO 80202; (303) 297–3111. You won't even need to leave your lodging to take in some of Denver's history. The Brown Palace Hotel is one of the oldest, most distinguished hotels in the region. Well-heeled travelers of the early 1900s were pampered at the Brown, and today there's no skimping on indulgence either. Business or pleasure travel becomes utterly enjoyable in the sophisticated environment of this classy hotel. Even the concierge will remember you long after your first visit. With its graceful nineteenth-century architecture, its more than one hundred years of history, and its reputation for excellence, the Brown attracts celebrities, politicians, and Denver's avant-garde. Treat yourself to luxury and surround yourself with elegance at this fine hotel.

DAY 2

Morning

BREAKFAST: One step in the door and you know you'll be treated royally at **Ellyngton's** in the Brown Palace Hotel (303–297–3111). The waitstaff here doesn't overlook a single detail. Selections from the menu include eggs Benedict, crab Benedict, and coffee brewed with water from the hotel's private well. Sunday brunch at Ellyngton's is famous for live jazz, good food, and Dom Pérignon.

If you can't get an overnight reservation at the Brown Palace, you'll want to at least walk through the exquisite lobby, or better yet, take a tour. Complimentary guided tours are available Wednesdays and Saturdays at 2:00 P.M. You can take a self-guided tour at any time. Stop at the concierge desk to pick up a brochure. For more information call the Brown Palace at (303) 297–3111.

To savor a taste of true Denver history, scout out historic **Larimer Square,** located between Fourteenth and Fifteenth Streets on Larimer. As Denver's oldest block, Larimer Street was at one time a disreputable and run-down area. Today Larimer Square thrives with unique shops, upscale restaurants, and refurbished brick Victorian buildings. Hanging flower baskets, open courtyards, and classical music playing from outdoor speakers add to Larimer Square's charm. From here you can take a horse-drawn carriage ride up the 16th Street Mall or through Lower Downtown.

For western furniture, cowboy stuff, and "cowkid" clothes, don't miss **Cry Baby Ranch** (1422 Larimer Square; 303–623–3979). This store is a great place to browse and remember the good old days when Roy Rogers was a superstar.

LUNCH: A few years ago the idea of salmon served with Fruit Salsa or Hunan Peanut Barbecue Sauce would have been considered overly exotic. Today **Cadillac Ranch** (1400 Larimer Square, Denver, CO 80202; 303–820–2288) succeeds with innovative dishes, as well as a few standbys. The menu here reads IN STEAK WE TRUST, and has items such as smoked prime rib, angel hair pasta with spicy buffalo sausage, and Route 66 Rotisserie Chicken. Sit on one of the saddle seats at the bar. Cadillac Ranch is

open from 11:00 A.M. to 11:00 P.M. Monday through Friday; from 11:00
A.M. to midnight Saturday; and from 10:00 A.M. to 11:00 P.M. Sunday.

Afternoon

For a close-up look at dinosaurs, visit **The Denver Museum of Natural
History** in City Park (2001 Colorado Boulevard, Denver; 303–322–7009).
Prehistoric Journey, the $7 million permanent exhibit at the museum,
chronicles prehistoric life in an animated process complete with life-size
dinosaurs and bellowing sound effects. The presentation captivates visitors as
they learn about the several-billion-year history of life on earth. On the other
museum floors, you'll see dioramas depicting animals in their habitats. The
Denver Museum of Natural History is open daily from 9:00 A.M. to 5:00 P.M.
except for Fridays, when hours are from 9:00 A.M. to 9:00 P.M. Admission is
$6.00 for adults, $4.00 for seniors and children ages three to twelve. A visit to
Gates Planetarium is included in the museum price. **IMAX Theater,**
located next to the museum, features films so realistic on its 4½-story screen
that you'll feel as though you're in the middle of the action.

THERE'S MORE

Cultural Connection Trolley. Get onboard and see the sights of Denver
   with a $3.00 all-day pass that is also valid on Light Rail and local RTD
   (Regional Transportation District) buses. Buy your ticket at several locations, including the RTD Market Street Station (at 16th Street Mall and
   Market Street), and the Ticket Bus (at 16th Street Mall and Curtis Street).
   The trolley runs during the summer months. For more information call
   (303) 299–6000. The City Connection combines information about major
   attractions, offers discounts on entrance fees, and has specially designed
   maps of downtown and metro Denver, along with a one-day pass for use
   on the trolley and RTD. Call (303) 388–1919 for information.
Molly Brown House Museum (1340 Pennsylvania Street, Denver, CO
   80203; 303–832–4092) was once the residence of the colorful character
   known as the "Unsinkable Molly Brown," whose place in history was
   firmly established when she survived the *Titanic* disaster of 1912. Today
   women clothed in 1900s period dress will escort you through this gorgeous Victorian mansion and historical landmark. The museum is open
   Monday through Saturday from 10:00 A.M. to 4:00 P.M. and Sunday from

noon to 4:00 P.M. A forty-five minute tour is available during museum hours; the last tour of the day begins at 3:30 P.M. Admission is $5.00 for adults, $3.50 for seniors, and $1.50 for children six to twelve. The museum is closed Monday during winter.

Black American West Museum and Heritage Center (3091 California Street, Denver, CO 80205; 303–292–2566) chronicles the lives of African Americans who settled the West, through an excellent collection of photographs, books, and artifacts. The museum is open weekdays from 10:00 A.M. to 5:00 P.M. and weekends from noon to 5:00 P.M. Admission is $3.00 for adults, $2.00 for seniors; $1.00 for persons ages thirteen to seventeen; 50 cents for children four to twelve; and free to children three and under.

Denver Firefighters Museum (1326 Tremont Place; 303–892–1436) has antique fire engines and firefighting equipment. You'll also learn the history of firefighting in Denver. The museum is open Monday through Friday from 10:00 A.M. to 2:00 P.M. and on Saturday during summer. Admission is $3.00 for adults and $2.00 for children ages two to sixteen.

Four Mile Historic Park (715 South Forest Street, Denver CO 80222; 303–399–1859) tells the story of pioneer life as it was on the plains in the late 1800s and early 1900s. This fourteen-acre farm has horses, chickens, and crops, as well as volunteers who demonstrate quilting, spinning, and other skills of the era. Four Mile Historic Park is open from 10:00 A.M. to 4:00 P.M. Wednesdays through Sundays and is closed Mondays and Tuesdays. Admission is $3.50 for adults, and $2.00 for seniors and persons ages six to sixteen.

SPECIAL EVENTS

April. Easter Sunrise Service is attended by thousands at Red Rocks Amphitheater, the spectacular outdoor arena located in the midst of towering red sandstone rocks. Take your stadium blanket and coffee and settle in for an inspiring service. For information call (303) 892–1505.

May. Cinco de Mayo attracts in excess of 200,000 people to Civic Center Park, where mariachi bands perform and vendors sell food and craft items.

July. During Buffalo Bill Days in Golden, celebrate the life and times of western hero Buffalo Bill with a Wild West show, burro races, a parade, and games. For information call (303) 279–3113.

September. Oktoberfest in Larimer Square highlights include beer, brats, strudel, oompah bands, and dancers decked in lederhosen. For more information call (303) 607–1276.

December. Denver boasts one of the world's largest outdoor Christmas displays when the City and County Building (1460 Cherokee Street) becomes an illuminated showpiece with thousands of multicolored lights. The decorations have been a Denver tradition for more than seventy years, and the lights have become a cherished custom for locals.

OTHER RECOMMENDED RESTAURANTS AND LODGINGS

Denver

Ruth's Chris Steak House (1445 Market Street, Denver CO 80202; 303–446–2233) specializes in U.S. prime beef that you can be assured will be prepared to perfection. Mouth-watering meals are served in the refined atmosphere of the sumptuous dining room. Ruth's Chris also serves seafood and a range of tempting desserts.

Strings (1700 Humboldt Street; 303–831–7310) has plenty of clout and cachet on the Denver restaurant scene. Come any night and you're likely to see businessmen in dark suits and women in cocktail dresses. The menu offers appetizers such as crab cakes and roasted mussels and entrees that include black pepper linguine and pan-seared mahimahi.

Pint's Pub (221 West Thirteenth Avenue, Denver, CO 80204; 303–534–7543) has a serious beer menu. Choose from twenty-five draught beers and a huge selection of single-malt scotch whisky. Wine lovers may be disappointed at the choice of two wines: red or white. The food menu offers broiled fish-and-chips, bangers and mash, and sheepherder's stew.

Lumber Baron Inn (2555 West Thirty-seventh Avenue, Denver, CO 80211; 303–477–8205 or 800–697–6552) was voted Denver's best place for a romantic night. Restored to the tune of $1 million, this ornate 3-story house is located minutes from downtown Denver. Rates begin at $125.

Adam's Mark Hotel (1550 Court Place, Denver, CO 80202; 303–893–3333) has recently expanded to feature more than 1,200 rooms. The hotel offers three ballrooms, convention facilities, and banquet space.

Embassy Suites (1881 Curtis Street, Denver, CO 80202; 303–297–8888) has more than 300 luxury guest suites and access to the adjacent Athletic

Club at Denver Place, which offers racquetball, squash, and basketball courts; an indoor swimming pool; and an indoor running track.

FOR MORE INFORMATION

Denver Metro Convention and Visitors Bureau, 1555 California Street, Denver CO 80202; (303) 892–1112 or (800) 645–3446. Request the free, 108-page color guide to Denver.

DENVER AND POINTS EAST

Lower Downtown (LoDo)

SPORTS TOWN AND MICROBREW CITY U.S.A.

1 NIGHT

*Professional football, hockey, baseball, and basketball
• Bicycling, golf • Brewpubs and billiards • Amusement park •
Tour of baseball park • Hot jazz*

Living it up in downtown Denver is sheer pleasure. Even seasoned travelers delight in this vibrant area that is the heartbeat of the city. Visitors to Denver's redeveloped Lower Downtown (LoDo) will find much to praise: art galleries, first-class dining, lively brewpubs, and a sophisticated yet easygoing charm.

As sports fans, Coloradans rank among the most loyal in the country. Denver is one of ten cities in the United States with all four major league sports: NFL Broncos, NBA Nuggets, NHL Avalanche, and MLB Colorado Rockies. Denverites are devoted sports participants as well as spectators. On any given day you'll see joggers, in-line skaters, bicyclists, and walkers.

Beer connoisseurs will have a field day downtown. As home to the largest brewpub in the United States (the Wynkoop Brewing Company), Denver boasts more than forty microbrews to sample.

As you explore and discover the charm of downtown Denver, it will lure you back time after time.

DAY 1

Morning

If you're traveling north on I–25, exit Auraria Parkway and follow the signs to **Lower Downtown.** Traveling south on I–25, exit Speer Boulevard South. Once you arrive downtown, let the valet at The Oxford Hotel (your

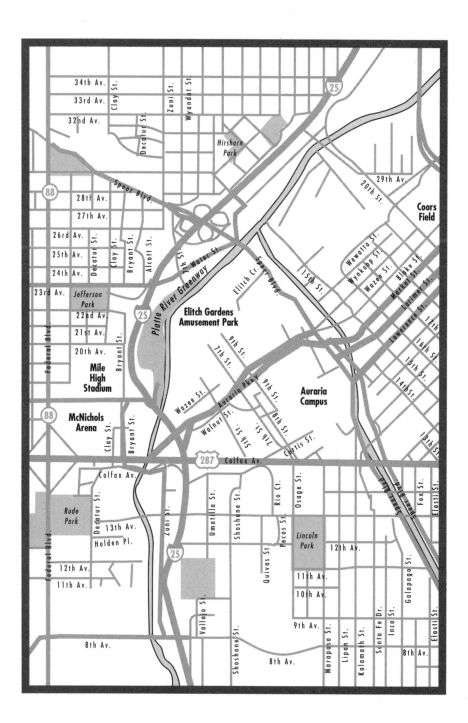

lodging for this evening; 1600 Seventeenth Street) park your car. Then forget about it for the weekend. You can walk, take the free Sixteenth Street Shuttle, or have the hotel's limousine take you where you want to go.

LUNCH: Beer is serious business at **Wynkoop** (that's WIN-koop) **Brewing Company,** located on the corner of Eighteenth and Wynkoop (that's WINE-koop); (303) 297–2700. Stop in and hoist a pint of Railyard Ale, have lunch, and relax in this trendy local favorite. Just don't plan on having an intimate conversation during Friday-evening happy hour, when this popular pub really gets lively. Laying claim to the titles of being Denver's first brewpub and North America's largest, the Wynkoop brewed and sold more than 5,000 barrels in 1995. When the business opened in 1988, founders pronounced the name "Win-Koop" rather than "Wine-Koop," like the street, and with a tongue-in-cheek attitude explained that they make beer, not wine. The pronunciation and the brewery's excellent reputation have stuck.

The Wynkoop chalks up another victory with its consistently excellent food. The menu ranges from basics such as fish-and-chips (dipped in Railyard Ale batter) to baked Atlantic salmon. Burgers, shepherd's pie, salads, and soup are also good selections. Billiards on the second floor attracts a huge pool-playing crowd, as well as a fair share of spectators. The handsome mahogany tables, exposed brick walls, and low lighting create the perfect ambience for an afternoon or evening game. You can also opt for shuffleboard, darts, or Foosball.

Afternoon

Walk to the **Tabor Center,** located at Sixteenth and Lawrence, and check out the stores and the architectural design of this unique, glass-enclosed, three-level shopping center. You'll find interesting vendor carts throughout the Tabor Center, as well as specialty shops and major retailers.

Cruise the **16th Street Mall,** an outdoor shopping district filled with cafes, food vendors, and clothing and souvenir stores. The mile-long mall has fountains, flowers, benches, and a passing parade of shoppers, business executives, and the occasional street entertainer. A free shuttle bus runs up and down the mall.

Get a behind-the-scenes look by touring **Coors Field,** home of the Colorado Rockies Baseball Club. Located on the corner of Twentieth and Blake Streets, this ballpark is not only handsome but also user-friendly. Tours are offered year-round and include visits to the club level, suite level, press area, visitors' clubhouse, and visitors' dugout. Call (303) 762–5437 to purchase tickets in advance.

DINNER: Morton's of Chicago (1710 Wynkoop, Denver, CO 80202; 303–825–3353) has perfected the formula of fine dining. Genteel, classy, and intimate, this restaurant tops the list. You'll find professional service, exquisite cuisine, and elegant surroundings at this first-class establishment that attracts the city's elite.

Start with an appetizer such as smoked Pacific salmon or sautéed wild mushrooms. The specialty of the house is beef, although the menu includes whole baked Maine lobster, lemon oregano chicken, and domestic rib lamb chops. Choose from entrees such as porterhouse steak, double filet mignon, and tenderloin brochette, cooked precisely to your liking. Save room for the Godiva hot chocolate cake with a liquid chocolate center, served with Häagen-Dazs vanilla ice cream. Morton's is open for dinner only.

Evening

For late-night conversation in a chic cigar room, stop in at **Trios Enoteca** (1730 Wynkoop Street; 303–293–2887). Enoteca is a Greek word meaning "wine library." This spot has a selection of more than sixty wines served by the glass as well as a few appetizers.

Jive the night away at **El Chapultepec** (1962 Market Street; 303–295–9126), the dive where President Bill Clinton stopped in to play a few notes on a borrowed saxophone when he was on the campaign trail in Denver. This funky, smoky bar is the coolest place in town to hear hot jazz. El Chapultepec has live music seven nights a week from 9:00 P.M. to 1:00 A.M. and is open daily from 7:00 A.M. to 2:00 A.M.

LODGING: The Oxford Hotel (1600 Seventeenth Street, Denver, CO 80202; 303–628–5400) offers a congenial retreat from the hustle and bustle of the city, and you'll find every amenity necessary for a secure and pleasant stay. Located in historic Lower Downtown Denver, The Oxford is within walking distance of Larimer Square, Coors Field, and numerous galleries and restaurants. Built in 1891 and renovated in 1983, this classic hotel is listed on the National Register of Historic Places. The lobby features marble floors, a gorgeous marble fireplace, and Baby Doe Tabor's piano. Enjoy a complimentary afternoon glass of sherry as you lounge in a wingback chair in the lobby. Rooms are decorated with English and French antiques, and the triple-sheeted beds are sheer indulgence. The hotel offers complimentary limousine service in the downtown area. Ask about special offers such as the Rockies Baseball Package or the Bubbles, Bed, and Breakfast Package, which, for $139 per couple, includes a deluxe room, a bottle of champagne, and breakfast in bed. Visit the full-service Oxford/Aveda Spa and Salon for a massage, or stop at The Oxford Club to work out with a personal trainer.

A walk through the **Cruise Room,** the restored bar next to the hotel's lobby, is a must. If you can find a seat, order a cocktail and enjoy the ambience of this local landmark, which is Art Deco at its finest.

DAY 2

Morning

BREAKFAST: **McCormick's Fish House** (303–825–1107), located in the same building as The Oxford, changes its menu daily, but you'll find entrees such as Denver omelets and Idaho rainbow trout from which to select. This popular restaurant, with its warm, wooden decor and comfortable streetside booths, is the perfect place to meet with friends or dine on your own. McCormick's is open daily from 6:30 A.M. to 2:00 P.M. for breakfast and lunch and from 5:00 to 10:00 P.M. for dinner. Brunch is served Sunday from 7:00 A.M. to 2:00 P.M.

At any time of the day, expect to find lots of action at **The Market** (1445 Larimer Street; 303–534–5140), an ideal spot for a midmorning cup of coffee and a pastry. Read the newspaper or people-watch at this Denver institution that buzzes.

If you're a literature lover, look no further. The **Tattered Cover Book Store** (1628 Sixteenth Street, Denver; 303–436–1070) has it all. This location is not as busy as the Tattered Cover Book Store in Cherry Creek, but it's just as wonderful. You can spend hours browsing the three floors of this incredibly well-stocked store. Don't miss the Travel Alcove on the first floor, which has a comprehensive selection of maps, globes, books, and comfortable couches. The Tattered Cover in LoDo is open from 9:00 A.M. to 9:00 P.M. Monday through Thursday from 9:00 A.M. to 11:00 P.M. Friday and Saturday, and from 10:00 A.M. to 6:00 P.M. Sunday.

LUNCH: You don't have to be a sports nut to enjoy the **Denver Chop-House and Brewery** (1735 Nineteenth Street, Denver; 303–296–0800). Located next door to Coors Field, the Denver ChopHouse is a great stop before going to a Colorado Rockies game, or any other time for that matter.

The microbrews are fresh, the potatoes are hand-mashed, and the pizzas are piled high. Call early for a reservation if you go on game day.

THERE'S MORE

Elitch Gardens Amusement Park (299 Walnut Street, Denver, CO 80204; 303–595–4FUN), in its new location near downtown Denver, has sixty-seven fun-filled acres. You'll find flower gardens, a 300-foot-tall tower with views of Denver and the Rocky Mountains, the Twister II Roller Coaster, and scads of other rides. Elitch Gardens has been in operation since 1890. The amusement park is open late May through early September, Sunday through Thursday from 10:00 A.M. to 10:00 P.M. and Friday and Saturday from 10:00 A.M. to 11:00 P.M. Admission is $19.95 for adults, $15.00 for seniors, and $9.95 for children ages three to seven. The fee allows unlimited rides.

Major league baseball. As one of two expansion teams added to the National League in 1993, the Colorado Rockies continue to break records for fan attendance. Coors Field, at Blake and Twentieth Streets, has been described as the best ballpark in the country. For Rockies tickets call (303) 762–5437. Ask about bargain seats in the "Rockpile."

Basketball. The Denver Nuggets professional basketball team plays at McNichols Arena and regularly hosts family evenings with special package deals. The season runs November through April. For ticket information call (303) 893–6700.

Football. Coloradans love their Denver Broncos, the 1998 Super Bowl Champions. If you're lucky enough to find a ticket to a game, you'll know why. Cheering the Broncos at Mile High Stadium on a crisp autumn afternoon with 76,000 other devoted fans is electrifying. For information call (303) 433–7466.

Hockey. Winner of the 1996 Stanley Cup, the Colorado Avalanche has also won the hearts of fans here. Hockey season runs from October through June. For tickets call (303) 893–6700.

Coors Brewery (Thirteenth and Ford Streets, Golden, CO 80401; 303–277–BEER) hosts free thirty-minute tours of its facility. You'll have a chance to sample Coors on tap. The brewery is open Monday through Saturday from 10:00 A.M. to 4:00 P.M.

Bicycling. Denver has an excellent trail system, with 415 miles of trails for bicyclists, walkers, and in-line skaters. Try the Cherry Creek Trail, which

runs from Confluence Park through downtown Denver to Cherry Creek
Reservoir. You can access the bike trail from ramps situated along Speer
Boulevard and First Avenue.

Golf. Inverness Hotel & Golf Club (200 Inverness Drive West, Englewood,
CO 80112; 303–799–5800) offers a championship golf course, tennis
courts, indoor and outdoor swimming pools, and upscale accommodations, all in a resort atmosphere. In addition, Denver's city golf courses are
a bargain. Reservations can be made by calling (303) 784–4000.

SPECIAL EVENTS

January. The National Western Stock Show and Rodeo brings out the cowboy or cowgirl in everyone. Rodeos, cattle auctions, livestock exhibitions,
and horse shows attract locals and visitors from around the country. Dress
in your western duds and join in the fun. The stock show takes place at
the Denver Coliseum, off I–70. Call (303) 297–1166 for information.

March. The St. Patrick's Day Parade in Denver is the city's largest annual
parade. Marching bands, horses, floats, and stagecoaches take to the streets
of downtown Denver to celebrate.

October. The Great American Beer Festival attracts beer lovers and beer
makers from around the world. Experts judge the top brews and award
gold, silver, and bronze medals in thirty-two categories. Taste a one-
ounce sample of nearly 1,000 different beers, including lagers, ales,
porters, and stouts. For information call (800) 645–3446.

OTHER RECOMMENDED RESTAURANTS AND LODGINGS

Denver

The Buckhorn Exchange (1000 Osage Street; 303–534–9505) is legendary
for its display of elk, buffalo, and bear trophies. As Denver's oldest restaurant, The Buckhorn Exchange offers choice beef, barbecued pork ribs, and
the occasional rattlesnake appetizer. You will need to loosen your belt a
notch or two here. Each February the restaurant celebrates Buffalo Bill's
birthday with a look-alike contest and other events.

Wazee Lounge and Supper Club (at the corner of Fifteenth and Wazee
Streets; 303–623–9518) has an atmosphere worthy of its steady stream of
clientele, whose members include artists, theatergoers, and social gatherers.
The black-and-white tile floor, mahogany bar, and stained-glass windows
above the bar create a classic 1930s mood. The Wazee claims to be the

"Source of the Best Pizza in the Civilized World." You can also choose from items such as a Philadelphia steak sandwich or a hot tuna sandwich on rye.

Hyatt Regency Denver (1750 Welton Street, Denver, CO 80202; 303–295–1234 or 800–233–1234) offers not only spacious accommodations but also a microbrewery walking tour. The package includes lodging at the Hyatt and free tasting at Breckenridge Brewery, Wynkoop Brewing Company, Champion Brewing Company, Rock Bottom Brewery, and the Denver ChopHouse.

Queen Anne Inn (2147 Tremont Place, Denver, CO 80205; 303–296–6666), fashioned in the Queen Anne style, offers both posh surroundings and convenient access to downtown Denver.

FOR MORE INFORMATION

Denver Metro Convention and Visitors Bureau, 1555 California Street, Denver, CO 80202; (303) 892–1112 or (800) 645–3446.

DENVER AND POINTS EAST

Stratton

THE ROAD LESS TRAVELED

1 NIGHT

Luxury B&B • Classic Car Museum • Golf
• Old-fashioned carousel
• Bike riding

If you've never considered heading east of Denver to vacation, the elegant Claremont Inn in Stratton may change your mind. As you motor through the vast flatland stretches, a couple of hours east of Denver, you will see a dignified structure standing tall on the prairie.

Luxurious, quiet, and classy, the Claremont can best be described as a destination B&B. This stylish inn offers all the amenities you could want and more. Rooms are private hideaways in themselves, and you can retreat here in grand comfort. Kick back in the sumptuous, red brocade chairs in the private Claremont Theater, or relax with a glass of cabernet and listen to classical music in the well-stocked, cozy wine cellar. Every inch of this inn is tastefully decorated, and you'll want to indulge in its sophistication.

When you're ready to explore, check out Stratton's Classic Car Museum. Take the inn's bicycle-built-for-two for a spin around town (population 650) or play a few holes of golf at the Stratton Municipal Golf Course. Ride the restored 1905 carousel and visit historic Old Town in nearby Burlington.

It doesn't take long to slow your pace and settle into a relaxed mood. You may want to simply admire the sunset from the inn's terrace or stroll the grounds. The peace and quiet of the wide open spaces are a prescription for urban stress, and before you know it you'll be scheduling your return trip.

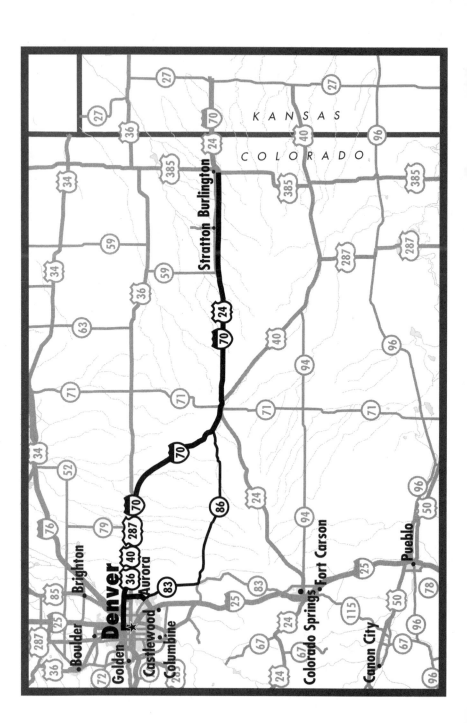

DAY 1

Morning

Take the **scenic route** from Denver south on Parker Road (Highway 83) and follow the Old Smoky Hill Trail in the midst of rolling meadows and ponderosa pines.

BREAKFAST: Eat at the western-style **Bandana's Cafe** (19552 East Mainstreet, Parker; 303–841–7179). The cafe is open daily for breakfast from 7:00 to 11:00 A.M. Monday through Friday and from 8:00 A.M. to noon on weekends. Try the Bullpen Burrito, *huevos rancheros,* or the delicious Parker Benedict. **KJ's Coffee** (10970 South Parker Road; 303–841–4975) is another breakfast option. Open daily from 6:30 A.M. to 6:00 P.M.

Across the street and east of Bandana's is **Mountain Man Nut and Fruit Company** (19565 Mainstreet; 303–841–0915). The gift store has a nice selection of nuts and fruits, candies, trail mixes, dried fruits, and chocolates. The store is open Monday through Friday from 9:00 A.M. to 6:00 P.M. and Saturday from 9:00 A.M. to 5:30 P.M; it's closed Sunday except during the Christmas season.

Continue south on Highway 83 until you reach Highway 86. Turn east at Franktown. For a short hike, detour south on Highway 83 about 4½ miles south of Franktown to **Castlewood Canyon State Park.** Parking is across the bridge to the south. Stop at the visitor center and purchase a $4.00 per vehicle pass. The park offers some easy hiking trails. For more information call (303) 688–5242.

Return to Franktown and continue east on Highway 86. You'll drive through the scenic Black Forest on a two-lane highway that has little traffic. You'll pass through the small towns of Elizabeth and Kiowa before intersecting with I–70 east about ten miles north of Limon.

Continue east on I–70 past Stratton 17 miles to Burlington.

Afternoon

Visit the **Kit Carson County Carousel and Old Town** in Burlington. From the Burlington exit take Lincoln Street to Rose Avenue; continue north on Fourteenth Street, and signs will direct you to the carousel.

The carousel was carved in 1905 by the Philadelphia Toboggan Company and is now a National Historic Landmark. A Wurlitzer Monster Military Band Organ plays tapes of marches, waltzes, and polkas. Rides are 25 cents per person, and the fully restored carousel operates from 1:00 to 8:00 P.M. daily, Memorial Day to Labor Day. For additional information write Kit Carson County Carousel Association, P.O. Box 28, Stratton, CO 80836.

Old Town in Burlington is a collection of historic buildings filled with antiques. During summer you'll find cancan shows, melodramas, and a soda fountain that serves floats and hand-dipped sundaes. Old Town is open year-round from 9:00 A.M. to 6:00 P.M. Monday through Saturday and from noon to 6:00 P.M. Sunday. For additional information call (800) 288–1334.

Return to Stratton via I–70 west.

DINNER: Claremont Inn, 800 Claremont Drive, Stratton; (719) 348–5125 or (888) 291–8910. Formal dinner at the Claremont is available on Saturday evenings and includes four courses, wine, and tea or coffee. The kitchen is supervised by innkeeper Dave Dischner, who trained at the Cooking School of the Rockies in Boulder, as well as in France and New York. Weather permitting, the staff will serve your gourmet meal on the terrace overlooking the plains of eastern Colorado. If the temperature is a bit chilly, you'll dine indoors, but you'll still have great views.

If you prefer, you can call ahead for a gourmet wine and cheese basket for dinner from the Claremont. A picnic of salads, fresh-baked crusty French bread, cold meats, cheeses, and a dessert such as chocolate mousse cake is available every evening except Saturday. You can also select a bottle of wine or cider from the wine cellar. Find a quiet spot on the terrace or the inn's backyard to enjoy your picnic.

LODGING: Claremont Inn Bed and Breakfast, 800 Claremont Drive, Stratton, CO 80836; (719) 348–5125 or (888) 291–8910. Hosts Dave and Sharon Dischner seem to have a sixth sense about their guests' interests, whether those be privacy, chatting about eastern Colorado, or needing a recommended route for a bicycle ride. This establishment is a class act, and you'll delight in any one of its seven lavishly decorated suites. Each room comes with a whirlpool tub and walk-in shower, thick bathrobes, a television, and a VCR.

The Colorado Room has expansive views of the wide-open spaces to the west and is decorated in a perfect blend of whimsy and good taste. Fish and bear accessories enhance this large suite decorated in a fishing lodge motif. The headboard of natural hickory graces the queen-size bed, and the fabric covering the deep-seated sofa (which makes into a queen sleeper) features fishing and hunting scenes. The hand-carved, hand-painted fish that hangs on the wall reads CLAREMONT INN, WORMS 5 CENTS.

The Out of Kansas Suite is decorated in a British Colonial motif with a four-poster bamboo queen bed, a sea-grass carpet, and a fanciful monkey lamp. The bathroom has a wooden cheetah standing guard and white mosquito netting over the tub.

The Waverly Room, recently featured in *Country Inns* magazine, is a favorite with guests. The room is so named because of the Waverly fabrics and wallcoverings. This suite has a blend of rose-colored florals, stripes, and plaids and includes a combination of antique and contemporary furnishings.

Ask about the **wine tastings** that take place in the Claremont's garden-level wine cellar. Here you can relax in the comfortable surroundings as you sip wines from around the world. The Claremont also hosts **Murder Mystery Weekends,** when guests dress in character and solve a whodunit plot. Each weekend features a different focus, such as a 1920s theme. Props, a script, and costumes are provided, and guests vote on their favorite actor, who is then awarded a complimentary night at the inn.

Rooms at the Claremont start at $89 Sunday through Thursday. Weekend rates begin at $119. Prices include a full breakfast.

DAY 2

Morning

BREAKFAST: Claremont Inn Bed and Breakfast. A pot of coffee and a newspaper will arrive at your doorstep in the early morning. Breakfast is served from 7:00 to 10:00 A.M. in the light-filled dining area near the kitchen. Huge windows provide prairie views as you enjoy fresh fruit, coffee, juice, muffins, and croissants. The entree may be an egg frittata with sausage or bacon; French toast; or scrambled eggs with fresh herbs, plus cheese and Belgian waffles. This sunny room, decorated in a floral and country motif, is a great breakfast location.

Take a spin through Stratton on the inn's unique side-by-side **bicycle-built-for-two.** Locals wave and smile as you pedal your way down Colorado Avenue.

LUNCH: Stop in at the family-owned Dischner's Super Valu (216 Colorado Avenue; 719–348–5518) to stock up on picnic items. Then head to **Stratton**

City Park, several blocks north of the Claremont. The park has a pool, tennis courts, a gazebo, and lots of areas in which to picnic or explore.

Return to Denver via I–70 west.

Afternoon

Stop in at **Denver International Airport** (DIA) for a self-guided tour of this incredible facility. Take Peña Boulevard from I–70 and follow the signs to DIA. The art displayed at DIA is one of the most impressive and largest public art programs in the country. Visitors will learn interesting details, such as the fact that the total area of DIA is 53 square miles and that 2.5 million cubic yards of concrete were used to construct five runways, taxiways, and aprons. Since you don't have to run to catch a flight, you can shop, dine, browse, and people-watch. Pick up a map at the Visitors Information Desk, or call ahead and it will be mailed.

THERE'S MORE

Weekend cooking classes are offered at the Claremont. Check in Friday evening and enjoy cocktails and a buffet supper. After breakfast Saturday morning, culinary techniques are taught in the state-of-the-art kitchen. You'll sample your efforts during a leisurely two-hour lunch and then return to class. A formal dinner is served in the evening. For information contact Claremont Inn Bed and Breakfast, 800 Claremont Drive, Stratton, CO 80836; (719) 348–5125 or (888) 291–8910.

Classic Car Museum (818 Colorado Avenue, Stratton; 719–348–5141), has more than fifty antique cars, trucks, and tractors. You'll see a 1957 Chevrolet two-door hardtop and a 1938 Twin City Tractor. The museum is open from 9:00 A.M. to 5:00 P.M. Monday through Saturday. Admission is $4.00 for adults, $2.00 for children ages eleven to fourteen, and free for kids ten and under.

Golf. The 9-hole course at the Stratton Golf Club (719–348–5412) is a fairly flat course, with views that stretch for miles.

SPECIAL EVENTS

June. Parker Country Festival. This festival celebrates summer with a pancake breakfast, live bands, a parade, a tractor pull, a bed race, a talent show, and carnival rides. For information call (303) 841–4268.

October. For the truly addicted ask about the Claremont Inn's Chocolate

Lovers' Weekend. Every meal (breakfast too) includes chocolate. This is a great couples' weekend, and you'll be able to indulge in fine chocolate, cuisine, and wine, all in the refined surroundings of this gracious inn. Call Claremont Inn Bed and Breakfast at (719) 348–5125 or (888) 291–8910.

December. The Claremont goes all out to welcome the holiday season with an 18-foot-tall Christmas tree, covered with 10,000 lights and countless ornaments. The dazzling creation stands in the center of the Great Hall. The entire house is decked for the holidays.

OTHER RECOMMENDED RESTAURANTS AND LODGINGS

Stratton

Golden Prairie Inn, north of I–70, Stratton; (800) 777–6042. This Best Western offers forty guest rooms with king and queen beds, an outdoor pool, and a lounge with shuffleboard. The Best Western Golden Prairie Inn Restaurant features home-style cooking.

FOR MORE INFORMATION

Stratton Chamber of Commerce, 700 New York Avenue, P.O. Box 419, Stratton, CO 80836; (800) 777–6042.

Burlington Chamber of Commerce, 415 Fifteenth Street, Burlington, CO 80807; (719) 346–8070.

Parker Chamber of Commerce, 19201 East Mainstreet, Parker, CO 80134; (303) 841–4268.

DENVER AND POINTS EAST

WaKeeney, Kansas

SUNFLOWERS, SUNSETS, AND PRAIRIES

2 NIGHTS

Peaceful country setting • Antiques • Fishing, golf, bike riding • Windmills

Kansas is as genuine as apple pie and the American flag. Folks here wave, greet you on the street, and welcome you like a long-lost friend.

Miles of prairie and wheat-covered fields show off their beauty in a subtle way. Pull over on a backcountry road and gaze at the sun setting on the horizon, as buttery light changes from pale orange to mauve. Kansas skies are not only beautiful and spacious but also unpolluted. Breathe in the clean air and listen to meadowlarks serenade. Instead of skyscrapers you'll see windmills and towering white grain elevators.

Notice on the map the vast space between large cities out here? This expanse of land is filled with country roads, cattle, farms and ranches, and acres of wheat-producing earth. You may not find the opera, sushi bars, or many celebrity types besides Bob Dole, but neither will you run into traffic jams or big-city crime. The Sunflower State is blissfully uncrowded.

In Kansas you'll find down-home cooking at its best. Cuisine here is basic and delicious—this is chicken-fried steak and pie a la mode country. Biscuits come laden with sausage gravy; bread is made from scratch; and corn on the cob is served practically fresh from the field.

Take time to visit Mount Sunflower, the highest point in the state. At 4,039 feet above sea level, the summit is little more than a bulge in the prairie and is located just a cow-pie's throw from eastern Colorado. You won't need survival equipment to bag this peak. In fact, you can complete the "ascent" in a ten-minute leisurely stroll. The most famous guest to date to climb the state's highest point is the late Charles Kuralt, who claimed

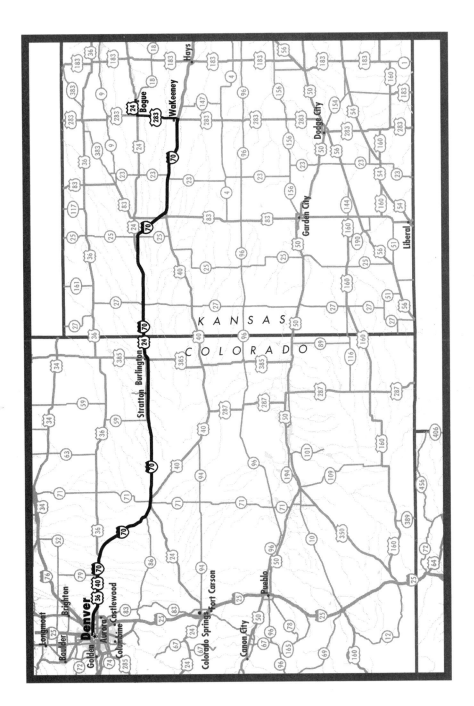

Mount Sunflower "my kind of mountain." You will too, as you stand on top
of Kansas in the middle of sagebrush-scented fields and all that big open sky.
This is America's heartland.

DAY 1

Morning

Travel east on I–70 for about 90 miles and exit at Limon (number 359).

BREAKFAST: Rip Griffin's Truck Stop is a legend, as far as I–70 travel
goes. Highway regulars would probably consider it bad luck to pass Limon
without a breakfast or coffee stop at Rip's. Order the Lumberjack Breakfast:
hamburger steak and two eggs. The gift shop has an assortment of goods,
from giant belt buckles to Patsy Cline tapes. Rip Griffin's is open twenty-
four hours a day every day of the year.

Bag a peak and climb **Mount Sunflower.** Kansas's highest point was
determined in 1961, the state's centennial year. Since then visitors from
around the world have "scaled the summit." Technically, to qualify as a
mountain there must be a 2,000-foot altitude gain, so Mount Sunflower is
not a mountain in the true definition of the word.

To get to Mount Sunflower, take the Kanorado exit south off I–70 and
set your trip odometer to zero. Travel south for 13.8 miles, then bear right
(the road changes to gravel at 6.5 miles). Follow the curvy road and continue south for approximately 8 miles. The total distance from I–70 is 21.8
miles. You will see signs to the trailhead as soon as you enter Wallace
County. For additional information and directions, contact landowners Ed
and Cindy Harold, Rural Route 1, Box 54, Weskan, KS 67762; (785)
943–5444.

Begin your walk (or cross-country ski) by crossing the cattleguard near the
trailhead. You won't see a sunflower in sight other than the one constructed of
old railroad ties that marks the "summit." Sign the guestbook and read some
of the comments, such as "Because it's here." One group whose goal was to
reach the highest point of each of the continental states within a month
climbed Mount Sunflower several years ago. In true Kansas form the party was
treated to showers, iced tea, and hospitality in the landowners' home.

Return to I–70 and continue east. The **Visitors Center,** several miles
east of Kanorado, has a wealth of brochures, maps, information, and coffee.

LUNCH: Crazy R, 1618 Main Street, Goodland, Kansas; (785) 899–3430.
This family-run cafe has great steaks, pork chops, hamburgers, and batter-fried

The Kansas prairie *stretches for miles.*

(photo by Sherry Spitsnaugle).

onions called Blooming Onions. The owner's father runs Johnnie's Meat Block, an old-fashioned butcher shop next door that provides meat for the restaurant. Crazy R is open from 11:00 A.M. to 11:00 P.M. Monday through Saturday and is closed Sunday.

Afternoon

High Plains Museum (1717 Cherry, Goodland, Kansas; 785–899–4595) chronicles life in the late 1800s and early 1900s, including the Dust Bowl era. Goodland is the home of America's first patented helicopter, and the museum houses a life-size automated replica. Open Monday through Saturday from 9:00 A.M. to 5:00 P.M. and Sunday from 1:00 to 4:00 P.M. Admission is free.

Continue on I–70 east and exit at Colby (number 53). Visit the **Prairie Museum of Art and History** (1905 South Franklin, Colby; 785–462–4590), located north of I–70. The museum boasts the biggest barn in Kansas and also has a one-room school, a country church, a 1930s farmstead, a sod house, and a doll collection. The museum is open from 9:00 A.M. to 5:00 P.M. Monday through Friday, and from 1:00 to 5:00 P.M. Saturday and Sunday; November 1 through March 30, the facility is closed Monday. The price for adults is $4.00; children six to sixteen are admitted for $1.00. Ask about senior discounts.

For a shopping excursion visit **Julie Adolph Interiors** (455 North Franklin, Colby; 785–462–6784). This delightful shop has an unusual selection of art, Oriental rugs, floral arrangements, and furniture. The store is open from 9:00 A.M. to 5:30 P.M. Monday through Saturday.

Continue east on I–70 and exit at Quinter (number 107). Travel south on Castle Rock Road about 22 miles to **Castle Rock,** a spiral-shaped limestone formation standing tall in the middle of the prairie. Castle Rock is a great place for children to run around, look at fossils, and explore the unusual rock formation. Return to I–70 via Castle Rock Road north.

DINNER: Q-Inn Restaurant (Quinter, Kansas; 785–754–3820) is located north off I–70. This family-run, friendly cafe serves some of the best food in the region. The fried chicken with mashed potatoes and gravy is almost as good as Mom's. Rolls come hot, fresh, and homemade. Choose catfish (also known as Kansas Seafood), buffalo chili, the salad buffet, or roast beef dinner. Pies—lemon, chocolate, and cherry, to name a few—are baked daily. Don't leave without a piece of German chocolate cake.

LODGING: You'll get no warmer welcome than the one from Dave and Mary Hendricks in their two-story cedar farmhouse, **Thistle Hill Bed and Breakfast** (Route 1, Box 93, WaKeeney, KS 67672; 785–743–2644). Rates range from $55 to $75. Each guest room in the antique-filled home is tastefully decorated in a Kansas theme. The Prairie Room pays tribute to family members who were early pioneers of Trego County. Mementos include a photo album from the 1800s full of ancestors' pictures and an original timber claim certificate from the 1900s that was awarded to Mary's great-grandfather.

The Sunflower Room is decorated around a hand-quilted sunflower spread designed and made by locals. This inviting room overlooks a peaceful scene of cattle roaming the prairie and a windmill turning in the breeze. The largest of the three guest rooms is the Oak Room, named for the stately oak tree visible from the picture window of this comfortable room, decorated with Old West artifacts and a queen bed made of weathered fence posts.

Hunters are welcome at Thistle Hill, and if they wish, breakfast is served before an early-morning departure. Pheasant season begins the second full weekend of November and continues through the end of January. One question often asked is how the B&B was named. According to Mary, tumbleweeds—the common name for the Russian thistle—blew in from the adjacent wheat stubble fields during a spring storm in such numbers that the driveway was blocked: "We were determined to have something good come from the mess, so we came up with Thistle Hill."

Mary has found more than one good use for the pesky native weed. In nearly every room of the home hangs a wreath made by Mary from the thorny troublemaker and symbol of the Kansas plains . . . the tumbling tumbleweed.

DAY 2

Morning

BREAKFAST: Thistle Hill Bed and Breakfast. Mary serves a country breakfast of eggs just gathered from the henhouse, juice, homemade muffins, and fresh coffee or herbal tea. Breakfast is served in the oak-floored dining room, complete with fresh lilacs on the table. In summer, visitors may prefer to eat in the screened-in porch area. Guests are welcome to explore the 620-acre working ranch.

Your first stop is **WaKeeney,** 7 miles east of Thistle Hill on I–70. Known as **Christmas City of the High Plains,** this town, with a population of 2,000, goes all out during the holiday season, when it decks the streets with fresh greenery, handmade wreaths, and more than 6,000 bulbs. A 35-foot tree stands at the intersection of Main Street and Russell Avenue, and a canopy of blue bulbs stretches from the top of the tree to evergreen-covered posts. Visitors can see the Christmas lights every evening from the first Saturday after Thanksgiving through New Year's Day. Many merchants have trees in their storefronts and Christmas items available year-round.

Take the first exit into WaKeeney and travel north 4 blocks to **Elk Dreamer Gallery** (202 South First; 785–743–2408). This attractive gallery has limited-edition prints by artists Bev Doolittle, James Bama, Bonnie Marris, and James Christensen. It also sells fine art books and pewter sculptures. Hours are Monday through Saturday from 10:00 A.M. to 5:00 P.M. Antiques lovers will not want to miss **Boeve's Coins and Antiques** (785–743–2116), located on the south side of I–70. Boeve's has an extensive selection of antique furniture, memorabilia, dishes, and coins.

Anybody who is anybody stops in at the **Donut Shop** (215 Main Street; 785–743–6494) sometime during the morning. This is where you'll get the news on weather, sports, and whose grandkids are visiting. Check the bulletin board for the article about WaKeeney published on the front page of the *Wall Street Journal*. You'll also find flyers about estate auctions and cattle sales. Pour a cup of coffee and introduce yourself to one of the locals. They love to visit with out-of-towners. The Donut Shop closes late morning.

Stop at **Always CHRISTmas** (124 North Main Street; 785–743–5587) and admire the Christmas trees exquisitely decorated by owners Robie Harries and Teresa Williams. Holiday ornaments, Santas, angels, and anything else you might need to deck your home for the season are available at this must-see shop. The store is open year-round Monday through Saturday from 10:00 A.M. to 7:00 P.M.

While you're browsing Main Street, visit **Gibson Pharmacy** (125 Main; 785–743–5753) and **Cleland Drug** (221 Main; 785–743–6321), both of which have an old-time soda fountain. Order a malt or cherry Coke and enjoy the relaxed pace.

Get away from interstate travel for the day and head north on Highway 283 to Hill City. The two-lane highway takes you past rolling hills and picturesque wheat farms. Continue to Bogue on Highway 24 east for 9 miles.

LUNCH: Gwen's Diner (304 Main Street, Bogue, Kansas; 785–421–3035) serves the best cinnamon rolls for miles around. Everyone in this small town, with a population of 150, knows each other, and sooner or later they all eat at Gwen's Diner. You won't have trouble finding the cafe on Main Street—it's where all the cars are parked. Owners Roger and Gwen Cooper have been in business since 1993, and the town is thrilled to have a place to congregate for coffee and home-cooked food. Depending on the day, you may find on the menu homemade chicken and noodles or meatloaf served with mashed potatoes and gravy. Ask Roger about his singing career. He's a regular on the Nashville scene and is quite a talented artist.

Afternoon

Return to Hill City on Highway 24 and continue 18 miles west to **Cottonwood Ranch Historic Site**, 0.5 mile north of the town of Studley. This ranch, which dates to the late 1800s, was recently dedicated as a state historic site by the Kansas State Historical Society. Today visitors can take a self-guided tour of five of the ranch's six original stone buildings, the house, washhouse, bunkhouse, stable, and shearing shed. Cottonwood Ranch is open to the public from 10:00 A.M. to 5:00 P.M. Wednesday through Saturday and from 1:00 to 5:00 P.M. Sunday. Admission is free. For more information call the ranch at (785) 627–5866.

Return to WaKeeney by traveling east on Highway 24 to Hill City and south on Highway 283.

DINNER: Sometimes you're in the mood for an old-fashioned burger, fries, and malt. **Dairy Queen** (521 Barclay Avenue, WaKeeney; 785-743-2160) will satisfy the craving. DQ is open 10:30 A.M. to 10:00 P.M. daily in summer and 10:30 A.M. to 9:00 P.M. daily the remainder of the year.

LODGING: Thistle Hill Bed and Breakfast.

DAY 3

Morning

BREAKFAST: Thistle Hill Bed and Breakfast.
Return to Denver via I-70 west.

THERE'S MORE

Trego County Historical Museum, located on the east side of WaKeeney on U.S. 283; (785) 743-2964. Whoever established this interesting museum put hours, heart, and soul into the project. Exhibits display pioneer life in western Kansas. Take time to read the newspaper articles about the tornado that swept through WaKeeney in 1951. The museum is open Tuesday, Friday, and Sunday from 1:30 to 4:00 P.M. Admission is free.

Golf. Big Creek Golf Course, WaKeeney (785-743-2617), is a 9-hole course with affordable fees. The view of a Kansas sunset as you finish the last hole is impressive. To get to Big Creek Golf Course, go south on Highway 283 for 2 miles; turn west and proceed 1 mile.

Cedar Bluff Reservoir, located in southern Trego County, is a favorite with locals and visitors for picnicking, camping, boating, and swimming. Miles of nature trails surround the lake. Fish for bass and walleye.

SPECIAL EVENTS

June. Biking Across Kansas. Rides begin at the Kansas–Colorado border and finish 500 miles later on the Colorado–Missouri border. Choose from itineraries such as the "Bedazzled Route" or the "Karefree Route." The week-long ride welcomes beginners and intermediate riders. Cyclists overnight in small towns along the way. The excursion is a wonderful way to experience the friendliness of this state. Numbers are limited and the trip has become popular with Kansans and out-of-staters, so register early. Call Larry or Norma Christie at (316) 684–8184.

August. Trego County Free Fair, WaKeeney. Ride the merry-go-round, eat a burger and a piece of homemade pie at the Scout Booth, and admire prizewinning vegetables and livestock.

November. WaKeeney Christmas Tree Lighting. Held late in the month. Locals and visitors gather on Main Street to sing Christmas carols, drink a cup of hot cider, and "ooh and ah" as the lights on the towering tree twinkle for the first night of the season. For information call the WaKeeney Chamber of Commerce at (785) 743–2077.

OTHER RECOMMENDED RESTAURANTS AND LODGINGS

Ogallah

Schreiner's Diner (Ogallah; 785–743–2907), located 7 miles east of WaKeeney off I–70, has a menu that changes daily, but you'll find Kansas favorites such as barbecued ribs or meatloaf served with mashed potatoes and gravy. Pies are made fresh daily. The restaurant is open from 7:30 A.M. to 5:00 P.M. every day except Sunday, when it closes.

WaKeeney

Budget Host Travel Inn (I–70 [exit 128] and Highway 283; 785–743–2121) is clean, well run, and conveniently located.

FOR MORE INFORMATION

Kansas Travel and Tourism, 700 Southwest Harrison Street, Suite 1300, Topeka, KS 66603; (800) 252–6727.

WaKeeney Chamber of Commerce, 216 North Main Street, WaKeeney, KS 67672; (785) 743–2077.

Colby Convention & Visitors Bureau, 350 South Range, Colby KS 67701; (800) 611–8835.

Sherman County Convention and Visitors Bureau, P.O. Box 628, Goodland, KS 67735; (888) 824–4222.

WESTERN
ESCAPES

Winter Park and the Fraser Valley

COOL, ESPECIALLY FRASER

1 NIGHT

Snowshoeing and snowtubing • Nordic skiing • Bicycling and hiking • Snowboarding camp • Four-wheel-drive tours • Spring Splash • Music festival

Getting to Winter Park via the gorgeous mountain drive or the popular Ski Train may be, as the saying goes, half the fun. Once you arrive in this western-style village, though, you'll find that the fun is really just beginning.

At 9,000 feet above sea level, the air is pure, thin, and guaranteed to clear your head. Thanks to the laid-back ambience of this congenial town, big-city stress is sure to take a tumble. Speaking of such, novice skiers are enthusiastically welcomed on the slopes. With runs named Shoo Fly and Moose Wallow, how could a beginner go wrong?

If you're a hotdogger, the black-diamond Outhouse run may be more your speed. Better yet, head over to Mary Jane, Winter Park's baby sister, and an incorrigible one at that. Affectionately known as "the Jane," these moguls are wild and wooly, just like the skiers the intimidating slopes attract. Mary Jane's reputation is one of abundant powder and steep terrain. Dubbed the First Lady of Adrenaline, Mary Jane is to be respected.

If you're a nonskier, no problem. Tour the mountain in a heated Sno-Cat and sip a cup of hot chocolate at the mid-mountain Snoasis Restaurant during the tour break. Or strap on a set of snowshoes and take a guided trip just beyond the slopes. You'll pass through silent forests and spectacular backcountry, and you're not apt to break any bones.

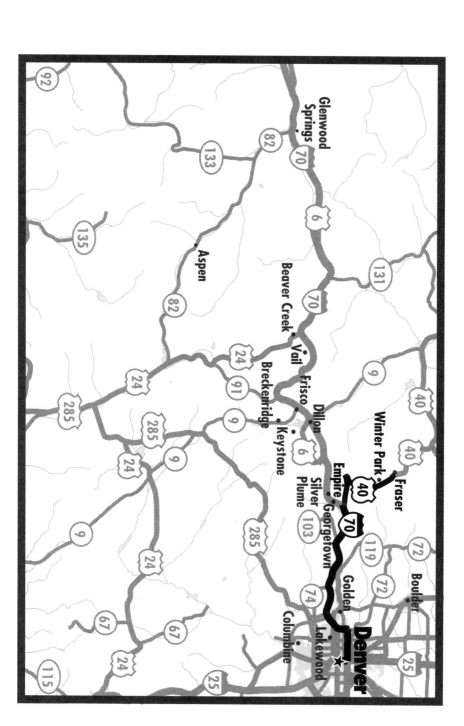

Ice skating, sledding, and Nordic skiing are available, and if you want to
feel like a kid again, snowtube down the slopes on an inflated rubber tube at
Fraser Valley Tubing Hill. Feet-first or head-first, it's a blast. Later bundle up
and steal away for a romantic, horse-drawn sleigh ride under a star-filled
evening sky.

Summer in Winter Park rivals ski season. Wildflowers grow in grand
style, and hikers and mountain bikers flock to the alpine meadows and lush
valleys. Flower boxes overflow with pansies, and the surrounding area is
transformed from a winter wonderland into a haven for cyclists, hikers,
anglers, and rafters.

Whether you choose January or July, cruising the bumps or lingering
over a French roast espresso, you'll bask in Winter Park's beauty and you'll
love all that big blue sky and sunshine.

DAY 1

Morning

Winter Park is located 67 miles northwest of Denver. Travel west on I–70
for 40 miles and take exit 232 to Highway 40. Continue on Highway 40
over Berthoud Pass into the town of Winter Park.

BREAKFAST: Before turning onto Highway 40, stop in Idaho Springs at
Marions of the Rockies (2805 Colorado Boulevard; 303–567–2925). To
get to Marions, take the first exit into Idaho Springs off I–70. The menu
includes eggs Benedict, breakfast burritos, and three-egg omelets. Marions is
open from 6:00 A.M. to 9:00 P.M. seven days a week; during winter the cafe
sometimes closes early on Sunday and Monday afternoons.

If you prefer, arrive via the Winter Park **Ski Train,** which pulls out of
Denver's Union Station weekends at 7:15 in the morning. Two relaxing
hours later you'll arrive 50 yards from the foot of the lifts at Winter Park. On
the train sip a cup of coffee and enjoy incredible views that you wouldn't
see from the highway. The train departs promptly at 4:15 P.M. the same day
and arrives in Denver at 6:15 P.M. If you plan to spend the night in Winter
Park, you will need to purchase full-fare tickets for both days.

A round-trip ticket (depart and return same day) is $35 for coach and $60
for club. The coach price offers reclining seats, as well as access to the snack
bar and the Cafe Lounge Car, where you can order a breakfast burrito, a
bagel, a cinnamon roll, coffee, and juice. Club-car rates include a continental

The moguls at Mary Jane *give skiers a thrill and a challenge.*
(photo by Byron Hetzler).

breakfast buffet, a private bar, and aprés-ski snacks on the return trip. You can purchase discounted lift tickets on the train. The Ski Train operates weekends mid-December through mid-April and also on some Fridays the months of December, February, March, and April. Reservations are essential. Call (303) 296–4754.

As the closest major ski resort to Denver and one of the most popular in the state, **Winter Park** has a devoted following. The ski area opened in 1940 with a simple rope tow and a long queue of enthusiastic people. Since then skiers have streamed to these slopes. With three interconnected mountains, superb snow, and diverse terrain, Winter Park Resort triumphs with outstanding green, blue, and black runs.

If you're not a skier, tour the mountain in comfort by **Sno-Cat.** You'll get a grand view, stories and interesting tidbits from the driver, and a stopover at the mid-mountain Snoasis Restaurant. Rides depart three times daily from the base of the lifts. Call the resort at (970) 726–5514, extension 1732, for a reservation. The price is $25 for adults and $22 for seniors.

LUNCH: Summer visitors can ride the **Zephyr Express Chairlift** to the 10,700-foot summit of Winter Park Mountain and have lunch at the **Lodge at Sunspot.** You'll have views of the Fraser Valley and the Continental Divide as you enjoy a sandwich or salad. Winter visitors can catch the free "Lift" bus in the Winter Park transportation circle to the base of Mary Jane mountain. The **Club Car** (970–726–8105) is a cozy restaurant that offers pastas and homemade soups. Enjoy lunch on the outdoor deck and watch the skiers and snowboarders.

Afternoon

Summer visitors will want to stroll, bike, or skate the paved **Fraser River Trail,** an easy-grade, 5-mile path between Winter Park and Fraser. You'll go through lush, wooded areas along the way.

If you'd prefer to see the countryside by vehicle, sign up for a guided tour with **Mad Adventures** (535 Zerex Street, P.O. Box 650, Winter Park, CO 80482; 970–726–5290 or 800–451–4844). The company offers a variety of tours, including a four-hour scenic trip to the 11,670-foot summit of Rollins Pass. You'll travel in an open-air, four-wheel-drive vehicle with a licensed guide.

Be sure to visit Winter Park's well-stocked shops and galleries, offering Southwestern jewelry, Native American art, and Colorado souvenirs.

DINNER: Dinner at the Barn (P.O. Box 171, Winter Park, CO 80482; 970–726–4923) features a catered meal served in a historic barn. During winter, you'll arrive at this eighty-acre ranch, located 5 miles from Winter Park, via horse-drawn sleigh. Dining takes place in horse stalls—don't worry; they're spotless—decorated with western antiques, such as old bits and bridles and harnesses. You'll dine by kerosene lamp on tables adorned with linen and china. The gourmet meal includes boneless chicken breast stuffed with sage dressing, wild rice, green beans amandine, biscuits with warm honey and butter, and, for dessert, homemade apple pie topped with caramel whipped cream. Winter rates are $49 per adult, plus gratuity. Bring your own alcoholic beverage if you wish.

During summer, Dinner at the Barn offers a Chicken and Ribs Barbecue and a tour of the ranch. You'll be treated to live entertainment with guitar, harmonica, washboard, or stumpfiddle music and possibly some cowboy poetry. The owners handle a lot of large groups in summer, but there are generally openings for individuals. Summer rates range from $17 to $36 per adult, depending on the package. Reservations are essential, and it's best to call or write as far in advance as possible.

LODGING: The **Foxwood** (P.O. Box 898, Winter Park, CO 80482; 970–726–0456 or 888–726–0456) is a log cabin tucked away on 8.5 acres, perfect for cross-country skiers and others seeking an escape from the usual ski condominiums. This mountain inn offers comfy rooms, private bathrooms with Jacuzzi tubs, a large living room with fireplace, and an outdoor hot tub. Foxwood is located 8 miles from Winter Park.

DAY 2

Morning

BREAKFAST: **Foxwood** features a hearty breakfast, with homemade bread, pancakes, fresh fruit, and an egg dish.

Depart Winter Park traveling northwest on Highway 40 headed for **Fraser**, the town that boasts about its reputation as "Icebox of the Nation." Fraser is the site on the weather map that has pictures of icicles next to its frigid temperature, which can plunge to well below zero. You will see signs on the east side of Highway 40 between Winter Park and Fraser for **Cozens Ranch House and Museum** (970–726–5488). Here you will get a glimpse of how the former sheriff of Central City lived. William Zane Cozens moved to the Fraser Valley in 1874 and operated a complex that included a hotel, dining room, and post office. Thanks to the Grand County Historical Association, today you can tour the restored ranch, which displays Cozens family artifacts. The museum is open Monday through Saturday from 10:00 A.M. to 5:00 P.M. and Sunday from noon to 5:00 P.M. Winter hours vary, so it's best to call ahead. Admission is $3.00 for adults.

LUNCH: **Crooked Creek Saloon** (401 Zerex Avenue, Highway 40, Fraser, CO 80442; 970–726–9250) is a typical mountain bar and can get boisterous during happy hour. The lunch crowd, however, behaves, and the food is tasty. Choose a Greek salad, fettuccine Alfredo, or an Awesome Fatboy Burger. The restaurant is open from 7:00 A.M. to 10:00 P.M. daily.

Afternoon

Return to Denver via Highway 40 and I–70 east.

THERE'S MORE

Summer skiing and snowboarding camp. Parsenn Bowl, at 12,060 feet above sea level, has snow late into the season. Die-hard skiers see no reason to squander a good snowpack, so Winter Park offers summer ski and snowboard camps, which begin in late-May. Call the Winter Park Competition Center at (970) 726–1590.

The **National Sports Center for the Disabled** (NSCD), founded by Hal O'Leary, is Winter Park's greatest gift. Originally created to teach young children with leg amputations to ski, the program has expanded to involve disabilities of many types. Today blind skiers and single and double amputees cruise the slopes. The center also offers a summer program for persons with disabilities. Activities include bicycling, hiking, camping, and rafting. For more information about the program, call the NSCD at (970) 726–1540 or (303) 780–6540.

Snowtubing. Go for it. Pounce onto a custom-made inner tube and soar down the slope. A rope tow will lug you and your tube back to the top so you can do it again. The **Fraser Valley Tubing Hill,** located at the south end of Fraser (970–726–5954), rents tubes weekends from 10:00 A.M. to 10:00 P.M. and weekdays from 4:00 to 10:00 P.M.

SPECIAL EVENTS

Late March and early April. Spring Splash brings out the Winter Park crowd. Spectators cheer as skiers and snowboarders negotiate a zany obstacle course that includes skiing or snowboarding across a 60-foot pond of icy water to reach the finish line. Skiers and snowboarders get discounted late-season ticket prices. An outdoor barbecue takes place daily on the deck of the mid-mountain Snoasis Restaurant. For information call Winter Park Resort Guest Services at (970) 726–5514, extension 1727.

July. American Music Festival is a two-day festival featuring a mixture of sounds from country to rock. Fans rave about this event that's a favorite with locals. Call the Winter Park and Fraser Valley Chamber of Commerce at (800) 903–7275.

August. Wine, Beer, & Food Festival. Enjoy sampling wine, beer, and gourmet cuisine in the alpine setting of Winter Park Resort. Other activities include winemakers' dinners, mountain biking, and a giant human maze. For more information call (970) 726–1540.

OTHER RECOMMENDED RESTAURANTS AND LODGINGS

Winter Park

Carvers Bakery and Cafe (95 Cooper Creek Way; 970–726–8202) is a favorite with those in the know. The atmosphere is relaxed and the food is excellent. You'll find breakfast selections such as whole wheat cinnamon rolls or granola with bananas, blueberries, and walnuts. The restaurant is open from 7:00 A.M. to 3:00 P.M. Sunday through Wednesday and from 7:00 A.M. to 9:00 P.M. Thursday through Saturday.

Deno's Mountain Bistro (78911 Highway 40, 1.5 miles north of the base of Winter Park Ski Area; 970–726–5332) serves a New York strip combo, grilled Atlantic salmon, pasta, and burgers. The restaurant is open from 11:00 A.M. to 11:00 P.M. daily.

Alpeggios, Highway 40, Winter Park, CO 80482; (970) 726–5402. This cozy restaurant serves authentic northern Italian and Mediterranean dishes, including such specialties as Veal Alpeggios and Penne Fantasia. Open daily from 5:00 to 9:30 P.M. Call for reservations.

Gasthaus Eichler Restaurant, 78786 Highway 40, Winter Park, CO 80482; (970) 726–5133 or (800) 543–3899. You'll find authentic German and European cuisine here. Many dishes are served with homemade spaetzle.

Iron Horse Resort Retreat, 100 Winter Park Drive, P.O. Box 1369, Winter Park, CO 80482; (970) 726–8801. This ski-in/ski-out facility has condominiums that range from studios to two-bedroom luxury units. Amenities include free local shuttle service, an on-site restaurant and lounge, a health club, an indoor/outdoor pool, hot tubs, and a ski shop.

Tabernash

Devil's Thumb Guest Ranch and Cross-Country Center, east of Fraser at 3530 County Road 83, P.O. Box 750, Tabernash, CO 80478; (970) 726–5633. This facility offers more than 90 kilometers of trails to cross-country ski. The ranch has cozy rooms and woodsy, backcountry charm. The on-site restaurant offers gourmet cuisine.

FOR MORE INFORMATION

Winter Park and Fraser Valley Chamber of Commerce, 78841 Highway 40,
   P.O. Box 3236, Winter Park, CO 80482; (970) 726–4221 or (800)
   903–7275 or, in Denver, (303) 422–0666.
Winter Park Central Reservations P.O. Box 36, Winter Park, CO 80482;
   (970) 726–5587 or (800) 729–5813.
Winter Park Resort, P.O. Box 36, Winter Park, CO 80482; (970) 726–5514.
Grand County Tourism Board, P.O. Box 208, Winter Park, CO 80482; (800)
   729–5821.

Georgetown

VICTORIAN CHARM

1 NIGHT

Narrow-gauge steam train • Walking tour
• Horse-drawn carriage ride • Romantic B&B inn
• Shopping • Christmas Market

Georgetown is one of Colorado's most beloved Victorian towns. This attractive, before-the-turn-of-the-century village charms at the outset. Gingerbread houses, flagstone sidewalks, and lovingly preserved churches create an elegant, bygone era.

The community traces its roots to the early gold prospectors who were tempted by rumors of fortune. Subsequently, miners unearthed silver deposits not far upriver at Silver Plume in the late 1800s. Shortly following the boom the Georgetown Loop Railroad was constructed.

Today you'll find a community devoted to the restoration and preservation of its heritage. The area also offers elegant B&B accommodations and hiking, biking, and skiing, all in the stunning setting of Colorado's Clear Creek Valley and the Arapaho National Forest.

The first two weekends of December, the town gussies up to greet the Christmas season. Smell the chestnuts roasting, listen to carolers serenade "Silent Night," and visit with Father Christmas.

DAY 1

Morning

From Denver travel west on I–70 for 45 miles and exit at Georgetown.

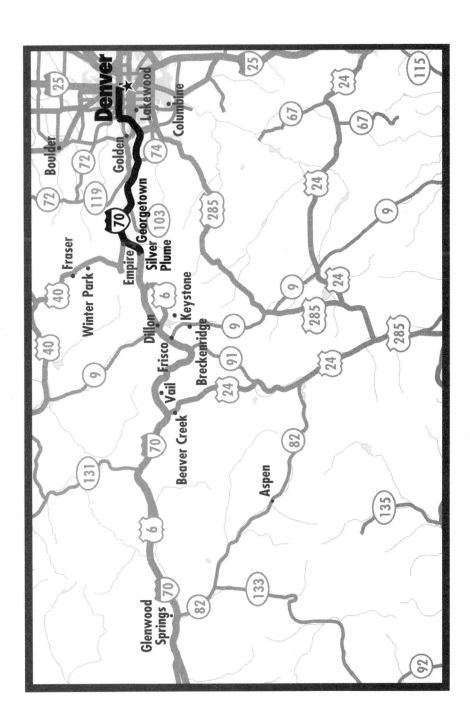

BREAKFAST: Save your appetite for a meal at **The Happy Cooker** (412 Sixth Street, Georgetown; 303–569–3166). The restaurant deserves a visit for its clever name, and the chef gets credit for the delicious Belgian waffles and homemade bread. Summer hours are 8:00 A.M. to 5:00 P.M. Monday through Friday and 8:00 A.M. to 6:00 P.M. Saturday and Sunday. Winter hours are 8:00 A.M. to 4:00 P.M. daily.

Stroll the streets of Georgetown and browse the shops, galleries, bookstores, and cafes. Be sure to visit **Georgetown Mercantile** (614 Rose, on the corner of Seventh and Rose Streets; 303–569–2109). The mercantile is housed in the St. James Hotel Building, which was built in 1875 before Colorado obtained statehood. This well-stocked store is a potpourri of treasures. You'll find old-fashioned tin boxes, candles, greeting cards, T-shirts, and much more. Georgetown Mercantile is open from 10:00 A.M. to 5:30 P.M. seven days a week.

For an outstanding selection of casual and ethnic clothing and handmade jewelry, shop at **Expeditions** (614 Sixth Street; 303–569–3322), upstairs from the Georgetown Gallery. Expeditions is open daily from 10:00 A.M. to 5:30 P.M.

Noel (612 Sixth Street; 303–569–2827) specializes in Christmas items. For shoppers interested in collectibles, Noel carries Lefton lighted houses, Fontanini nativity sets, and House of Hattan. Noel is open daily from 10:00 A.M. to 5:30 P.M. **Powder Cache Antiques** (612 Sixth Street; 303–569–2848), located upstairs from Noel, sells western Americana and antiques. The owner displays his personal collection of mining artifacts in the **Mining Museum,** located inside the store. Admission is free. Powder Cache Antiques and the museum are open from 10:00 A.M. to 5:00 P.M. daily.

Take a **self-guided walking tour** of the 5-square-block downtown. Pick up a map at the **Community Center,** located at Sixth and Argentine Streets (303–569–2840). Originally the town bakery and later the Clear Creek County Courthouse, this building today houses an excellent visitor information center.

From the Community Center continue south to the **Hamill House** (305 Argentine Street; 303–569–2840). This restored structure was the home of silver tycoon William Arthur Hamill, who was one of the richest men in the county. The building, which is now operated by Historic Georgetown, Inc., exhibits 1880s furnishings. Admission is $5.00 for adults and $3.00 for seniors and students; children under six are admitted free. Open from 10:00 A.M. to 4:00 P.M. daily, Memorial Day through September, and from noon to

4:00 P.M. on weekends only, October through December. Closed January 1 until Memorial Day.

You won't want to miss the grand **Hotel de Paris,** at Sixth and Taos Streets (303–569–2311). The hotel opened in 1875 and today is a museum operated by the National Society of Colonial Dames of America. This lovely old building was modeled after a French inn. The builder, Louis Dupuy, a Frenchman who arrived in Georgetown as a miner, longed to have a bit of his homeland in Colorado. Open from 10:00 A.M. to 4:00 P.M. daily Memorial Day weekend through September and from noon to 4:00 P.M. on weekends during winter. Admission is $3.50 for adults; discounts are available for seniors and children.

Of special note is the **Georgetown Gallery** (612 Sixth Street; 303–569–2218), which features Colorado artists and has an impressive selection of pottery, oils, and pastels. Georgetown Gallery is open from 10:00 A.M. to 5:00 P.M. daily in summer. Winter hours are from 11:00 A.M. to 4:30 P.M., except on Tuesday and Thursday, when the gallery closes.

LUNCH: The New Place, 715 Seventh Street; (303) 569–2552. Locals call this restaurant the Place. The cafe serves delicious Mexican food, starting with homemade chips and salsa. The roasted red pepper and goat cheese quesadilla is listed as an appetizer, but you can make a meal from this selection. Chile rellenos and tamales rate high honors. Dessert includes flan, bread pudding with tequila sauce, fruit rellenos, and fried ice cream.

Afternoon

After lunch it's "all aboard" the **Georgetown Loop Railroad.** Sit back and take in the incredible scenery as you wind through the woods, twist and turn on sharp curves, and cross Clear Creek several times. The 1920s narrow-gauge steam locomotive (restored in 1975) crosses Devil's Gate Bridge and stops at Silver Plume. Here you can visit the Lebanon Silver Mine. Slip on a hard hat and admire the old silver mine as a guide talks about mining methods in the 1800s. The round-trip train ride lasts an hour, and if you tour the mine, the trip will take two and a half hours.

The train departs from both Devil's Gate boarding area and the Silver Plume Depot (exit 226 off I–70). Tickets are available at the Old Georgetown Station and the Silver Plume Depot. The train runs daily, rain or shine, from Memorial Day through Labor Day; during September the train runs on Saturdays and Sundays only. For tickets contact Georgetown Loop Railroad,

Old Georgetown Station, 1106 Rose Street, P.O. Box 217, Georgetown, CO 80444; (303) 670–1686. A round-trip ticket is $11.95 for adults and $7.50 for children ages three to fifteen. The price of the mine tour is $4.00 for adults and $2.00 for children ages three to fifteen.

Mountain-bike enthusiasts can take a combination bike-train tour, with uphill transportation on the locomotive and a guided bike ride down. Tour costs begin at $45. Bike rentals and helmets are available. Call **Trails and Rails Downhill Mountain Bike Tours** in Georgetown at (303) 569–2403 or on the Denver line at (303) 670–1686.

Visit the **Georgetown Energy Museum** (600 Griffith Street; 303–569–3557), where you will see waterwheels and generators that were installed in 1906 and still produce electric power. The plant also operates as a museum and is open to the public Memorial Day weekend through September from 10:00 A.M. to 4:00 P.M. The facility is closed except by appointment the remainder of the year.

Arrive at dinner in comfort and style via horse-drawn carriage. Contact **Rutherford Carriage Service** at (303) 569–2675.

DINNER: Raven Hill Mining Company, 612 Sixth Street, Georgetown; (303) 569–2209. This restaurant serves barbecued pork, smoked bratwurst, and baby back ribs, among other excellent selections. Save room for peach cobbler or Margarita Key Lime Pie. The Raven serves buffalo prime rib after 5:00 P.M. on weekends. Open 11:00 A.M. to 9:00 P.M. daily.

LODGING: Alpine Hideaway, P.O. Box 788, Georgetown, CO 80444; (800) 490–9011 or (303) 569–2800. This luxuriously peaceful B&B is the ideal place to celebrate a special occasion. The Alpine Hideaway offers privacy and comfort in a sumptuous setting. Each of the three elegant guest rooms has a gas fireplace, a Jacuzzi tub for two, and mountain views. The Country Irish Room, located on the second floor, displays photos of innkeeper Dawn Janov's prizewinning Arabian horses. This room has a king-size bed and a vaulted ceiling with skylight. The dreamy Mountain Contemporary Room boasts a romantic four-poster iron bed and private entry to an outdoor garden with a swing, hammock, and waterfall. The bathroom is decorated in black-and-white tile and offers such extras as gold fixtures and a bidet. The Scandinavian Room features a ceramic fireplace.

ESCAPE TWO

WESTERN

DAY 2

Morning

BREAKFAST: Janov refers to her B&B as a "bed and basket." Breakfast at the **Alpine Hideaway** is indeed an occasion. At a prearranged time a gourmet basket of food and a carafe of coffee, tea, or hot chocolate appear at your doorstep. The basket holds items such as bacon quiche, pistachio banana bread, and a plate of fresh kiwi, grapes, and mango. Presentation is superb. Fresh flowers, cloth napkins, and heart-shaped cheeses help create the detailed array. Dining in the privacy of your room is a relaxed way to begin the day.

Motor along the 22-mile loop on **Guanella Pass Road,** a Scenic and Historic Byway (CRs 381 and 62) that twists through Arapaho National Forest. The byway climbs to 11,600 feet through lush aspen and spruce forests to the broad, windswept tundra. The route gains elevation almost immediately but can be driven with an ordinary vehicle, even though the road is not paved the entire way. Park at the top of Guanella Pass and take in the exhilarating air and dramatic scenery. At Guanella Pass you'll get views of Mount Bierstadt, Grays Peak, and Mount Wilcox. On the descent you'll pass alpine lakes, spruce forests, and, if it's summer or autumn, quaking aspen trees. Schedule two hours for this route.

On your return trip to Denver via I–70, stop at **Tommyknocker Microbrewery & Pub** (1401 Miner Street, Idaho Springs; 303–567–2688). Its Maple Nut Brown Ale is an excellent brew. Order a buffalo burger or the buffalo meatloaf served with mashed potatoes and gravy. Open daily from 11:00 A.M. to 10:00 P.M.; the bar stays open until 2:00 A.M.

THERE'S MORE

Skiing. Loveland Ski Area is located 12 miles west of Georgetown on I–70 near the east entrance to Eisenhower Tunnel. Loveland Valley and Loveland Basin (the two connected areas that make up the ski area) offer skiers one of the longest ski seasons in the state, extending from mid-October through mid-May. This family-friendly resort offers day care, a rental shop and ski school, and a bar and restaurant. Snowboarders are welcomed here, and they can let loose on the spacious runs. Loveland Basin is the more demanding of the two ski areas.

Fishing. Georgetown Lake, located at the east end of Georgetown, is packed with cutthroat and rainbow trout. The mountain setting makes this lake an excellent spot to drop a line and contemplate the day away.

Hiking. Pavilion Point, a favorite with railroad buffs, is a historic footpath that follows a portion of the Argentine Central Railroad bed. The easy trail is about 1 mile one-way and is a good picnic spot. You'll get views of the train, Silver Plume, and Georgetown. Drive south from Georgetown on Guanella Pass Road 2.5 miles to Waldorf Junction (Forest Road 248). Turn right and travel 1.2 miles.

Cross-country skiing. Whatever can be hiked in the summer can usually be skied in the winter. Numerous trails in the Arapaho National Forest welcome Nordic skiers with good snow conditions, well-marked paths, and peaceful touring. Check with the Clear Creek Ranger District Office (303–567–2901) at exit 240 off I–70 for maps, weather conditions, and advice on skiing or hiking. The ranger office is open 8:00 A.M. to 5:00 P.M. Monday through Saturday during the winter and seven days a week during the summer.

Mountain biking. Bike the six-mile path to the ghost town of Waldorf. The trail begins 2.5 miles south of Georgetown along Guanella Pass Road.

SPECIAL EVENTS

July. Traditional Independence Day celebration includes a parade, a barbecue, bucket brigade races, fireworks, and old-fashioned merrymaking. Drive to Silver Plume for the ice cream social and street dance.

December. The holidays come to life during the first two weekends of December during Christmas Market, a glorious outdoor festivity that celebrates the season in a Victorian fashion. The festival takes place from 10:00 A.M. until dusk.

OTHER RECOMMENDED RESTAURANTS AND LODGINGS

Georgetown

The Renaissance, 1025 Rose Street, Georgetown, CO 80444; (303) 569–3336. This restaurant specializes in northern Italian cuisine. The menu offers veal, wild game, and an extensive wine list.

Hardy House Bed & Breakfast Inn, 605 Brownell Street, Box 156, Georgetown, CO 80444; (303) 569–3388 or (800) 490–4802. Sit by the potbellied stove in the nineteenth-century parlor or soak in the outdoor hot tub after a day of sightseeing. Breakfast includes anything from eggs Benedict served on Sundays to waffles, pancakes, or quiche Monday through Saturday. Ask about the romance package, which includes a night's stay in the Victoria Suite, a horse-drawn carriage ride, dinner at a local restaurant, champagne, chocolates, flowers, and breakfast in your room.

Empire

Peck House Hotel and Restaurant, about 5 miles northeast of Georgetown on U.S. 40, off I–70, exit 232; (303) 569–9870. This lodging is billed as Colorado's oldest continually operated hotel and offers eleven well-appointed rooms. Antiques and pictures of the Peck family decorate the parlor. The Peck House Restaurant serves an exceptional Sunday buffet, complete with champagne, quail, salmon, pastries, and other appetizing selections.

FOR MORE INFORMATION

Georgetown Information Center, 404 Sixth Street, Georgetown, CO 80444; (800) 472–8230.

Historic Georgetown, Inc., 305 Argentine, P.O. Box 667, Georgetown, CO 80444; (303) 569–2840 or, in Denver, (303) 674–2625.

Georgetown Chamber of Commerce, P.O. Box 444, Georgetown, CO 80444; (800) 472–8230 or (303) 569–2888.

Clear Creek Ranger District Office, P.O. Box 3307, Idaho Springs, CO 80452; (303) 567–2901.

Summit County

THE PERFECT MOUNTAIN GETAWAY

1 NIGHT

Mountain-bike Dirt Camp • Llama lunch hike • Gondola rides • Sailing on Lake Dillon • Snowshoe tour • Fly fishing • Snow Sculpture Championships

This multimountain, multiresort area offers powder skiing, a renowned culinary school, mountaintop gourmet dining, and much more.

Summit County encompasses four ski areas, four towns, and three resorts. Breckenridge is the oldest settlement, followed by Dillon, Silverthorne, and Frisco. Victorian street lamps and architecture enhance Breckenridge, which was once a one-road community made up of hardy settlers and gold-seeking prospectors. Locals later realized the area's other commodity of "white gold," and ski areas sprouted to accommodate the downhill craze. Summit County soon boasted Breckenridge, Arapahoe Basin (affectionately known as A-Basin, or the Legend), Keystone, and Copper Mountain.

In the summer the area becomes a playground for bicyclists, golfers, and trekkers. When is the last time you took a llama to lunch? Let a llama carry the load as you hike to a beautiful picnic site with 360-degree views of the Rockies. With activities that range from conventional to extraordinary, it's little surprise that visitors flock to this mountain getaway.

DAY 1

Morning

Summit County is located 70 miles west of Denver via I–70. To get to Keystone, take the Dillon/Silverthorne (exit 205) and travel 6 miles south on U.S. Highway 6.

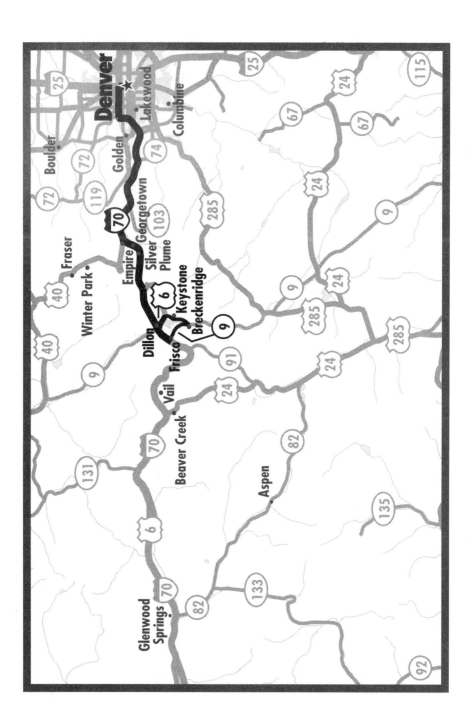

Skiers will want to head directly to the slopes. Gladed terrain, broad basins with colossal snow cover, and green or black diamonds are yours for the asking.

Arapahoe Basin tops out at 13,050 feet above sea level. A-Basin is a favorite with die-hard skiers, thanks to its late season and festive atmosphere. With only 10 percent of the terrain designated as easy, A-Basin may not be the place for a beginner, but it's pure enchantment for the intermediate to expert skier. Nearly vertical terrain and long chutes (not to mention an out-door barbecue at the top of Exhibition Lift) are enough to satisfy hard-core mogul-seekers. A-Basin is located east of Keystone on Highway 6, at the base of Loveland Pass. For information call (970) 468–0718 or (888) 272–7246.

With more than 2,000 acres of skiable terrain, **Breckenridge Ski Area** offers moguls for the advanced skier and nearly horizontal slopes for the rookie. Beginners may wish to avoid Hades and Devil's Crotch runs and stay on Flapjack. Peaks 8, 9, and 10, which are part of the Ten Mile Range, may have lackluster titles, but the high-altitude mountains are anything but bor-ing. Skiers will find plenty of opportunities to break into a high speed on the steep slopes. Breckenridge Ski Area is 70 miles west of Denver via I–70 (exit 203) and 9 miles south on Highway 9. For more information call (800) 404–3535.

Copper Mountain Resort offers good skiing stats, with an annual snowfall of 255 inches and 350 acres of "extreme skiing." Copper is a great place for beginners to gain confidence and also offers an outstanding chil-dren's ski school. On the other end of the scale, guided extreme-skiing tours are available for dauntless experts. Club Med stationed itself here with the only ski village in North America. Copper is located about 6 miles south-west of Frisco. For information call (970) 968–2882 or (800) 458–8386.

Nighttime-skiing devotees rave about the twilight runs at **Keystone,** billed as the largest night-skiing single-mountain operation in the country. Lift tickets are valid until 9:00 P.M., so you can ski well after the sun sets. Chances of snow here? One hundred percent. Keystone has the largest snowmaking operation in North America. As the pacesetter in making snow, Keystone continues to improve on its already successful Mother Nature–enhancing efforts. Accommodations at Keystone are well-designed, and the resort commits itself to guest service and fine cuisine. Racing enthu-siasts will want to ask about Keystone's Mahre Training Center, which offers coaching, lift tickets, and a session with Phil or Steve Mahre, the twin

Summit County *offers miles of biking trails.*

(photo by Sherry Spitsnaugle).

Olympic medalists. Keystone is located east of Dillon on Highway 6. For information call (800) 404–3535.

Nonskiers can try **ice skating** or **ice hockey.** Keystone Lake in Keystone Village is the largest maintained outdoor ice rink in North America. Rent skates or ice hockey equipment at the rental shop near the lake.

To arrange a guided **snowshoe tour,** plan a **fly-fishing** trip (year-round), or shop for the latest in outdoor clothing, stop at **Summit Guides** (970–468–8945) located near the lake. Spend time browsing the **shops** next to Keystone Lake. You'll find everything from gourmet chocolate to T-shirts.

LUNCH: Alpenglow Stube, P.O. Box 38, Keystone, CO 80435; (800) 354–4386. Treat yourself to the Stube Skiers Buffet at North America's highest gourmet, award-winning restaurant. The buffet is a feast of freshly smoked meats, homemade soups, and fresh bread. The Stube is located at the top of North Peak in The Outpost Lodge. Nonskiers can ride two gondolas to the restaurant for $10 per person. The Alpenglow Stube also serves dinner, with entrees such as wild game grill, pan-seared tuna, and duck breast.

Afternoon

During the warm months have lunch at **Pizza on the Plaza** (970–496–3729), located next to the Keystone Activities & Dining Center in Keystone Village. This restaurant has a selection of pasta, pizza, and sandwiches.

Summer visitors will want to cruise the paved bike path. Pick up a map at the Keystone Activities & Dining Center, located in Keystone Village, directly behind Keystone Lodge. **Sports Shaq,** (970–496–4245) located near Keystone Lake, rents bicycles, paddleboats, canoes, kayaks, and in-line skates.

Set sail on **Lake Dillon.** Take a cruise aboard a 25-foot sailboat with an experienced guide. Your skipper will take you on a ninety-minute tour of the lake. The price is $24.50 for adults and $21.00 for children twelve and under. Call Keystone Activity Center at (800) 354–4386.

Keystone Resort offers a **weekly cooking class** where guests don a chef's hat and apron, participate in hands-on training and preparation of an evening meal, then feast on the five-course dinner. Certified Executive Chef Bob Burden conducts the class. Price is $50 per person. For more extensive culinary training, enroll in the four-day workshop. The resort's award-winning chefs lead the classes. Call (800) 354–4386.

DINNER: Keystone Ranch, 1437 Summit County Road 150, Keystone, CO 80435. Located 3 miles from Keystone Village, this elegant, 1930s ranch homestead offers a phenomenal dining experience. You will be pampered by the professional waitstaff as you savor six courses of gourmet Colorado cuisine. Nibble on the sun-dried-tomato bread as you review the extensive wine list. The fixed-price menu offers appetizers such as chilled pheasant and Piney Ridge venison, followed by soup, salad, sorbet, and an entree of elk with wild mushrooms, roast rack of lamb, or tenderloin of beef, among others. Ask your waiter if you can relocate to the living room for dessert, a grand finale that includes Grand Marnier soufflé or chocolate demitasse. This cozy room, with its roaring fire and comfy couches, is the ideal place to linger over a glass of port, espresso, and after-dinner conversation. An elk antler chandelier adds to the rustic charm. Dinner reservations are handled through Keystone Activity Center, (800) 354–4386.

LODGING: Keystone Resort, Box 38, Keystone, CO 80435; (800) 404–3535. Choose Keystone Lodge in the village or a condominium in a more secluded area. The lodge has a complete workout facility. Luxury home rentals are also available.

DAY 2

Morning

BREAKFAST: Edgewater, located on the second floor of **Keystone Lodge,** has a breakfast buffet that includes waffles, egg dishes, and pastries. Outside dining is available in the summer. The restaurant serves breakfast from 6:30 to 10:30 A.M. daily and is open for lunch until 2:00 P.M.

A splendid way to see the countryside in summer is on horseback. **Keystone Stables** (970–496–3550) can arrange a one-hour or a full-day ride. If you prefer to travel by auto, contact **Tiger Run Tours** (970–453–2331) to go exploring in a four-by-four off-road vehicle. During winter the company offers snowmobile tours.

LUNCH: Hop on the gondola to the top of **Keystone Mountain** to rendezvous with the llamas. The animals carry lunch as you hike with a guide on the intermediate 1-mile path to the picnic site. Lunch includes items such as chicken fajitas, fresh fruit salad, and strawberry shortcake. The price is $37 for adults and $25 for children ages six to twelve; minimum age is six. The llama lunch is available July 4 through Labor Day weekend. For reservations call the Keystone Activity Center at (800) 354–4386.

Winter visitors will want to feast on the "Skier's Lunch" at **Ski Tip Lodge** (on Montezuma Road, 1 mile east of Keystone Village; 970–496–4950). The buffet includes soups, salads, and fresh bread, served in the cozy setting of a log lodge. Call for the winter schedule and reservations.

THERE'S MORE

Dirt Camp. "Take your mountain bike to school." Professional mountain-bike racers teach basic riding techniques to beginners and advanced skills to accomplished riders. Sign up for a two-hour, half-day, or two-day clinic at Keystone. Call (800) 711–DIRT.

Women's Mini Spa at Keystone Resort. This four-day session offers activities such as hiking and biking in the Colorado Rockies. Participants also attend low-fat-cooking classes and learn relaxation techniques. For more information call (800) 438–7251.

SPECIAL EVENTS

January. Early every January spectators swarm to Breckenridge to watch teams from around the world compete in the International Snow Sculpture

Championships. Squads sculpt colossal pieces of art—some stunning, others whimsical—from twenty-ton blocks of snow at this crowd-pleasing event. Call (970) 453–6018.

Breckenridge Ullr Fest. Another week with partying on the agenda is this creative celebration, held in late January, that honors the mythical Norse god of winter. The festivities include a parade, ice skating, and a visit by Ullr himself. Call (970) 453–6018.

April. Breckenridge Beach Daze. Spring is welcomed in style beginning April Fools' Day with a parade and crowning of the Town Fool. With snowfall at generally the heaviest of the season, conditions delight skiers. Call (970) 453–6018.

Eenie Weenie Bikini Contest. Men and women ski or snowboard on Copper Mountain's Main Vein ski run for prizes in this zany competition. For information call (970) 968–2882, extension 7885.

May. Annual Taste of Breckenridge. Wine, cuisine, and competition. This town knows how to throw a party, and the Annual Taste is no exception. Chefs gather and rival for the desired Chef's Hat. Call (970) 453–6018.

September. Taste of Keystone and Colorfest Open Golf Tournament. Feast on the best of the best, enjoy fabulous fall colors, and play a few rounds of golf. For dates call the Keystone Activity Center at (800) 354–4386.

OTHER RECOMMENDED RESTAURANTS AND LODGINGS

Keystone

Ski Tip Lodge, P.O. Box 38, Keystone, CO 80435; (970) 496–4950 or (800) 222–0188. This rustic retreat was once a stagecoach stop. Today the intimate lodge provides the perfect escape for a romantic weekend. You won't be distracted by television or the telephone. The lodge also operates as a restaurant, with four-course dinners, lunch during the winter, and Sunday brunch in the summer. Breakfast is included with lodging. Ski Tip Lodge is on Montezuma Road, 1 mile east of Keystone Village.

Sleigh-ride dinner at **Soda Creek Homestead** (800–354–4386). Bundle up for the brisk trip via sleigh pulled by Belgian draft horses to this restored 1880s homestead. Guests can choose steak, chicken, or vegetable kebab for dinner.

Breckenridge

The Village at Breckenridge, 535 South Park Avenue, Breckenridge CO 80424; (970) 453–2000 or (800) 800–7829. This ski-in/ski-out complex has 455 units, ranging from studios to three-bedroom suites. The lobby features an elk-antler chandelier, antique showshoes on the wall, and an upright piano. Cozy up next to the fireplace in the library just off the lobby. From Denver take I–70 west to Frisco, turn south on Highway 9, and drive 9 miles to the town of Breckenridge.

The Allaire Timbers Inn, 9511 Highway 9 South Main, P.O. Box 4653, Breckenridge, CO 80424; (970) 453–7530 or (800) 624–4904. This rustic log inn offers ten guest rooms, each with private bath and mountain views. Enjoy views of Ten Mile Range as you relax in the outdoor spa.

Mi Casa Restaurant, 600 South Park Place; (970) 453–2071. This popular après-ski spot serves great margaritas, chunky salsa and chips, and fish tacos. The atmosphere is lively and the bar is packed.

Frisco

Galena Street Mountain Inn, First Avenue and Galena Street, P.O. Box 417, Frisco, CO 80443; (970) 668–3224 or (800) 248–9138. Each of the inn's fifteen guest rooms offers down comforters and mountain views. A complete gourmet breakfast is included.

FOR MORE INFORMATION

Summit County Chamber of Commerce, P.O. Box 214, Frisco, CO 80443; (970) 668–5800 or (800) 530–3099.

Breckenridge Resort Chamber, 555 South Columbine Street, Box 1909, Breckenridge, CO 80424; (970) 453–2913 or (800) 221–1091.

Keystone Resort, Box 38, Keystone, CO 80435; (800) 222–0188.

Copper Mountain Resort Chamber, P.O. Box 3003, Copper Mountain, CO 80443; (970) 968–6477.

Vail and Beaver Creek

A WINTER AND
SUMMER PLAYGROUND

2 NIGHTS

*Betty Ford Alpine Gardens • Music festival • Pedestrian
mall • Fine dining • High-altitude golf • World-class
shopping • Ski museum • Gondola*

Vail is the quintessential ultraopulent resort. As one of the world's newer
playgrounds, Vail is synonymous with class, glorious mountain scenery, and
the good life.

Styled after the likes of European resorts, Vail Village feels like a reproduction of a charming ski town in Bavaria. A-frame bungalows, large
wooden clock spires, and the occasional "*S'il vous plait*" create an international flavor here more prominent than in any other area of the state.

Vail's little sister, nearby Beaver Creek, has followed the trendsetter's
footsteps to become as fashionable an area. Some observers say Beaver
Creek has emerged as an equal to the well-to-do Vail. The slopes of Beaver
Creek rate the same in panache, and the luxurious accommodations are
second to none.

Hollywood types descend on Aspen rather than Vail, but you will still
hear the occasional report of a glitterati-sighting.

In relation to the history of Colorado, Vail is an infant. Nearly four
decades old, Vail became a ski area before it became a town. Today, first-class
restaurants thrive in Vail and Beaver Creek, and you will want to indulge in
the superb sustenance. Jagged, snowcapped peaks of the spectacular Gore
Range tower above Vail and Beaver Creek, creating a year-round picture-
perfect scene.

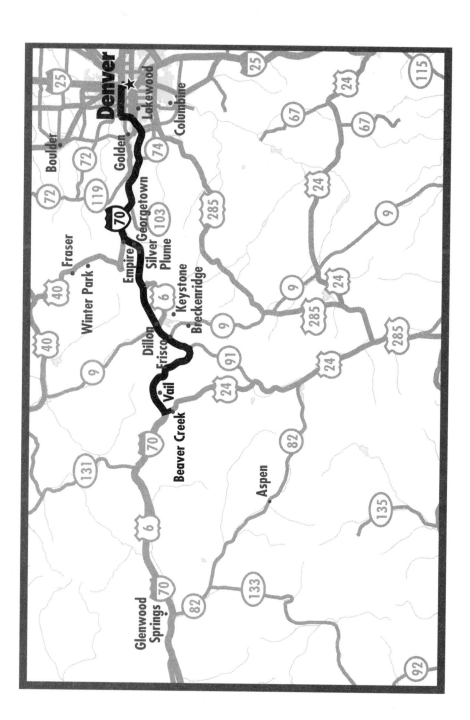

DAY 1

Morning

From Denver travel 100 miles west on I–70 to Vail. Take the Vail Village exit (number 176) and follow signs to the public parking just north of the village.

LUNCH: Red Lion, located at the top of Bridge Street in Vail Village; (970) 476–7676. Sit on the outdoor patio and enjoy Cajun catfish, three-alarm chili, or barbecued baby back ribs as you watch the parade of shoppers stroll by.

Afternoon

After lunch, join the crowd in browsing the upscale boutiques, galleries, and sports shops of **Vail Village.** The pedestrian mall, with its geranium-filled planters and stylish bistros, is a destination of its own. You'll no doubt see fur-clad, diamond-covered women, and you will hear not only French but a smattering of Spanish, Japanese, or Swedish as you meander down the cobblestone pathway or linger in one of the outdoor cafes.

You can purchase anything from a snowboard to a full-length mink coat in these few blocks. The **Alaskan Shop,** located in the Lodge Promenade (184 East Gore Creek Drive, Vail, CO 81657; 970–476–3750), has a good selection of sculptures and art.

You don't have to be a skier to ride the **Eagle Bahn high-speed gondola at Lionshead.** This supersophisticated gondola travels at 19.7 feet per second, ascending the mountain in just eight minutes. Speed is just the beginning. The twelve-passenger cabin comes with heat, so you will commute to the summit in comfort. At the top sits the colossal **Eagle's Nest Adventure Ridge,** which offers both day and night activities. Tube, sled, snowmobile, snowshoe, snowboard, ice skate, or watch the action from the **Blue Moon Bar.** You can rent ice skates, snowshoes, sleds, and even snow boots and snowsuits. For information call (970) 476–9090. During summer take a mountain bike on the gondola and ride down, or rent a bike at the top.

DINNER: Game Creek Club, located in Vail's Game Creek Bowl; (970) 479–4280. Ride in a Sno-Cat-drawn sleigh from Eagle's Nest on Vail Mountain to the Game Creek Club for an evening of gourmet dining, surrounded

by snow-covered evergreens. Chef Paul Forzacca creates a culinary extravaganza for guests at this superb restaurant. You'll feast on a multicourse dinner
that, depending on the season, may include smoked rainbow trout, five-spice
roasted duck, barbecue-grilled swordfish, or pan-roasted Colorado striped
bass. Guests may opt to stay overnight at the Game Creek Club Chalet. Call
in advance for dinner reservations and additional information.

LODGING: Hyatt Regency Beaver Creek, 50 West Thomas Place, P.O.
Box 1595, Avon, CO 81620; (970) 949–1234 or (800) 233–1234. Located
just steps from the slopes, this ski-in/ski-out lodge sits in the heart of Beaver
Creek. Standard rooms are spacious, with mountain views. Suites have a gas
fireplace, a towel warmer, and lush terry robes. Extras include a complete spa
facility, six whirlpools beneath a waterfall, and a huge outdoor fireplace
where guests gather for cocktails in the evening. The hotel has so many
wood-burning fireplaces that a full-time firetender is employed to keep the
hearths stoked. Of special mention is the storyteller who mingles with guests
in the lobby and shares tales of Beaver Creek in the early days. This engaging
gentleman, who is in his early seventies, dresses in a cowboy hat, crisp white
shirt, leather vest, red bandanna, and cowboy boots. He is in the hotel Thursday through Saturday from 4:00 to 7:00 P.M. Prices at the Hyatt change with
the seasons; the best rates are in spring and fall. To get to the Hyatt, travel
west from Vail on I–70 for 8 miles and take the Avon exit south to the
Beaver Creek entrance. You will pass through a guard gate before entering
the resort area.

DAY 2

Morning

BREAKFAST: The **Patina** in the Hyatt (970–949–1234) is convenient, and
the morning buffet is hearty. Request a made-to-order omelet or eggs Benedict. A cold buffet with granola, muffins, and fruit is another option. The
outdoor terrace is the perfect place for that endless cup of coffee. The restaurant serves breakfast from 7:00 to 10:30 A.M.

   If skiing is an indispensable part of your vacation, you'll love this getaway.
Choose the excitement of **Vail Mountain.** Its immense terrain stretches
over 3,150 vertical feet, making it the largest single ski mountain in the
country. Skiers may also want to try the great bumps of **Beaver Creek.**

Vail attracts skiers and visitors *from around the world.*

(photo by Chan Christiansen).

Summer activities run the gamut from golf to river rafting. With **nine 18-hole courses** in the Vail Valley, you'll find plenty of variety.

Beaver Creek Resort Golf Club, at the foot of Beaver Creek Mountain, offers views of the surrounding ranges in the White River National Forest. For information call (970) 845–5775.

Cordillera has two 18-hole courses: one "mountain course" and a "valley course" that each provide views of the Sawatch and Gore Mountain Ranges. For information call (970) 926–5100.

Eagle-Vail Golf Course, located between Vail and Beaver Creek, has reasonable fees. Contact Eagle-Vail Golf Course, 0431 Eagle Drive, Avon CO 81620; (970) 949–5267.

River rafters can contact **Timberline Tours** (P.O. Box 131, Vail, CO 81658; 970–476–1414 or 800–831–1414) for float trips on the Colorado, Arkansas, and Eagle Rivers.

LUNCH: Golden Eagle Inn (located on Beaver Creek Plaza, next to the new outdoor ice rink; 970–949–1940) serves Florida blue crab cakes with asparagus and smoked chicken fettuccine, as well as a wide selection of other entrees.

If you are in Vail at lunchtime, try **Garfinkel's** (970–476–3789), located next to the Eagle Bahn Gondola in Lionshead. Its menu says SKI HARD-- PARTY HARDER. Here you'll find pool, Foosball, sports on television, beer on tap, and menu choices such as BLT on Texas toast and chicken quesadilla.

Afternoon

At an altitude of 8,200 feet, the **Betty Ford Alpine Gardens,** located in the **Gerald R. Ford Park,** are the highest public alpine gardens in the world. The botanical gardens are named for Mrs. Ford's contributions to the Vail Valley. Nearly 500 varieties of plants and flowers are featured in the gardens, which are open from "dawn to dusk, snowmelt to snowfall." Admission is free. The Betty Ford Alpine Gardens are located at the east end of Vail Village along the Gore Creek walking path. For additional information contact Vail Alpine Garden Foundation, 183 Gore Creek Drive, Vail, CO 81657; (970) 476–0103.

Another excellent outdoor experience is a visit to the **Vail Nature Center** (601 Vail Valley Drive, Vail, CO 81657; 970–479–2291). Walk the quiet trails of seven acres of mountain vegetation with an experienced naturalist. Visit the interpretive center and inquire about special programs that include a Wildflower Walk, a Beaver Pond Tour, and a Morning Bird Walk. Other classes include Flyfishing and Stream Ecology, as well as Nature's Medicine Chest and Pantry, in which participants learn about plants used to create many modern medicines. The center is open late May through early October from 9:00 A.M. to 5:00 P.M. daily. Admission is $1.00 for persons ages seven and older.

To see memorabilia from the famous Tenth Mountain Division, visit the **Colorado Ski Museum and Colorado Ski Hall of Fame** (231 South Frontage Road, Vail, CO 81658; 970–476–1876). This is one of several museums in the country dedicated to the history of skiing. The museum is open from 10:00 A.M. to 5:00 P.M. Tuesday through Sunday; closed during May and October.

DINNER: Beano's Cabin, Beaver Creek Mountain, Beaver Creek; (970) 949–9090. Take a horse-drawn wagon ride to this luxury log-cabin restaurant located on Beaver Creek Mountain. In winter, you will arrive via Sno-Cat-drawn sleigh. Tucked away in the Larkspur Bowl, this cozy restaurant serves wood-fired pizzas, homemade soups, and fresh-baked bread, along with an array of tempting gourmet entrees. Sunday brunch at Beano's is superb. The restaurant is open from December through April and from June through late September. Horseback rides and horse-drawn wagons depart from the Beaver Creek stables; or you can arrive by shuttle van, which departs from the covered bridge in Beaver Creek.

LODGING: Hyatt Regency Beaver Creek.

DAY 3

Morning

BREAKFAST: The Dancing Bear, located in the West Vail Lodge, exit 173 off I–70; (970) 476–2290. Bagels, multigrain pancakes, and eggs Benedict top the list for breakfast, served from 7:00 to 11:00 A.M. weekdays and until noon on weekends.

Return to Denver via I–70 east.

THERE'S MORE

Gerald R. Ford Amphitheater, located next to Gore Creek east of Vail, is an open-air theater that hosts the Bolshoi Ballet Academy, in addition to free concerts, in the summer. Call (970) 476–2918.

The Chapel at Beaver Creek offers the following Sunday services: Presbyterian at 8:00 A.M., Baptist at 9:30 A.M., Lutheran at 11:00 A.M., and Catholic Mass at 5:30 P.M. The chapel is located on Elk Track Road immediately south of Beaver Creek Village. A mountaintop service (11:30 A.M. in summer and 12:30 P.M. in winter) takes place at the top of Beaver Creek Mountain. Visitors arrive via chairlift. Skier access is next to the small bridge over Beaver Creek, across from Centennial Express chairlift. For more information call (970) 845–9449.

Minturn. Located 7 miles west of Vail via Interstate 70, this town (population approximately 1,300) retains its down-to-earth atmosphere but is slowly updating its image. What used to be a drugstore is now an art gallery.

SPECIAL EVENTS

April. Taste of Vail Après-Ski Event is a palate-pleasing list of activities that include port wine seminars, cooking demonstrations, winemaker dinners, and a mountaintop picnic. For additional information call Vail/Beaver Creek reservations at (800) 622–3131 or Taste of Vail at (303) 479–0220.

Colorado Microbrewery Tasting draws beer lovers from around the state. Held annually at the Hyatt Regency Beaver Creek, this event is informative and entertaining. Call (970) 949–1234.

July through August. Bravo! Colorado. Music fills the valley during these well-attended concerts, held at the Ford Amphitheater, at the Vail Interfaith Chapel, and in Beaver Creek. Contact Bravo! Colorado, 953 South Frontage Road #104, Vail, CO 81657; (970) 827–5700.

September. Vail Mountain School Home Tour. Visit elegant homes in Vail and the surrounding area. For information call (970) 476–3850.

October. Annual Vintners of Colorado Food and Wine Tasting. A seminar, reception, and four-course dinner complemented by Colorado wines highlight this event, held at the Hyatt Regency Beaver Creek. A port/cigar tasting takes place the same weekend. You'll feel oh-so-genteel as you sip a glass of rich port and puff a Macanudo next to the roaring fire in the Hyatt's Crooked Hearth. Representatives from port and cigar companies enlighten guests on the traditions and etiquette. For details call (970) 949–1234.

OTHER RECOMMENDED RESTAURANTS AND LODGINGS

Vail

Daily Grind, 288 Bridge Street, Vail, CO 81657; (970) 476–5856. With strong coffee, excellent pastries, and a clientele that includes locals, this cafe is one you won't want to miss.

Sweet Basil, 193 East Gore Creek Drive, Vail, CO 81657; (970) 476–0125. Lunch is a better bargain than dinner at this popular restaurant, but you can be assured that whenever you dine here, the food and service will be outstanding. Sweet Basil offers seasonal specials such as mushroom appetizers and chocolate truffles in the autumn, when mushrooms are abundant.

Vail Cascade Hotel & Club, 1300 Westhaven Drive, Vail, CO 81657; (970) 476–7111. This ski-in/ski-out property has a ski valet to provide a fast route to the top of the mountain for its guests. During summer the hotel offers bicycle rentals as well as indoor and outdoor tennis courts. **The Cascade Club and Spa** offers aerobics and fitness classes, racquetball, steam rooms, and full-body massages.

Vail Athletic Club Hotel & Spa, 352 East Meadow Drive, Vail, CO 81657; (970) 476–0700. Located in the heart of Vail Village, this hotel offers a full athletic club and spa.

Edwards

Lazy Ranch Bed & Breakfast, P.O. Box 404, Edwards, CO 81632; (970) 926–3876. Feed the chickens and the horses, and enjoy the country atmosphere of this homey B&B located 10 miles west of Vail.

Beaver Creek

The Charter (P.O. Box 5310, Beaver Creek, CO 81620; 800–525–6660 or 970–949–6660) has luxury condominiums for rent, as well as a complete spa facility on-site. This lodge makes the ideal home away from home.

FOR MORE INFORMATION

The Chamber of Commerce, P.O. Box 1437, Avon, CO 81620; (970) 949–5189.

Eagle Valley Chamber of Commerce, P.O. Box 964, Eagle, CO 81631; (970) 328–5220.

Vail Valley Tourism and Convention Bureau, 100 East Meadow Drive, Vail, CO 81657; (800) 525–3875 or (970) 476–1000.

Vail/Beaver Creek Reservations, P.O. Box 7, Vail, CO 81658; (800) 622–3131 or (970) 949–5750.

Glenwood Springs

RELAXATION IN THE ROCKIES

1 NIGHT

*Hot springs • Historic hotels • Fishing • Vapor caves
• Firefighter memorials • Brewery*

Located at the foot of spectacular Glenwood Canyon and next door to the Colorado River, Glenwood Springs boasts the world's largest natural outdoor hot springs pool. And what a lagoon it is! Relax in the steamy, soothing waters as you gaze out onto the mountainous backdrop.

Before becoming known for its resort atmosphere, this area was the meeting place for the Utes, who called the region Yampah, meaning "big medicine." Today you can indulge in a massage or herbal Jacuzzi at the Yampah Spa and Vapor Caves.

The town's Hotel Colorado is known for its historic stateliness. When Theodore Roosevelt stayed here in 1905 after hunting bear in the area, the grand lodge came to be called the Little White House of the West. One story says that hotel maids fashioned a bear from fabric after Roosevelt's unsuccessful hunt, hence the origination of the teddy bear. The Hotel Denver, located across from the train station, began as a boardinghouse. Today, the renovated lodge has its own brewpub.

The region offers a wealth of sports activities that include golf, rafting, and fishing during summer, and skiing, snowmobiling, and ice fishing during winter. A nighttime visit to the hot springs is a good end to any day.

DAY 1

Morning

From Denver head west on I–70 for 158 miles to Glenwood Springs. You'll travel the recently finished (at a cost of $490 million) four-lane interstate

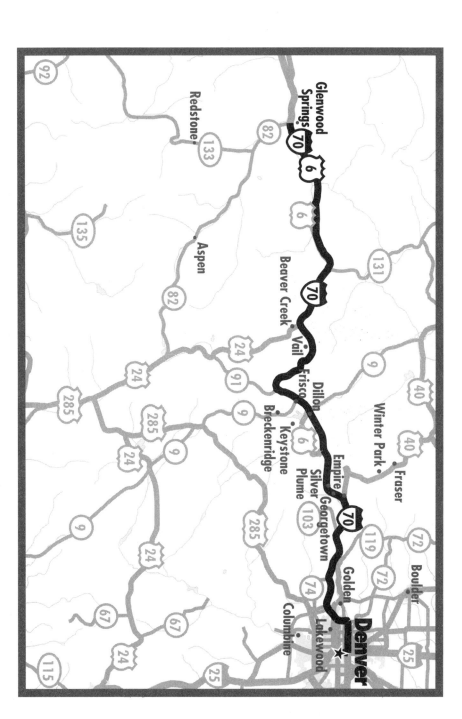

through Glenwood Canyon. This 18-mile stretch is billed as one of the most remarkable and beautiful roadways ever built.

LUNCH: Hot Springs Pool Restaurant, 401 North River Street, Glenwood Springs, CO 81601; (970) 945–7131. This casual restaurant has daily specials that change, but you might find grilled cheese with seven-bean soup or cream of potato soup. Other choices include roast beef dinner, stuffed baked potatoes, and cheeseburgers. The restaurant is open from 7:00 A.M. to 3:00 P.M. daily.

Afternoon

After lunch, sunbathe in the grassy area near the **Hot Springs Pool** or, if it's winter, soak in one of the two steamy pools and watch snowflakes fall. The larger pool is maintained at 90 degrees Fahrenheit and the smaller pool at 104 degrees.

Every six hours some three and a half million gallons of water from the springs refill the large pool. Kids love the water slide ($4.00 for eight rides). At the Hot Springs Athletic Club, guests can use the indoor Jacuzzi, play racquetball, or lift weights for an additional fee.

The pools are open every day of the year (except when they are being cleaned) and have been since 1888. Hours are 9:00 A.M. to 10:00 P.M. during the winter and 7:30 A.M. to 10:00 P.M. during summer. A daily pass is $7.25 for adults and $4.75 for children ages three to twelve. For more information call (970) 945–7131.

Across from the Hot Springs Pool is the **Glenwood Springs Center for the Arts** (970–945–2414), which exhibits work by local artists. Hours are Monday through Friday from 10:00 A.M. to 4:00 P.M. and Saturday and Sunday from noon to 4:00 P.M.

Visit the two **Storm King Mountain Memorials,** honoring the four-teen firefighters who lost their lives while battling a fire in nearby South Canyon on July 6, 1994. A sculpture of three firefighters is located at Two Rivers Park in Glenwood Springs; take Sixth Street west to Devereaux Road and turn left to Two Rivers Park. The other memorial is a trail located 2 miles outside the city, at the scene of the blaze. To reach the trail, take I–70 west from Glenwood Springs to the Canyon Creek exit (number 109); drive east for 0.5 mile, park, and hike the 1.5-mile trail at the base of Storm King Mountain.

DINNER: Glenwood Canyon Brewing Company, located in the Hotel Denver, 402 Seventh Street; (970) 945–1276. This restaurant and pub are

The train rolls into this *picturesque town twice a day.*

(photo by Sherry Spitsnaugle).

housed on the site of a turn-of-the-century bottling plant. Exposed brick and large windows create a pleasant atmosphere in both the bar and the restaurant. Handcrafted beers on tap include Hanging Lake Honey Ale (made with local honey) and Vapor Cave India Pale Ale. For starters try the canyon quesadilla or the macho nachos. In brewery tradition brewpub bread bowls include soup or stew served with bread. The Wisconsin Cheddar cheese beer soup is delectable. Other choices include grilled salmon filet, baked baby back ribs, and Maine lobster soft tacos. Authentic old-fashioned root beer made with local honey is available. The brewery opens at 11:00 A.M. daily.

LODGING: Hotel Colorado, 526 Pine Street; (800) 544–3998 or (970) 945–6511. This dignified lodging, with its 128 rooms, counts among its visitors American presidents, William Howard Taft and Theodore Roosevelt. The hotel is ideally located, adjacent to the Hot Springs Pool. Many rooms are decorated with period antiques. Ask to see the penthouse suites on the fifth floor—you'll have to climb the stairs to see the two bell-tower suites, but doing so is worth the effort.

DAY 2

Morning

BREAKFAST: The **Grand Lobby** in the Hotel Colorado has traditional breakfast fare, as well as nontraditional items, including a breakfast quesadilla, and smoked trout and a bagel. The restaurant serves breakfast from 7:00 to 11:00 A.M. daily.

Walk the short distance from Hotel Colorado to the **Yampah Spa and Vapor Caves** and sweat out your cares in the 115-degree steam caves. Pamper yourself with a European body wrap, a mud bath, an herbal facial, or a rose petal masque. Rest in the solarium after your massage. The Vapor Caves are open from 9:00 A.M. to 9:00 P.M. seven days a week. Admission to the caves is $8.75. To make an appointment for a massage, contact Yampah Spa and Vapor Caves, 709 East Sixth Street, Glenwood Springs, CO 81601; (970) 945–0667.

Stories say that famous gunman **Doc Holliday** came west to Glenwood Springs in 1887 searching for a cure for his tuberculosis, but the disease was already in an advanced stage. Holliday died at age thirty-five, supposedly in bed with his boots on at the Glenwood Hotel. Today you can visit the **grave of the legendary gunslinger.** The trail to Holliday's grave begins at Twelfth Street and Bennett Avenue. From there it's an easy 0.5-mile hike to the historic Linwood Cemetery. Look for the signs leading to Holliday's grave. Anonymous donors often leave a deck of cards or a whiskey bottle on the site.

LUNCH: Daily Bread Cafe and Bakery, 729 Grand Avenue; (970) 945–6253. Breads and pastries baked from scratch highlight the menu at this restaurant. The spinach salad satisfies even the grandest appetite. Other options include taco salad, tuna grill, and a bacon, mushroom, and onion burger. Save room for a piece of peach or chocolate Kahlúa pecan pie. The cafe is open from 7:00 A.M. to 2:00 P.M. Monday through Friday, from 8:00 A.M. to 2:00 P.M. Saturday, and for breakfast only, from 8:00 A.M. to noon Sunday.

Afternoon

On the way back to Denver via I–70, hike **Hanging Lake Trail,** which you can reach from the Hanging Lake Rest Area 11 miles east of Glenwood

Springs in Glenwood Canyon. This easily accessible hike is one of the most popular in Colorado. Plan on an hour to hike the 1-mile trail. Hanging Lake, canyon cliffs, and waterfalls are the rewards. Be sure to bring your camera.

For a special dinner on the return trip to Denver, dine at **The Fort** (19192 Route 8 at U.S. 285, Morrison, CO 80465; 303–697–4771). Though this restaurant can seat more than 300 guests, you'll still be able to have a romantic dinner at a fireside table. Buffalo is a preferred choice, but you can also order elk, salmon, prime rib roast, or fresh rainbow trout. Recite the Mountain Man's Toast (on the back of the restaurant's business card) with the correct hand gestures and your first cocktail is on the house. If you're celebrating a birthday or anniversary, the waiter will bring a piece of chocolate cake and a candle and take your picture to send home with you. Take C–470 east to 285 south, and follow Route 8 to the restaurant. The Fort is open for dinner only. Reservations are recommended.

THERE'S MORE

Amtrak. Take the train from Denver's Union Station to Glenwood Springs. The five-and-a-half-hour trip takes passengers through fabulous scenery and more than thirty-five tunnels. For a schedule call Amtrak at (800) 872–7245.

Sunlight Mountain Resort. This small resort, 10 miles southwest of Glenwood Springs off Highway 82, offers friendly service and affordable rates. You can rent downhill or cross-country gear, take lessons, and enjoy a day on the slopes for much less than it would cost at many other resorts. Many lodges offer a package deal with lift ticket included. Take Highway 82 south (also known as Grand Avenue) from Glenwood Springs to Four Mile Road (County Road 117). Signs will direct you to the ski area. Additionally, shuttles run regularly from town to the resort. For information call Sunlight Mountain Resort at (800) 445–7931 or (970) 945–7491.

Redstone. This small rural town has Victorian homes, antiques shops, art galleries, and boutiques along its single main street. To reach Redstone, drive 12 miles south on Highway 82 to Carbondale and continue west on Highway 133 to Redstone.

Frontier Historical Museum, 1001 Colorado Ave, Glenwood Springs; (970) 945–4448. The museum holds the bedroom furnishings from Colorado's legendary couple Horace and Baby Doe Tabor. Admission is

$3.00 for adults; children under twelve get in free. From May through September the museum's hours are 11:00 A.M. to 4:00 P.M. Monday through Saturday. From October through April its hours are 1:00 to 4:00 P.M. Monday, Thursday, Friday, and Saturday.

River rafting. Spend a half-day or an entire day in a raft on the Colorado River or the Roaring Fork River. Contact Rock Gardens Rafting, Inc., 1308 County Road 129, Glenwood Springs, CO 81602; (970) 945–6737.

Snowmobiling. The Sunlight to Powderhorn Trail, a recreational trail, runs from Sunlight Mountain Resort all the way to Powderhorn near Grand Junction. The trail is well groomed and well marked. For rentals and information call Rocky Mountain Sports, 2177 300th R, Glenwood Springs, CO 81601; (970) 945–8885.

Fishing. Stop in and talk shop with the staff at Roaring Fork Anglers (2022 Grand Avenue; 970–945–0180). Whether it's the Crystal, Eagle, Fryingpan, Colorado, or Roaring Fork, these guides know the river like an old friend.

SPECIAL EVENTS

June. Glenwood Springs' Strawberry Days began in 1897. It's the city's biggest and most popular happening, and you won't want to miss the free strawberries and ice cream.

June–August. Summer of Jazz. On Wednesday evenings musicians gather to put on a show of blues, Dixieland, and jazz. The show starts at 6:30 at Two Rivers Park, Highway 6 and Two Rivers Park Road. For information call (970) 945–6589.

OTHER RECOMMENDED RESTAURANTS AND LODGINGS

Glenwood Springs

Calder's Market (730 Grand; 970–945–2055) is the place locals socialize over gourmet java and a pastry.

Wildrose Bakery (310 Seventh Street, across from the train depot; 970–928–8973) offers fresh bread, pastries, quiche, coffee, and tea.

Nineteenth Street Diner, 1908 Grand Avenue; (970) 945–9133. Order a Philly Cheesesteak, then adjourn to the bar to watch some sports on the television at this casual restaurant.

Florindo's, 721 Grand Avenue, Glenwood Springs; (970) 945–1245. This restaurant specializes in northern and southern Italian cooking. Daily specials change, but you'll always find an excellent selection of pastas and seafood. Lunch is served from 11:30 A.M. to 3:00 P.M. Monday through Friday.

Sopris Restaurant and Lounge, located 5 miles south of Glenwood Springs on Highway 82; (970) 945–7771. This restaurant has an extensive wine list and fresh seafood, steak, and veal. Open from 5:00 P.M. daily.

Hotel Denver, 402 Seventh Street, Glenwood Springs; (970) 945–6565 or (800) 826–8820. Built in 1906, this lodge is located directly across from the train station and offers special weekend package deals.

Redstone

Redstone Castle, 0058 Redstone Boulevard, Redstone, CO 81623; (970) 963–3463 or (800) 643–4837. Antiques, feather comforters, a library, and views of the Crystal River grace this B&B. If you can't book a night here, try to schedule a tour. Tickets are $10 per person and can be purchased at either the Redstone Country Store (located at the south end of Redstone Boulevard; 970–963–3408) or the Three Sisters Bookstore (located at the north end of Redstone Boulevard; 970–963–2551). The guided tour lasts an hour and a half and is given Saturdays and Sundays at 1:30 P.M. To reach Redstone, drive 12 miles south on Highway 82 to Carbondale and continue west on Highway 133. Redstone Castle is located 1 mile south of the town of Redstone.

Redstone Inn (82 Redstone Boulevard, Redstone, CO 81623; 970–963–2526 or 800–748–2524) offers lodging and a restaurant. Dine on Brie-stuffed mushrooms for an appetizer and continue with wood-roasted chicken or Colorado prime rib.

Pie Plate Cafe, 373 Redstone Boulevard, Redstone, CO 81623; (970) 963–8347. Enjoy Egg McRedstone--otherwise known as ham and eggs-- or quiche of the day. The Pie Plate Cafe is open from 8:00 A.M. to 4:00 P.M. daily.

FOR MORE INFORMATION

Glenwood Springs Chamber of Commerce, 1102 Grand Avenue, Glenwood Springs, CO 81601; (970) 945–6589.
Central Reservations; (888) 445–3696.

Aspen

ONE OF THE WORLD'S MOST BEAUTIFUL SETTINGS

2 NIGHTS

Maroon Bells • World-famous music festival • Art galleries •
Shopping • Fine dining • Victorian architecture

Aspen is indeed the place to schmooze, schuss, and cruise the après-ski hot spots, but this famous town is also a cultural mecca and recreational paradise.

Visit during the summer months when the Aspen Music Festival is in full swing and you'll get a taste of everything from classical to opera as melodies permeate idyllic afternoons. Raft the rivers, climb the mountains, or uncover that elusive bargain in one of the trendy boutiques. If this is your first visit to Aspen, you'll be impressed by the area's awesome beauty. Snowcapped peaks, Victorian homes, and tree-lined streets welcome you to this region that combines jet-setters, celebrities, longtime residents, and tourists.

On the slopes, Aspen's runs rate as world-class. Off the slopes, Aspen is a bona fide community with year-round residents, town festivals, and Friday-night little league games. Nonetheless, the allure lies in the charisma and splendor of this well-known area.

DAY 1

Morning

Aspen is located 220 miles from Denver. Drive west on I–70 to Glenwood Springs and then southeast on Highway 82 to Aspen.

BREAKFAST: Petra Cafe, 507 Taos Street, Georgetown; (303) 569–2443. This quiet Victorian town, located forty-five minutes west of Denver, makes a

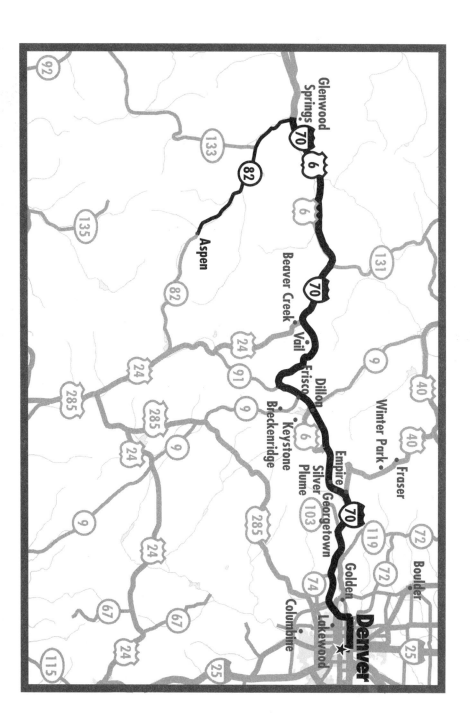

perfect morning stop. Breakfast at the Petra is exceptionally good. You'll find omelets, fruit bowls, and baked goods, as well as a pleasant courtyard for outdoor dining.

From Georgetown continue west on I–70, and southeast on Highway 82 from Glenwood Springs.

When you arrive in Aspen, stop at the **Aspen Chamber Resort Association** (425 Rio Grande Place; 970–925–1940). From Main Street turn north onto Mill Street. Turn right onto Rio Grande Place and immediately turn right into the parking circle. The center is open from 8:00 A.M. to 5:00 P.M. Monday through Friday; closed weekends year-round.

LUNCH: Boogie's Diner (534 East Cooper Avenue; 970–925–6610) has appetizers such as Chubby Checker Chicken Fingers and Boogie's Baltimore Chicken Wings. Entrees include the Monster Mash Meat Loaf Dinner; Elvis's Favorite, "The Hound Dog"; and macaroni and cheese. Indulge in Ben & Jerry's ice cream for dessert.

Afternoon

Art lovers can explore to their heart's content in Aspen's more than forty galleries. Pick up the complimentary copy of *Aspen Magazine's* Gallery Guide, which has a map and listings. You'll find a superior selection of photography, paintings, sculpture, jewelry, weavings, and more. **Footloose and Fancy Things** (240 Mill Street; 970–925–9155) has a selection of handmade moccasins, jewelry, belts, and a large collection of original E.S. Curtis photogravures.

To see exhibits from local and nationally acclaimed artists, visit the **Aspen Art Museum** (590 North Mill Street; 970–925–8050). The museum is housed in a former hydroelectric plant on the banks of the Roaring Fork River. The museum is open from 10:00 A.M. to 6:00 P.M. Wednesday, Friday, and Saturday and from 10:00 A.M. to 8:00 P.M. Thursday.

As you're cruising the galleries, you will want to "power shop" the exquisite boutiques, recreational stores, and bookshops that Aspen offers. **Mountains & Streams** (424 East Cooper Avenue; 970–925–5580) has an extensive selection of outdoor clothing.

DINNER: Soft lighting, fresh flowers, classical music, a roaring fireplace, and black-checked tablecloths on white linen set the scene for a romantic dinner at **Jack's Restaurant at the Sardy House** (128 East Main Street; 970–920–2525). Service is impeccable in this cozy dining room that seats twenty-two, and cuisine is equally superb. Begin with an appetizer, such as the smoked trout and spinach salad, and move on to one of many succulent entrees, such as seared Chilean sea bass or grilled caribou tenderloin. For dessert splurge on bananas Foster or ginger crème brûlée. The table by the bay window is a favorite. Reservations are recommended. Jack's is open for breakfast from 7:30 to 10:30 A.M. daily and until noon on Sunday; for dinner, from 5:30 until the last seating, at 9:30 P.M. Closed for lunch.

LODGING: Aspen Square Condominium Hotel, 617 East Cooper Avenue, Aspen, CO 81611; (970) 925–1000. Located in the heart of Aspen, this lodging is ideal for a stay of several nights. Rooms feature a wood-burning fireplace, a four-poster bed, ski storage, a fully stocked kitchen, and a balcony. You will want to take advantage of the free parking (a scarce commodity in Aspen), workout room, outdoor pool, and Jacuzzi.

DAY 2

Morning

BREAKFAST: Located steps away from the Aspen Square Condominium Hotel is **Poppycock's** (609 East Cooper Avenue; 970–925–1245). This busy restaurant specializes in affordable breakfasts and terrific smoothies.

"**First Time on Skis**" is a program offered by Ski Schools of Aspen that is the best deal going for rookies. Participants get three days of lift tickets, lessons, and ski rentals for $159 without equipment and $189 with equipment, in addition to a "guarantee" that they'll ski top-to-bottom on Buttermilk Mountain or from the top of Two Creeks to the base of Fanny Hill on Snowmass. If not, Day Four is free. Call **Aspen Skiing Company** at (970) 925–1220 or (800) 525–6200.

Novice snowboarders will want to sign up for the one- to three-day **snowboarding package,** in which class size is limited to three persons. Packages include instruction, lift tickets, and equipment. Call **Aspen Skiing Company** at (970) 925–1220 or (800) 525–6200.

If skiing is not on your agenda, there are numerous other options.

Take a **walking tour of Aspen** and learn about the historic past of this community. Originally the area was hunting land for the Ute Indians and later prospered with silver mining in the late 1800s. Call **Aspen Historical Society** at (970) 925–3721 for information.

The **Silver Queen Gondola,** at the base of the ski area, lifts riders to the 11,212-foot summit of Aspen Mountain in twenty minutes. At the top are views of the town of Aspen. The gondola is open 10:00 A.M. to 4:00 P.M. daily, mid-June through August, and weekends the first half of June and the month of September. A round-trip ride is $18.00 for adults, $12.00 for persons ages thirteen to nineteen, and $6.00 for children ages three to twelve. Ask about free concerts, nature walks, and high-altitude Frisbee golf at the summit.

LUNCH: In winter, skiers and nonskiers alike can ride the Silver Queen Gondola to have lunch at **Sundeck Restaurant** (970–920–6335) located at the top of Aspen Mountain. Relax on the outdoor deck as you enjoy the views and lunch items such as elk chili or pizza. The Sundeck serves lunch from 11:00 A.M. to 3:30 P.M. daily.

Afternoon

Among the most photographed peaks in North America, **Maroon Bells** is located just outside Aspen. On the nearly 100 miles of trails, you can spend hours taking pictures and hiking this scenic area. Cars are not allowed on Maroon Lake Road between 8:30 A.M. and 5:00 P.M. June through Labor Day and weekends in September. If you are visiting at that time, plan to take the Roaring Fork Transit Authority shuttle to the base of the mountains. The driver gives an interesting history of the area and points out places where avalanches have occurred. If you drive your car to Maroon Bells, take Highway 82 from Aspen for 1 mile west and turn left at the ASPEN HIGHLANDS sign.

As home to Aspen's art community, the **Wheeler Opera House** (320 East Hyman Avenue; 970–920–5770) has been restored to its original Victorian splendor. The 3-story building is both a museum and a state-of-the-art performance center. This showpiece structure features velvet stage curtains, a red carpet, and lavish period furnishings. Take a tour, or better yet, attend a ballet, opera, or theater performance. The Wheeler Opera House is located on the corner of Mill Street and Hyman Avenue Mall and is open for free tours from 9:00 A.M. to 5:00 P.M. every day of the year.

DINNER: Lucci's (508 East Cooper Street; 970–925–8866) offers an array of Italian fare, including everything from classic minestrone soup to veal shank braised in white wine and cooked in tomato-garlic sauce. You'll dine by candlelight on a red-checked tablecloth. For dessert try the tiramisù or the restaurant's own version of chocolate "moose."

LODGING: Aspen Square Condominium Hotel.

DAY 3

Morning

BREAKFAST: Main Street Bakery Cafe, 201 East Main Street; (970) 925–6446. Hardwood floors, alfresco dining on the patio, gourmet jams, and fresh-baked scones, croissants, and muffins help make this restaurant a favorite. Try the corned-beef hash, breakfast burrito, pancakes with fresh fruit, or homemade granola with a cup of Aspen Blend coffee. Main Street Bakery is open from 7:00 A.M. to 9:30 P.M. daily.

Return to Denver via Highway 82 west to Glenwood Springs and I–70 east.

THERE'S MORE

Rocky Mountain Institute, 1739 Snowmass Creek Road, Old Snowmass, CO 81654; (970) 927–3851. This world-famous think tank was created with research in mind. Free guided tours are conducted Tuesdays and Fridays at 2:00 P.M.; visitors can take a self-guided tour anytime from 9:00 A.M. to 4:30 P.M. Monday through Friday. To get to the institute from Aspen, drive north on Highway 82 for 14 miles to Old Snowmass and go left. Follow Snowmass Creek Road for 1.7 miles.

River rafting. For a trip down the Roaring Fork, contact **Colorado Riff Raft** (555 East Durant Avenue, P.O. Box 4949, Aspen, CO 81612; 800–759–3939 or 970–925–5405). Cruise the Pinball Rapids and the Raft Ripper Rapids on the Arkansas River. Another rafting company is **Blazing Adventures** (800–282–7238 or 970–925–5651).

Ashcroft mining town. Located 13 miles from Aspen in the Castle Creek Valley, Ashcroft once boasted 2,500 residents in its heyday as a mining camp in the late 1800s. Today you can tour the old buildings and hike the nearby trails. To get to Ashcroft from Aspen, follow Highway 82 west to Castle Creek Road. Turn left and travel on Castle Creek Road for 12 miles. For information call the **Aspen Historical Society** at (970) 925–3721.

SPECIAL EVENTS

June. The *Food & Wine* Magazine Classic at Aspen is one of the largest and most prestigious events of its kind. The world's leading chefs and wine experts gather to participate in cooking demonstrations, wine and food tastings, and seminars. Call (888) 794–6397.

June–August. Aspen Music Festival and School. An impressive roster of visiting conductors and guest artists highlight this renowned event, which attracts musicians, students, and audiences. For a complete calendar call (970) 925–3254 or the concert hotline at (970) 925–3172.

July. The annual Independence Day Parade brings out the entire community for a parade and old-fashioned fun. For information call (970) 925–1940.

July–August. Aspen Theatre in the Park. Experience contemporary theatre in an intimate outdoor setting. For tickets call (970) 920–5070.

OTHER RECOMMENDED RESTAURANTS AND LODGINGS

Aspen

Jimmy's: An American Restaurant and Bar, 205 South Mill; (970) 925–6020. Enjoy a cocktail on the outdoor deck. The menu includes burgers, steaks, and ribs. Open daily from 3:30 P.M. to 2:00 A.M.

Flying Dog Brew Pub, 424 East Cooper Avenue; (970) 925–7464. Enjoy a pint of the brewpub's best-seller, Doggie Style Ale, as you look over the menu, which includes basic pub-grub fare.

Sardy House, 128 East Main, Aspen, CO 81611; (970) 920–2525 or (800) 321–3457. The parlor of this B&B summons guests to relax in the inviting, velvet-covered sofas and chairs. Furnishings are classy and comfortable, and you'll find his-and-her terry robes in your room, as well as a towel warmer, feather comforter, and cherry-wood armoire. Breakfast is served on the patio outside next to the pool or in the antique-filled dining room.

T-Lazy-7-Ranch, 3129 Maroon Creek Road, Aspen; (970) 925–4614. Located in a beautiful area on the road to Maroon Bells, the T-Lazy-7 is a great place to get away from it all. Enjoy snowmobiling in winter and horseback riding in summer. The ranch offers a western party Wednesdays and Thursdays that features a cook-your-own ribeye steak dinner, a sleigh ride, and a live country band.

Snowmass Village

Snowmass Lodge & Club, P.O. Box G-2, Snowmass Village, CO 81615; (800) 525–0710 or (970) 923–5600. This accommodation offers a full-service resort atmosphere with all the amenities you'll need for a skiing or a nonskiing vacation. A restaurant, an athletic club, racquetball, an indoor swimming pool, a golf course, indoor tennis courts, and shuttle service to the town of Aspen and the ski areas of Aspen and Buttermilk Mountains are available.

Carbondale

Mt. Sopris Inn, 0165 Mt. Sopris Ranch Road, P.O. Box 126, Carbondale, CO 81623; (970) 963–2209 or (800) 437–8675. This comfortable B&B is located on fourteen acres near the Crystal River.

FOR MORE INFORMATION

Aspen Chamber Resort Association, 425 Rio Grande Place, Aspen, CO 81611; (970) 925–1940 or (800) 262–7736.

Aspen Central Reservations, 425 Rio Grande Place, Aspen, CO 81611; (888) 290–1324.

Aspen Skiing Company, P.O. Box 1248, Aspen, CO 81612; (970) 925–1220 or (800) 525–6200.

Snowmass Resort Association, P.O. Box 5566, Snowmass Village, CO 81615; (970) 923–2000 or (800) 598–2003.

ᴱˢᶜᴬᴾᴱ ˢᴱⱽᴱₙ

WESTERN

Grand Junction and the Grand Valley

WILD, WOOLY, AND WONDERFUL

2 NIGHTS

Winery tours • Dino-digging • Colorado National Monument • Art on the Corner • Fine dining • Outdoor recreation

This up-and-coming, visitor-friendly community may take you by surprise. Emerging from its reputation as primarily an agricultural and industrial area, Grand Junction is also recognized for its cultural savvy and commitment to the arts. Add to this the glorious red canyons of Colorado National Monument and an area so rich in fossils that it delights dino lovers of all ages and you have a treasure trove of an excursion.

Stroll the tree-lined sidewalks of Main Street Mall and you'll see how Grand Junction is cultivating its image. Enjoy shaded streets, galleries, water fountains, historic structures, boutiques, and a cordial atmosphere. The Art on the Corner outdoor exhibit features more than four dozen impressive sculptures.

Winemakers have taken a liking to the region's fertile, fruit-producing land and have successfully established a half-dozen wineries in the valley. Drive from vineyard to vineyard and sample a chardonnay, cabernet, Riesling, or fruit wine. You'll be astounded at the incredible scenery that sprawls over this beautifully rugged countryside.

Best of all may be the dinosaur bones and tracks that survived in the Grand Valley. The fossils fascinate any adult or child in a T-Rex tizzy. Wanna-be paleontologists can explore to their heart's content.

Grand Junction makes the perfect jumping-off spot for any number of outdoor adventures. Set up base camp for a few days in this area and you'll have an almost infinite list of sites to uncover.

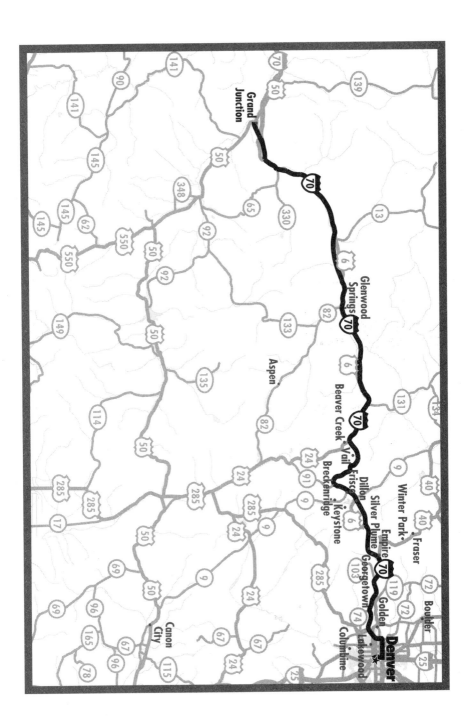

Local wineries *grow their own grapes.*

(photo by Sherry Spitsnaugle).

DAY 1

Morning

Travel west on I–70 to Grand Junction, located 258 miles from Denver.

BREAKFAST: Home on the Range Cafe (2700 Colorado Boulevard, Idaho Springs; 303–567–0518) was named "Best Breakfast on Your Way to the Mountains" by a local paper. Potato pancakes, biscuits and gravy, and breakfast burritos are favorites. If you order the pancake soufflé, plan on forty-five minutes for baking time. To get to Home on the Range, take the first exit into Idaho Springs and travel west on Colorado Boulevard; the cafe is on the north side of the street, several blocks after you enter town. The restaurant is open from 7:00 A.M. to 3:00 P.M. Monday and Tuesday and from 7:00 A.M. to 9:00 P.M. Wednesday through Saturday; closed Sunday.

When you arrive in Grand Junction, stop at the **visitor center** (740 Horizon Drive; 970–244–1480) to stock up on maps and information. This new facility has an exceptional display of photographs of the area. The staff here is eager to welcome visitors and answer questions. Be sure to pick up a map of the local wineries.

Take a jaunt downtown to admire the **Art on the Corner** outdoor sculptures, located on Main from First to Seventh Streets. Many of the works are available to purchase. The community votes every year for one sculpture that then becomes part of the permanent display.

LUNCH: Crystal Cafe, 314 Main Street, Grand Junction, CO 81501; (970) 242–8843. This family-run restaurant has been a success since the day it opened. Ceiling-size skylights create a light, airy setting, and cuisine here is second to none. Anyone seeking incredible desserts has come to the right place. Other guaranteed items include quiche of the day served with salad garnish, homemade soup of the day, and the grilled eggplant sandwich. For dessert choose Lila's fresh lemon tart with whipped cream or Marsha's double chocolate cake a la mode with hot fudge. Crystal Cafe serves breakfast from 7:00 to 10:15 A.M. daily. The lunch seating is from 11:00 A.M. to 1:45 P.M. daily.

Afternoon

A few doors down from Crystal Cafe is **Dinosaur Valley** (362 Main Street; 970–241–9210). This museum is a dinosaur devotee's heaven. Children love to excavate for "dinosaur bones" in the Kiddie Quarry. Volunteers are available to answer questions about the latest fossil discoveries. The museum is open daily from 9:00 A.M. to 5:00 P.M. Memorial Day through Labor Day. The remainder of the year, the hours are from 10:00 A.M. to 4:30 P.M. Tuesday through Saturday.

Next, visit the **Western Colorado Center for the Arts** (1803 North Seventh Street; 970–243–7377). The gallery has a collection of Native American tapestries, as well as contemporary art. The museum is open daily from 9:00 A.M. to 5:00 P.M. Admission is $2.00 for adults; free for those under twelve.

When you're ready for a break, stop at **Jitters Espresso Cafe & Bakery** (504 Main Street; 970–245–5194) and sip a cup of tea or gourmet java. The Espresso Milk Shake is a sure thing. Decor here is 1950s vintage.

The **Museum of Western Colorado** (248 South Fourth Street; 970–242–0971) chronicles the geologic and cultural history of western Colorado. Pottery, Ute baskets, and artifacts are displayed. The museum is open Monday through Saturday from 10:00 A.M. to 4:45 P.M. Memorial Day through Labor Day, and Tuesday through Saturday from 10:00 A.M. to 4:45 P.M. the remainder of the year. Admission is $2.00 for adults and $1.00 for ages two to seventeen.

To see lifelike dinosaur replicas that rumble and move, visit **Dinamation's Dinosaur Discovery Museum** (550 Crossroads Court, Fruita, 8 miles west of Grand Junction; 970–858–7282 or 800–DIG–DINO). Visitors are visually transported to the Jurassic period with the help of robotic, snarling creatures that will have your skin crawling and the kids running for cover. The believable Utah Raptor sends tremors through the crowd as it attacks another robotic reproduction. Stand on the earthquake simulator and feel the plate tectonics tremble as you begin to comprehend how the earth has been transformed through time. Hands-on exhibits are outstanding.

Dinamation's Dinosaur Discovery Museum is open seven days a week year-round. Hours are 9:00 A.M. to 5:00 P.M. Monday through Saturday and 10:00 A.M. to 5:00 P.M. Sunday. Admission is $5.00 for adults and $3.50 for kids and seniors; children ages two and younger are admitted free.

Let the kids tag along with paleontologists as they conduct their on-site research. **Dinosaur Discovery Expeditions** offers several-day sessions in the summer months that include accommodations, meals, transportation, equipment, and instruction about excavation. Inquire about Family Dino Camps by calling (800) DIG–DINO.

DINNER: Dolce Vita, 336 Main Street, Grand Junction; (970) 242–8482. This stylish eatery offers an urban atmosphere and creative cuisine. You could make a meal from the appetizers alone, but you won't want to miss out on the incredible entrees. Begin with nachos Italian-style or the *bruschetta,* which is grilled bread with garlic, roma tomatoes, basil, and olive oil topped with goat cheese. Next feast on Linguine Dolce Vita, a wonderful combination of shrimp, mushrooms, garlic, pine nuts, spinach, and pasta, or choose grilled marinated chicken breast, served with garlic mashed potatoes and vegetables. Dolce Vita is open from 11:00 A.M. to 10:00 P.M. Monday through Friday and from 11:30 A.M. to 10:00 P.M. Saturday; closed Sunday.

LODGING: Los Altos, 375 Hillview Drive, Grand Junction, CO 81503; (970) 256–0964 or (888) 774–0982. This exceptional B&B completed in 1997 indulges guests in luxurious decor and comfort. Each of its six rooms has a private bath and views of the spectacular Grand Valley. Of special mention is the Vista Suite, popular with honeymoon couples. This romantic suite features a gas fireplace, a king-size bed, a reading room, and two outdoor decks.

Nothing, it seems, has been overlooked in this spacious, light-filled room. Candles sit next to the oversize tub in the rose-colored bathroom, and brass racks hold luxuriant towels. A huge walk-in closet is perfect for a several-night stay. Rates range from $80 to $150 depending on the room and season.

DAY 2

Morning

BREAKFAST: Los Altos innkeepers Lee and Young-Ja Garrett go out of their way to ensure that you don't leave on an empty stomach. Breakfast may include pancakes or an egg casserole, along with homemade muffins, fresh fruit, and coffee or tea.

Morning is a glorious time to be at **Colorado National Monument,** when the pastel orange of the sky is at its most radiant. Millions of years of weather have created a theatrical exhibition of the forces of nature here. Sheer ridges, muted hues, and rugged textures characterize the maze of ravines and majestic landscape.

Golden eagles, bighorn sheep, mountain lions, chipmunks, and squirrels reside here. Encompassing 32 square miles, Colorado National Monument offers short walks and day trips or longer backcountry junkets. Hike the easy 1-mile-round-trip **Canyon Rim Trail,** which parallels a cliff edge, to enjoy a view of **Wedding Canyon.**

Monoliths, rock spires, and desolate mesas provide the backdrop for not only hikers but Nordic skiers and horseback riders. For a trail ride check with **Rim Rock Adventures** (970–858–9555). It offers hour-long or half-day rides into Devil's Canyon. Ask about the evening saddle-horse and pack-mule rides and scrumptious cookouts.

Drive the 23-mile **Rim Rock Drive,** which serves as the main road through the park and provides access to the visitor center and picnic area. From the road you can see much of the monument, but it would be a shame not to get out of the car and enjoy the breathtaking scenery. Stop at the **visitor center,** located 4 miles from the west entrance, for information about the geology and history of the monument, along with maps and a slide show. Rangers are on hand to suggest trails. Summer campfire programs are available. To get to the west entrance, take I–70 west to Fruita and follow the signs. To reach the east entrance, follow Monument Road west from downtown Grand Junction. Admission is $4.00 per vehicle for a seven-day pass.

For more information contact Colorado National Monument, Fruita, CO 81521; (970) 858–3617.

LUNCH: Picnic at one of several areas in Colorado National Monument.

Afternoon

Even if you're not a wine connoisseur, visiting the local **wineries** is an excellent choice for the afternoon. Travel east from Grand Junction on U.S. 6 about 12 miles to the small farming town of Palisade. Stop at the **Palisade Chamber of Commerce** (309 Main Street; 970–464–7458) for information and a map.

Begin at **Carlson Vineyards** (461 35 Road, Palisade; 970–464–5554). This mom-and-pop operation distinguishes itself with not only its excellent peach, plum, and cherry wines but also its wit. Ask for a sample of the Tyrannosaurus Red, made with Colorado grapes. The winery offers tours and samples year-round every day from 11:00 A.M. to 6:00 P.M.

The oldest winery in the state is **Colorado Cellars** (3553 East Road, Palisade; 800–848–2812). This winery produces about 15,000 cases of wine a year. The tasting room is open from 9:00 A.M. to 4:00 P.M. Monday through Friday and from noon to 4:00 P.M. Saturday.

Plum Creek Cellars (3708 G Road; 970–464–7586), located just outside Palisade, is open daily from 10:00 A.M. to 5:00 P.M. for samplings. Taste the 100 percent Colorado-grown wines, including pinot noir, merlot, sauvignon blanc, and Riesling.

Confre Cellars (3701 G Road, Palisade; 970–464–7899) produces honey wine—also known as mead—and has a well-stocked gift store. The winery offers tours and tastings daily from 10:00 A.M. to 5:00 P.M.

Grande River Vineyards (787 Elberta Avenue, Palisade; 970–464–5867) specializes in chardonnay and red and white Bordeaux-style blends. Tasting room hours vary.

Canyon Wind Cellars (3907 Highways 6 and 24, Palisade; 970–464–0888) has a beautiful setting, especially if you visit during the fall harvest, when the grapes are ready to be picked. Tours and tastings are available by appointment.

DINNER: Gladstones, 2531 North Twelfth Street, Grand Junction, CO 81501; (970) 241–6000. Begin with an appetizer of fresh Maine mussels or peel-and-eat shrimp, and move on to an entree such as Gladstones' specialty of prime rib or Australian lobster tail. Desserts include Kentucky bourbon chocolate chip pecan pie and chocolate mousse.

LODGING: Los Altos Bed and Breakfast.

DAY 3

Morning

BREAKFAST: Los Altos Bed and Breakfast.
Return to Denver via I–70 east.

THERE'S MORE

Cross Orchards Historic Farm (3073 Patterson/F Road; 970–434–9158) gives a sense of early farm life. In the late 1800s this apple orchard ranked as one of the largest and most productive in the United States. Wander the grounds and view exhibits that include plows, wagons, and old farming tools. The gift shop sells novelties and food items. Cross Orchards is open daily May through October from 10:00 A.M. to 4:00 P.M., as well as for special events throughout the year. Admission is $4.00 for adults, $3.50 for seniors, $2.00 for children ages six to twelve, and $1.00 for kids ages three to five; children under two are admitted free.

Powderhorn Resort. Located 35 miles east of Grand Junction; (970) 268–5700. Small, friendly, and accommodating, this ski resort offers two restaurants, a lodge, ski rentals, and a lounge. Snowmobilers can undertake the 120-mile recreational trail connecting Powderhorn Resort to Sunlight Mountain Resort in Glenwood Springs. The well-maintained track crosses White River and Grand Mesa National Forests.

Rock climbing. For personalized instruction with a qualified guide, contact Vertical Horizons Guides, P.O. Box 9031, Grand Junction, CO; (970) 245-8513. Owner-director Kris Hjelle has been climbing for more than twenty years.

Grand Junction Symphony. Enjoy outstanding classical performances with talented musicians and guest artists. For a schedule call the symphony at (970) 243–6787.

Adobe Creek Golf Course, 876 18½ Road, Fruita, CO 81521; (970) 858–0521. This 18-hole course offers affordable greens fees and a country club atmosphere.

SPECIAL EVENTS

April. Fruita Fat Tire Festival. Held late in the month. Join bicyclists for excursions along Kokopelli's Trail, which runs all the way to Moab, Utah. There's also plenty of carbo-laden food.

July. Dinosaur Days. This week-long festivity celebrates the mammoth creatures in a creative way, with dinosaur parades, concerts, and some silliness too.

August. Palisade Peach Festival. Celebrate the peach season at this several-day event, held late in the month, when the famous western slope peaches are ripe and juicy.

September. Colorado Mountain Winefest. Held late in the month. Grand Junction and Palisade host this three-day event dominated by wine tastings, celebrations of the grape, and gorgeous fall colors.

OTHER RECOMMENDED RESTAURANTS AND LODGINGS

Grand Junction

Rockslide Brewery, 401 Main Street; (970) 245–2111. Here you'll find Big Bear Stout, Rabbit Ears Amber Ale, and a menu that includes buffalo wings, a Philly steak sandwich, burgers, and pizza.

The Winery, 642 Main Street; (970) 242–4100. This restaurant is an excellent choice for a romantic dinner. The specialty here is steak, but choices also include orange-marinated swordfish, king crab, and salmon. Open 5:00 to 10:00 P.M. daily.

The Hilton, 743 Horizon Drive, Grand Junction, CO 81503; (970) 241–8888 or (800) 445–8667. This property has 264 rooms, tennis courts, a pool, and a fitness room.

FOR MORE INFORMATION

Grand Junction Visitor & Convention Bureau, 740 Horizon Drive, Grand Junction, CO 81506; (970) 244–1480 or (800) 962–2547.

Museum of Western Colorado, 248 South Fourth Street, Box 20000–5020, Grand Junction, CO 81502; (970) 242–0971.

Colorado National Monument, Fruita, CO 81521; (970) 858–3617.

Palisade Chamber of Commerce, 309 South Main Street, Palisade CO 81526; (970) 464–7458.

SOUTHERN
ESCAPES

Colorado Springs

PIKES PEAK GRANDEUR

2 NIGHTS

Historic luxury resort • U.S. Air Force Academy •
Manitou Springs • Garden of the Gods • Hiking
• Horseback riding • Pikes Peak and the World's
Highest Cog Railway • Mountain zoo

Tourists flock to Colorado Springs in numbers reaching up to six million annually, and it's no secret why: The area offers a mild, dry climate and a magnificent landscape, along with countless attractions.

The elegant Broadmoor, with its breathtaking mountain location, superb service, three 18-hole championship golf courses, world-class spa, and fine restaurants, is reason enough to visit this city. Add to this Pikes Peak, Cheyenne Mountain Zoo, and Garden of the Gods and you'll find more than enough to explore.

Nature provides many of the enticements that lured explorers long ago and captivate visitors today. One look at the 14,110-foot summit of Pikes Peak on a cloudless Colorado day will leave you in awe. More than a century ago, Katharine Lee Bates was so inspired by the magnificent view that she wrote the celebrated words to "America the Beautiful."

The glorious Pikes Peak region indeed brings to mind the phrases "spacious skies" and "purple mountain majesties."

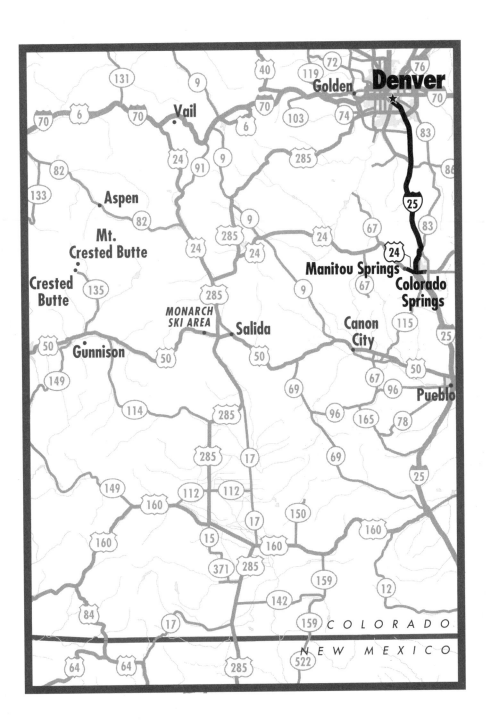

DAY 1

Morning

Take I–25 south from Denver for 70 miles of incredible views. You'll pass pine forests, and if you're fortunate you'll catch a glimpse of snowcapped Pikes Peak. Hold off for breakfast until you arrive at your classy digs at The Broadmoor. Exit at Circle Drive (number 138). Circle Drive turns into Lake Avenue, and The Broadmoor is located at the end of the road. Signs will direct you to the hotel.

BREAKFAST: Espresso Broadmoor is a favorite with guests for its relaxed setting and shining brass espresso machine. Try the vegetable quiche or a fresh-baked ham and cheese croissant. The cafe is located around the corner from the main lobby of The Broadmoor and is open from 6:30 A.M. to 10:00 P.M. daily.

Next, check with the concierge about a **tour of The Broadmoor.** As one of the country's most elegant resorts, this 3,000-acre property, which sits at the foot of Cheyenne Mountain, features everything from tennis courts to its own lake, as well as a state-of-the-art Spa and Fitness Center.

After your tour, head to what is billed as the most visited attraction in the area, **Garden of the Gods** (1805 North Thirtieth Street; 719–634–6666). To get to Garden of the Gods, take U.S. Highway 24, turn north on Ridge Road, and follow the signs. Garden of the Gods is open year-round, and admission is free.

The unusual red sandstone formations, which were molded by wind and water over millions of years, were declared sacred grounds to the Ute, Arapaho, and Cheyenne Indians. The area provides a dramatic backdrop for a late-morning hike, bicycle tour, or horseback ride. **Academy Riding Stables** has a horse suited to each rider's abilities and will give guided tours of the park. Rides are available throughout the summer months. Call Academy Riding Stables at (719) 633–5667 for information.

For details on hiking or biking, check with **Garden of the Gods Visitors Center.** The center is open from 8:00 A.M. to 8:30 P.M. during summer and from 8:30 A.M. to 5:30 P.M. in winter. At the center you can also learn more about the geology, vegetation, and history of the area. Naturalists are available during the summer months to guide walks around the park.

Learning the names of the unique formations is as much fun as admiring the boulders themselves. Look for **Balanced Rock,** the **Kissing Camels,** and **Toothsome Rocks.** The region is recognized worldwide for its chal-

The Broadmoor *sets the standard for luxury and service in the West.*
(photo by Bob McIntyre, McIntyre Photography).

lenging climbs, and you may see technical rock climbers inching up the
sandstone walls.

LUNCH: Marigold Cafe and Bakery (4935 Centennial Boulevard;
719–599–4776) has a menu that changes daily, but you'll find fresh-baked
pastries and items such as cream of chicken soup, Greek salad, and beef stew.
The restaurant serves breakfast and lunch only and is open from 6:00 A.M. to
5:00 P.M. Monday through Friday and from 7:00 A.M. to 5:00 P.M. Saturday.
Marigold Cafe is closed Sunday.

Afternoon

Glen Eyrie Castle (3820 North Thirtieth Street, Colorado Springs;
719–594–2477 or 800–944–4536) is a huge estate that was built by the

founding father of Colorado Springs, General William Palmer, for his wife. The property contains riding stables and nine reservoirs in addition to the castle. The mansion boasts twenty-four fireplaces and is listed on the National Register of Historic Places.

Visitors can indulge in the **Formal Victorian Tea** (Sunday only; $12.25; includes tour) or the **Cream Tea,** served Monday through Saturday ($9.50; includes tour). Afternoon tea, scones with Devonshire cream, a truffle, fresh fruit, and a slice of pound cake are served in the Music Room. Tours begin at 1:00 P.M., and admission is $5.00. Glen Eyrie is located just north of Garden of the Gods. Reservations are essential for tours or tea.

Visit the **Colorado Springs Fine Arts Center** (30 West Dale Street; 719–634–5581). This fine gallery and museum houses a world-class collection of art, including works by Charles Russell, Georgia O'Keeffe, and John James Audubon. International touring exhibits are also showcased in this Art Deco building. Admission is $3.00 for adults, $1.50 for seniors and students, and $1.00 for children ages six through twelve; children ages six and under are admitted free.

DINNER: Phantom Canyon Brewing Company, 2 East Pikes Peak Avenue, Colorado Springs, CO 80903; (719) 635–2800. Traditional pub grub of the best kind is served here, and you can wash down those beer-battered fish-and-chips with an excellent ale or stout. Feast on London broil of flank steak with roasted garlic mashed potatoes and creamed spinach and leeks, or beer-braised pot roast with mashed potatoes and gravy. Try a Queen's Blonde Ale, Phantom India Pale Ale, or Zebulon's Peated Porter, all of which are brewed on-site. Billiards are available upstairs, and you're likely to meet a local or two who frequent this preferred place to quaff a cold one. The microbrewery is open 11:00 A.M. to midnight on weekdays and 11:00 to 1:30 A.M. Saturday and Sunday.

LODGING: The Broadmoor, 1 Lake Avenue, Colorado Springs, CO 80906; (800) 634–7711. This famous resort is a tourist attraction all by itself. Service is impeccable, and the amenities at The Broadmoor are nothing less than first-class. Rooms are luxurious, and many offer splendid views of Cheyenne Mountain and the resort's Cheyenne Lake.

Spencer Penrose opened the pink-stucco, elaborately decorated hotel in the early 1800s to become none other than a world-class resort. The intricate chandeliers, marble fountain, and curved staircase helped to create an

Italian Renaissance style. The Broadmoor soon secured a reputation as one of the most superb hotels of its day, appealing to VIPs of all types. Since its grand opening in June 1918, this showpiece of the Rockies has hosted numerous presidents, dignitaries, and movie stars. Former guests include U.S. Presidents Hoover, Eisenhower, Nixon, Reagan, and Bush; foreign notables Margaret Thatcher and the King of Siam; and celebrities Bob Hope, Bing Crosby, John Wayne, and Jimmy Stewart.

During the winter season, from November to April, rates run from $170 for a double to $315. May through October the rates start at $280 for a double and go up to $425.

DAY 2

Morning

BREAKFAST: Feast on pan-seared filet of mountain trout or on eggs and a cheese buttermilk biscuit at the **Lake Terrace Dining Room,** located on the mezzanine level of The Broadmoor as you look out onto Cheyenne Lake.

Today's agenda begins with a sojourn to the awe-inspiring and majestic backdrop to Colorado Springs, **Pikes Peak.** If you're feeling energetic and fit, you can arrange to hike to the summit, but you'll want to schedule two days to finish the 26-mile round-trip. For information on hiking, visit the office of Pike National Forest (601 South Weber Street; 719–636–1602).

There are easier ways to reach the summit, mainly in the comfort of your car or via **Pikes Peak Cog Railway.** Either way you'll want to have a jacket. At 14,100 feet the air is thin and chilly and has half the oxygen found at sea level.

The 9-mile route takes a little more than three hours round-trip, including a forty-minute stopover at the top. On the trip up you may spot deer or other animals and there will be several photo stops. Little can compare to the panoramic vista from the summit. You can view Denver to the north, the Sangre de Cristo Mountains to the south, and the Great Plains to the east.

LUNCH: The appropriately named **Summit House** offers a snack bar and shopping, or you may wish to wait and have lunch in Manitou Springs.

To reach the depot take I–25, then exit 141 west on U.S. 24 for 4 miles; turn onto Manitou Avenue West and proceed 1.5 miles to Ruxton Avenue;

turn left and drive about 0.5 mile to 515 Ruxton Avenue, Manitou Springs. Admission from April through June is $21.50 for adults, $10.00 for children ages five through eleven, and free for children under age five who are held on an adult's lap. Prices increase slightly for the months of July and August. For additional information write Pikes Peak Railway, Box 351, Manitou Springs, CO 80829, or call (719) 685–5401.

For a breezier trip down, try a bicycle descent. **Challenge Unlimited** drives clients (kids, Grandma, Mom and Dad) by van to the summit and escorts them down as they ride bikes on the 20-mile ride. Say "Wheeeee!" Twenty-one-speed mountain bikes, helmets, cold-weather gear, and all other necessary equipment is provided. The ride up in the van takes an hour, and the descent on bikes takes about two and a half hours. Contact Challenge Unlimited, 204 South Twenty-fourth Street, Colorado Springs, CO 80904; (800) 798–5954.

Spend some time in **Manitou Springs,** a small artists' community with attractive Victorian homes, gift shops, and galleries. Health-seekers arrived in this town in the late 1800s to "take the cure" by drinking water from the mineral springs. Home to Manitou Springs Mineral Water, this National Historic District is a good place to spend the afternoon exploring on your own or taking the free walking tour offered by the local Chamber of Commerce, 354 Manitou Avenue, Manitou Springs, CO 80829; (719) 685–5089.

Named for the clamor the wind makes as it blows through the tunnels, **Cave of the Winds** is both impressive and touristy. Still, if you are fascinated by stalagmites, stalactites, subterranean chambers, and narrow passageways, you've come to the right place. Cave of the Winds (719–685–5444) is located off Highway 24, north of Manitou Springs on Serpentine Drive.

For wanna-be spelunkers there's a special **Explorer Tour.** You can venture with a flashlight, crawl on elbows and knees on the slippery surface, and get as muddy as you want. Cost is $60 per person. Children under thirteen are not permitted on the Explorer Tour, and children ages thirteen to seventeen must be accompanied by a parent or guardian.

For the less daring there is the forty-minute **Discovery Tour,** which departs every fifteen minutes. Admission is $10.00 for adults, $5.00 for children ages six through fifteen, and free for children six and under. Cave of the Winds is open daily. Hours are 9:00 A.M. to 10:00 P.M. from May 1 through Labor Day weekend. Hours are 10:00 A.M. to 5:00 P.M. from Labor Day to May 1.

DINNER: The **Penrose Room at The Broadmoor.** This luxurious restaurant specializes in gourmet cuisine in an elegant, romantic setting. A three-piece orchestra serenades as you choose from the elaborate menu selection of Pan-Seared Foie Gras, Chateaubriand (carved tableside), Roasted Rack of Colorado Lamb, Maine Lobster, and dessert soufflé.

Evening

Top off the evening with a visit to **The Broadmoor's Golden Bee.** Located on the lower level of the International Center at The Broadmoor, this authentic nineteenth-century English pub is ideal for sipping a yard-long schooner of beer and singing old-time favorites with the ragtime pianist. The crowd is merry, the honky-tonk is loud, and the mood is festive. Patrons are often given a stick-on "bee" to wear. Don't miss this distin-guished-by-day, boisterous-by-night pub.

LODGING: The Broadmoor.

DAY 3

Morning

LATE BRUNCH: If it's Sunday, you'll want to enjoy the incredible brunch in **The Broadmoor's Lake Terrace Dining Room.** Live classical piano music filters throughout the dining area, and artistic ice sculptures decorate the tables. You'll find a buffet-style extravaganza, featuring cold poached salmon, fresh fruit, a carving station offering a variety of meats, and a large dessert selection. The Broadmoor's acclaimed bananas Foster is a treat.

After breakfast stroll around the peaceful lake or strike up a game of ten-nis. **The Broadmoor's Spa and Fitness Center** staff will arrange for a multitreatment program to fit your needs, whether you're in the mood for maximum relaxation or maximum workout.

Cheyenne Mountain Zoo (4250 Cheyenne Mountain Zoo Road; 719–633–9925) is poised on the slopes just above The Broadmoor. This unique mountain zoo, which focuses on the plights of many endangered species, is regarded as one of the most superior in the country and is home to more than 800 animals. You'll find Siberian tigers, black leopards, hippos, and Mexican gray wolves. At 6,800 feet above sea level, the zoo provides sensa-tional views of Colorado Springs and the surrounding area. The zoo is open daily Memorial Day weekend through Labor Day weekend from 9:00 A.M. to

5:00 P.M. and the remainder of the year from 9:00 A.M. to 4:00 P.M. Adults pay $6.75 for entrance, seniors pay $5.75, and children ages three to eleven are admitted for $3.75; children two years of age and under are admitted free.

LUNCH: Picnic at the zoo or take advantage of the snack bar.

Afternoon

On your way back to Denver via I–25 north, visit the **U.S. Air Force Academy.** Take exit 156B off I–25. Shortly after entering the grounds, you'll see an imposing B-52 bomber on display. Stop at the **Barry Goldwater Air Force Academy Visitor Center,** open daily in summer from 9:00 A.M. to 6:00 P.M. and in winter from 9:00 A.M. to 5:00 P.M. Here you can pick up a map for a self-guided tour of the grounds. The gift shop has displays and films about the history of the academy.

You can walk to the **Cadet Chapel** from the visitor center. The chapel, which is an architectural marvel, has seventeen spires that rise 150 feet into the sky. The public is welcome to visit Monday through Saturday from 9:00 A.M. to 5:00 P.M. and Sunday from 1:00 to 5:00 P.M. Sunday services are held at 9:00 and 11:00 A.M., and the public is welcome to attend. For information call (719) 333–4515.

THERE'S MORE

Pikes Peak International Raceway, located in Fountain, 15 miles south of Colorado Springs on I–25 (exit 123), is a 1-mile oval track that is among the finest in the world. When the announcer proclaims, "Gentlemen, start your engines," get ready for the high-powered Indy cars to roar. The world-class facility also has stock car, sports car, and motorcycle races, which run May through September. For a schedule and tickets, call (800) 955–7223.

ProRodeo Hall of Fame and American Cowboy Museum, 101 Pro Rodeo Drive; (719) 528–4764. Cowboys and cowgirls alike will get a kick out of this museum, which contains an excellent exhibit of western art, photographs, and displays of cowboy and rodeo gear. Admission is $6.00 for adults, $5.00 for seniors, and $3.00 for children ages six through twelve; children under six are admitted free.

The North American Aerospace Defense Command (NORAD)
hosts tours of the underground fortress several times a month, but public
visits are limited and booked solid, so you will want to call months in
advance for a reservation. The facility is entombed deep within
Cheyenne Mountain and was constructed to endure a nuclear attack.
Call (719) 474–2241.

U.S. Olympic Complex, 1 Olympic Plaza, Colorado Springs; (719)
578–4618. Stop at the visitor center and the U.S. Olympic Hall of Fame
for a guided tour of this thirty-six-acre complex, the elaborate training
center for more than half of the U.S. Olympic sports. You'll see five
sophisticated gymnasiums and a weight-training room on the tour, as
well as the Indoor Shooting Center, which has two 50-meter ranges.
Proceeds from merchandise sold at the visitor center help support the
athletic programs. Summer hours at the complex are Monday through
Saturday from 9:00 A.M. to 5:00 P.M. and Sunday from 10:00 A.M. to
5:00 P.M. Winter hours are Monday through Saturday from 9:00 A.M. to
4:00 P.M. and Sunday from noon to 4:00 P.M.

SPECIAL EVENTS

March/April. Easter Sunrise Services at Garden of the Gods. This spring
tradition is an impressive sight as worshippers gather in the dramatic setting of these awesome formations. The inspirational service is well worth
requesting that 5:00 A.M. wake-up call.

July. Pikes Peak Hill Climb. Held on the Fourth of July. The annual "Race to
the Clouds" is the second oldest auto race in America, right behind the
Indianapolis 500. Former winners of the rigorous event are Bobby Unser
(he has won the Hill Climb thirteen times), Al Unser, Mario Andretti,
Rick Mears, and Roger Mears. Contact Pikes Peak Hill Climb Association, 135 Manitou Avenue, Manitou Springs, CO 80829; (719) 685–4400.

August. Pikes Peak or Bust Rodeo. Billed as Colorado's largest outdoor
rodeo, this event, held early in the month, draws big names in the prorodeo circle. The city decks out in western wear and welcomes cowboys
and cowgirls with foot-stompin' enthusiasm.

Pikes Peak Marathon is considered to be one of the world's most demanding. The race is a great spectator sport--unless, that is, you're into gruel-
ing runs. If that's the case, you'll want to compete.

OTHER RECOMMENDED RESTAURANTS AND LODGINGS

Colorado Springs

Flying W Ranch. Located north of Garden of the Gods, the Flying W will satisfy any cravings for a western setting and authentic barbecue. You'll also be entertained by the Flying W Wranglers. Reservations are required. Call (800) 232–FLYW or (719) 598–4000.

The Hearthstone Inn, 506 North Cascade Avenue, Colorado Springs, CO 80903; (719) 473–4413 or (800) 521–1885. This nonsmoking B&B is elegantly furnished with antiques, overstuffed chairs, and a wood-burning fireplace in the parlor. Some rooms have a view of Pikes Peak, while others feature a private porch. A full gourmet breakfast is included.

The Antlers Doubletree Hotel, 4 South Cascade Avenue, Colorado Springs, CO 80903; (719) 473–5600 or (800) 528–0444. This comfortable hotel offers a complete range of services and a microbrewery. Judge Baldwin's Brewing Company, Colorado Springs' first microbrewery, serves not only a specialty ale brewed on-site but burgers, pastas, and soups. Atmosphere is casual. Lunch and dinner are served here daily, and breakfast is available Sunday morning.

Room at the Inn, 618 North Nevada Avenue, Colorado Springs, CO 80903; (800) 579–4621. This 1896 classic Queen Anne, 3-story home has a wraparound porch, a turret, a gabled roof, and seven rooms, each with private bath. Afternoon tea and a snack are available, and a full breakfast is served on the veranda, weather permitting. During the cooler months enjoy breakfast in the comfort of the antique-filled dining room. Rates begin at $85.

FOR MORE INFORMATION

Colorado Springs Convention & Visitors Bureau, 104 South Cascade, Suite 104, Colorado Springs, CO 80903; (719) 635–7506 or (800) 888–4748.

Colorado Springs Chamber of Commerce, 2 North Cascade Avenue, Suite 110, Colorado Springs, CO 80903; (719) 635–1551.

Manitou Springs Chamber of Commerce, 354 Manitou Avenue, Manitou Springs, CO 80829; (719) 685–5089.

Salida and the Upper Arkansas Valley

REDISCOVER SOUTHERN COLORADO

1 NIGHT

Fish hatchery • Snowboarding • Sno-Cat tours • Scenic tram •
Rockhounding • Fishing, golf, horseback riding •
Snowshoe/wine-tasting tour • Mountain biking

If outdoor recreation is a significant element of your getaway, then life just got sweeter. Natural beauty and quiet isolation dominate this vast region. With more 14,000-foot mountains than any other location in Colorado, the Sawatch Mountain Range is one step short of heaven for climbers. Rafters and kayakers love to shoot the Class III rapids of the Arkansas River. Golf enthusiasts will appreciate Salida's 9-hole course, with views of the Collegiate Peaks.

The small town of Salida may be missing the excitement of the state's more opulent resort areas, but visitors will find a homespun hospitality. Here a hot night on the town might be a soak in the Salida Hot Springs Pool.

One of the best things about the Upper Arkansas Valley is its spectacular landscape. Salida is surrounded by the Pike and San Isabel National Forests, offering abundant backcountry areas to explore. One thing is certain: There is something to suit every outdoor lover.

DAY 1

Morning

Salida is located 157 miles southwest of Denver. Follow U.S. 285 south to Poncha Springs, then travel east on U.S. 50 5 miles to Salida. Monarch Ski &

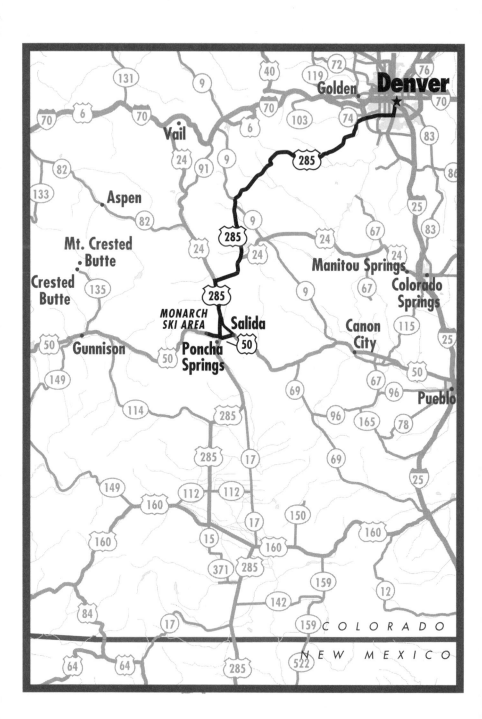

Snowboard Area is located 21 miles west of Salida on U.S. 50.

LUNCH: For a no-nonsense meal and a bit of local gossip on the side, eat at **Country Bounty** (413 West Rainbow Boulevard on Highway 50, Salida, CO 81201; 719–539–3546). Chicken-fried steak and mashed potatoes, a hot roast beef sandwich, fried chicken, and Rocky Road Pie are specialties of the house. Open daily from 6:00 A.M. to 8:00 P.M.

Afternoon

Having recently changed its name from Monarch Ski Corporation to **Monarch Ski & Snowboard Area,** this resort recognizes the increasing interest in winter's fastest-growing sport. "Shredders" are welcomed and indulged with **Meadows Terrain Park,** a snowboarders-only area designed with input from local snowboarders. Monarch Ski & Snowboard Area holds several snowboarding competitions throughout the season, including the Big Air and Boardercross events.

Downhill skiers will be equally pleased. Mountains are bold and steep, and the area is legendary for its powder. Annual snowfall is 350-plus inches, and the ski area boasts about its absence of snow-making equipment. The resort has a special "snowline," giving callers the latest snowpack report: (800) 228–7943.

Adventurers interested in a day in the backcountry with a guide can take advantage of **Monarch's Great Divide Sno-Cat Tours.** For $125 per day guests travel by Sno-Cat to Monarch's 900 acres of above-timberline terrain to ski or snowboard on the Continental Divide. Participants learn about backcountry safety before heading out on their adventure into untamed territory. For more information call (888) 996–7669.

Discover the serenity of the backcountry and spend a day on **cross-country skis.** Nordic skiers will find an ample number of secluded trails to explore and are welcome on designated groomed trails at the ski area. The resort rents telemark equipment as well as snowboarding gear. Monarch Ski & Snowboard Area is located 21 miles west of Salida on U.S. Highway 50. For additional information call (888) 996–7669.

Summer activities include a ride on the **Monarch Scenic Tram** to the 12,012-foot summit for incredible views from the observation tower. Telescopes are available, and maps identify the peaks. A round-trip ticket is $6.00 for adults, $5.00 for seniors, and $3.00 for children. The tram operates daily mid-May through late September from 9:00 A.M. to 4:00 P.M. For more information call (719) 539–4789.

Snowboarders "catch some air" *at Monarch Ski & Snowboard Area.*
(photo by Chris O'Connell).

Other summer pastimes include an afternoon at **Salida Golf Club** (404 Grant Street, Salida, CO 81201; 719–539–1060). This 9-hole course has views of the Collegiate Peaks, as well as some challenging holes that wreak havoc upon even the best golfers.

Rafters can float through **Brown's Canyon** with **Noah's Ark** (P.O. Box 850, Buena Vista, CO 81211; 719–395–2158). The company is located 6 miles south of Buena Vista on Highway 285. A half-day trip covers 10 miles on the Arkansas River, and you'll bounce through eight moderate rapids. A full-day trip consists of lunch and a few more rapids than the half-day outing, including Seidell's Suckhole, a Class IV. The price for a half-day is $33.50 per person; for a full day, $62.00 per person. Youth rates are available. Multiday excursions are another option. The company can accommodate all levels of rafting experience. Rafting season is from mid-May to the end of August.

Two other companies that lead raft trips are **Arkansas Valley Expeditions** (P.O. Box 100, Salida, CO 81201; 800–833–RAFT) and **Wilderness**

Aware (P.O. Box 1550, Buena Vista, CO; 800–462–7238 or 719–395–2112). Many consider the **Arkansas River** to be one of the finest fishing rivers in the state. Without a doubt this area is a natural destination for anglers. Rewards are not only drop-dead-gorgeous scenery but the prospect of landing a sizable rainbow trout. **Browner's Guide Service** (228 North F Street, Salida, CO 81201; 800–288–0675 or 719–539–4506) will arrange a guided fly-fishing trip that includes either walk-and-wade fishing or float fishing. For additional information contact the Division of Wildlife Office (7405 Highway 50, Salida; 719–539–3529).

Visitors are welcome to observe daily activities that might include feeding, sorting, or moving fish at **Mount Shavano Trout Hatchery and Rearing Unit** (7725 County Road 154, Salida, CO 81201; 719–539–6877). Four million fish, including brown, rainbow, and cutthroat trout, as well as kokanee salmon, are hatched annually at this location. Guided tours are available during summer. The facility is located 0.5 mile northwest of Salida on Highway 291 and is open from 8:00 A.M. to 4:30 P.M. every day of the year. Admission is free.

Take a trail ride into the backcountry of Sawatch Range. **Mount Princeton Riding Stables** (15870 County Road 162, Nathrop, CO 81236; 719–395–6498) provides a horse suited to every rider's ability.

Rockhounds will find Colorado's richest mineral and gem locations in the upper Arkansas River Valley, west of Salida. For information pick up a brochure at the Chamber of Commerce (406 West Rainbow Boulevard, Salida; 719–539–2068).

Mountain bikers can stop at **Otero Cyclery** (108 F Street, Salida; 719–539–6704) for both dual- and front-suspension mountain-bike rentals (helmet included) and information on trails in the area. Request a complimentary copy of *The Mountain Bike Guide,* which has maps and descriptions of area trails.

DINNER: **Cliffhanger's Restaurant and Bar** at Monarch Mountain Lodge (719–539–2581) specializes in good food at an affordable price. Chef David Asher has put together a menu that includes baby back ribs and a whiskey chicken sandwich. Homemade soups vary daily, but you may find clam chowder, chicken mushroom, or cheesy ham and potato soup. The restaurant is casual and is open for dinner only from 5:00 to 9:00 P.M. Sunday through Thursday, and from 5:00 to 11:00 P.M. on Friday and Saturday.

LODGING: **Monarch Mountain Lodge,** 1 Powder Place, Monarch, CO 81227; (719) 539–2581 or (800) 332–3668. The lodge has an outdoor hot tub, a sports bar, and a massage therapist. Ask about "Ski & Stay" packages, which include a lift ticket to Monarch Ski & Snowboard Area and a room at Monarch Mountain Lodge.

DAY 2

Morning

BREAKFAST OR LUNCH: Drive to Poncha Springs, 5 miles west of Salida, for Sunday brunch at the **Jackson Hotel** (6340 Highway 285, Poncha Springs, CO 81242; 719–539–4861). Brunch features pancakes, biscuits and gravy, and *huevos rancheros*. Best of all, you'll be serenaded with live hammer dulcimer music. Brunch is served from 9:30 A.M. to 2:00 P.M. Sunday. Lunch at the Jackson Hotel is equally good. Order the Turkey Terrific, a sandwich made from fresh roasted turkey, cornbread stuffing, and cranberry sauce. The Mexican food tastes homemade, and the green chile is superior. Don't miss the Mexican flan de vanilla. The restaurant is open for lunch from 11:30 A.M. to 2:00 P.M. every day except Wednesday, when it closes.

If you can't schedule a meal at the Jackson Hotel, stop to see this historic building, one of the oldest in Chaffee County. Rooms are no longer available, but you'll want to tour the antique-filled parlor and guest rooms. Built in 1878 as a stage stop, Jackson Hotel's claim to fame is that Jesse James, Billy the Kid, Susan B. Anthony, and other legendary figures stayed here. The guest registry is on display in Denver at the Natural History Museum. Ask about the diamond dust mirror and the 1874 solid rosewood Weber piano, which was hauled here by oxcart. The builder of the hotel, Hank Jackson, designated in his will that these items are never to leave the premises. Don't miss the bullet hole in the staircase, the result of a Jesse James shootout.

Return to Denver via Highway 285.

THERE'S MORE

Mountain Spirit Winery, 15750 County Road 220, located 12 miles west of Salida; (719) 539–1175. This family-run winery is located on a five-acre farm in apple orchard country. Stop for a tour and a sample of the cherry wine. During July and August the winery hosts Mountain Spirit Evening, when guests are treated to gourmet food, live music, and wine. A popular winter event is the snowshoe/wine-tasting tour.

Llama trekking. Full-day and multiday hikes are offered by Spruce Ridge Llama Treks (4141 County Road 210, Salida, CO 81201; 719–539–4182). You'll travel through national forests as llamas haul the gear. All equipment is provided.

Mount Princeton Hot Springs. Three outdoor swimming pools, two indoor hot tubs, and natural rock pools attract crowds to this location. Overnight accommodations and dining are also available. For more information contact Mount Princeton Hot Springs, 15870 County Road 162, Nathrop, CO 81236; (719) 395–2447.

Salida Hot Springs Pool. Soak in the hot mineral springs or swim in the 25-meter lap pool. Summer hours are from 1:00 to 9:00 P.M. daily. Winter hours are from 4:00 to 9:00 P.M. Tuesday through Thursday and from 1:00 to 9:00 P.M. Friday through Sunday. Located at Centennial Park, 410 West Rainbow Boulevard, Salida, CO 81201; (719) 539–6738.

Ghost Railroad Tour. For a unique excursion contact Colorado Historic Adventures (331 Columbine #C, Golden, CO 80403; 303–278–7380). Colorado has hundreds of abandoned railroads, including the Denver South Park and Pacific. The Alpine Tunnel, considered by many to be the highlight of the South Park, is located about an hour from Salida. A guide will escort you on a custom-designed half-day, one-day, or multiday tour as you follow the route of one of Colorado's historical ghost railroads.

Visit the **Salida Museum,** located next to the Chamber of Commerce,n at 406 West Rainbow Boulevard. This museum displays mining, railroad, and early settler memorabilia. Open Memorial Day through Labor Day from 11:00 A.M. to 7:00 P.M.

SPECIAL EVENTS

June. FibArk (First in Boating on the Arkansas). This international raft and kayak race attracts kayakers, spectators, and the entire Salida community for a long weekend of music, a parade, and the highlight: a 26-mile kayak race from Salida to Cotopaxi. For details call (719) 539–7254.

July. The town sponsors an old-fashioned Fourth of July celebration, complete with street dancing, a chili cook-off, fireworks, and music.

The Aspen-Salida Music Festival held early in July features a series of concerts that include performances from the Aspen concert series.

November. Christmas Mountain USA. Held the end of the month. More than 3,000 bulbs illuminate Salida's Tenderfoot Mountain to begin the holiday season.

December. On New Year's Eve skiers and snowboarders carry lighted torches as they weave their way down the mountain in a celebration that begins at 4:00 P.M. Fireworks follow.

OTHER RECOMMENDED RESTAURANTS AND LODGINGS

Salida

First Street Cafe, 137 East First Street; (719) 539–4759. This cafe is located in one of the oldest buildings in Salida's historic downtown. The cafe serves breakfast, lunch, and dinner and offers a breakfast burrito, a salad bar, and lemon garlic chicken. Summer hours are 8:00 A.M. to 10:00 P.M. Monday through Saturday and 10:00 A.M. to 3:00 P.M. Sunday. Winter hours are 8:00 A.M. to 7:00 P.M. Monday through Thursday and 8:00 A.M. to 10:00 P.M. Friday and Saturday.

The River Suites at Monarch Shadows, 16724 Highway 50 West, Salida, CO 81201; (719) 539–6953 or (800) 464–6953. Situated 10 miles from Monarch Ski & Snowboard Area and 9 miles from Salida, this first-class accommodation offers suites with a wood-burning stove, a private hot tub, a television, and a complete kitchen. The two-bedroom suite can accommodate six adults. Rates range from $125 to $175 and change with the seasons.

Mosca

Inn at Zapata Ranch, 5303 Highway 150, Mosca, CO 81146; (800) 284–9213 or (719) 378–2356. This secluded guest ranch, located about 90 miles south of Salida, offers a championship 18-hole golf course, fine dining in the lodge's restaurant, and rustic, comfortable guest rooms.

FOR MORE INFORMATION

Greater Buena Vista Area Chamber of Commerce Visitors Center, 343 South Highway 24, P.O. Box 2021, Buena Vista, CO 81211; (719) 395–6612.

Heart of the Rockies Chamber of Commerce, 406 West Rainbow Boulevard, Salida, CO 81201; (719) 539–2068.

Chaffee County Visitors Bureau Hotline; (800) 831–8594.

For information on camping, hiking, and other national forest activities, contact the Salida Ranger District Office, 325 West Rainbow Boulevard, Salida, CO 81201; (719) 539–3591.

Gunnison

HOSPITALITY ON THE WESTERN SLOPE

2 NIGHTS

*Taylor Reservoir • Old mining towns •
Cumberland Pass • Pristine backcountry • Blue Mesa
Reservoir • Pioneer Museum*

Gunnison captures the essence of the Old West and offers a welcome contrast to fast-paced resorts. Here the daily whistle blows at noon in small-town tradition, streets are wide, and folks say "Howdy." In this neck of the woods, Cattlemen's Days is the social highlight of the summer.

As gateway to Gunnison National Forest, the town of Gunnison sits in the heart of some of the state's most dramatic wilderness. Unspoiled, vast, and ideal for outdoor recreation, the Gunnison Valley begs to be hiked, biked, four-wheeled, fished, and explored.

Gunnison is the perfect place to set up base camp. The town offers good shopping, superior restaurants, and a sunny disposition. You're as likely to see a rancher driving a truck filled with bales of hay as you are a college student with a daypack cruising on a bicycle.

You'll encounter an interesting history here and virtually unlimited access to pristine wilderness. And you will be welcomed with genuine hospitality.

DAY 1

Morning

To get to Gunnison, take U.S. Highway 285 traveling southwest from Denver to Poncha Springs. Continue west on U.S. Highway 50 into Gunnison. Plan on a three-and-a-half- to four-hour drive from Denver.

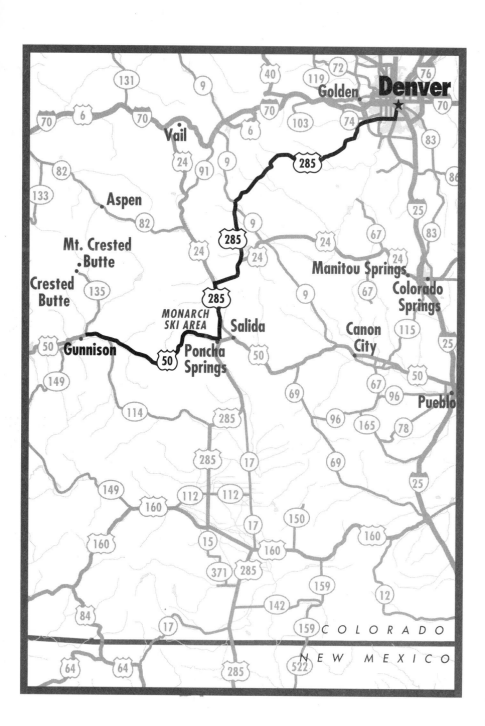

Your first stop in Gunnison is the **Visitor Center and Chamber of Commerce** (500 East Tomichi Avenue; 970–641–1501), where you can stock up on maps and brochures. The office is open seven days a week from 8:00 A.M. to 7:00 P.M. Memorial Day through Labor Day and Monday through Friday from 8:00 A.M. to 5:00 P.M. the rest of the year. Be sure to pick up the brochure *Ghosts of a Town: 20 Circle Tour Trips of the Gunnison Country.*

Across the street from the visitor center is **Jorgensen Park,** where you can in-line skate during the summer and play ice hockey when the weather turns cold. Equipment rentals are available at the city's warming hut located at the park.

LUNCH: Stuff yourself for next to nothing at the **Blue Iguana** (303 East Tomichi Avenue, Gunnison; 970–641–3403), where the most expensive item on the menu is about $6.00. Decor consists of red vinyl tablecloths, a giant chile pepper in the dining room, and a menu painted on the wall. Choices include a build-your-own burrito for less than $2.00 and combination plates for a couple of dollars more. A popular hangout for students attending Western State College, the Blue Iguana has picnic tables both inside and out. The restaurant is open from 11:00 A.M. to 10:00 P.M. Monday through Saturday and is closed Sunday.

Afternoon

For an introduction to town, take the 2.5-mile, self-guided **walking tour** of historic Gunnison with the help of a map and brochure available at the visitor center. The pamphlet lists interesting tidbits about properties that include commercial businesses and private residences. On the route you'll see Gothic Revival architecture, the first stone house in Gunnison, and the oldest existing church in town.

Spend some time browsing the shops along Main Street. For the ultimate in outdoor wear, visit **Cottonwoods** (111 North Main, Gunnison; 970–641–4728). This eclectic store sells everything from gourmet jams to fishing vests and also has a coffee counter where you can get an espresso to go. Snowshoes are available to rent here during winter.

To shop at a unique store that sells designer western-style furniture, you'll need to drive to the edge of town. **Back at the Ranch** (100 Spencer Avenue, Gunnison, CO 81230; 970–641–0727) is worth the mileage. This fashionable store is packed with cowboy art and distinctive home furnishings.

You'll find an exceptional display of area memorabilia at **Pioneer Museum** (East Highway 50, Gunnison; 970–641–4530). In addition to antique cars and wagons, you'll see old saddles, an arrowhead collection, and ranch machinery that dates to the early days. The museum is open Memorial Day through Labor Day from 9:00 A.M. to 5:00 P.M. Monday through Saturday; the museum is closed the remainder of year. Admission is $4.00 for adults and $1.00 for children ages six to twelve.

DINNER: The aroma of roasted garlic tantalizes your senses when you walk in the door at **Garlic Mike's Italian Cuisine** (2674 North Highway 135, Gunnison; 970–641–2493), 2 miles north of Gunnison on Highway 135. The restaurant is named after the owner's son, not to be confused with the chef, whose name is also Mike. Italian dining doesn't get much better. From the red-checked tablecloths to the immense stone fireplace and bustling open kitchen, this cafe exudes charm. Some of the choices from the menu are Filetto di Salmon al Forno con Formaggio, Sirloin Steak Gorgonzola, and Lasagne da Campania. Desserts include Chocolate Truffle Cake, Chocolate Mousse, and Tiramisù Cake, among others. Weather permitting, dine outside on the pleasant riverfront patio. The hours change with the seasons, so call ahead.

LODGING: The **Mary Lawrence Inn** (601 North Taylor, Gunnison, CO 81230; 970–641–3343), built in 1885 and renovated in 1989, offers guests a homey atmosphere amid antiques, handmade quilts, and Victorian charm. In the early 1900s Mary Lawrence, a teacher and school administrator, operated the building as a boardinghouse. Today you'll find homemade goodies in the cookie jar, a large deck where guests gather in the late afternoon, and an inviting sun porch filled with comfy chairs and magazines. Each of the five guest rooms has a private bath. This inn is particularly kid-friendly and offers two-room suites. Rates range from $69 to $109 depending on the room and season.

DAY 2

Morning

BREAKFAST: Mary Lawrence Inn. Join other guests in the sunny dining room at the fourteen-person oval table for a full breakfast that may include Asparagus Eggs Benedict or Gingerbread Pancakes with Nectarine Cream Sauce.

Plan ahead for a picnic lunch and stop at **Farrell's Restaurant** (310

Gunnison National Forest *offers acres of wilderness.*

(photo by Sherry Spitsnaugle).

North Main Street; 970–641–2655) to pick up a sandwich, coleslaw, and a giant chocolate chip cookie or two. Food here is prepared from scratch, and you'll find a selection of fresh breads and pastries.

Take Colorado 135 north out of Gunnison to Almont to begin a **loop tour of old mining towns.** The brochure *Ghosts of a Town: 20 Circle Tour Trips of the Gunnison Country,* from the visitor center, guides you on a trip through towns that thrived during the gold rush of the late 1800s. Roads are narrow and often have only one lane, but you won't need a four-wheel-drive vehicle. Much of this route is closed in winter, so ask about road conditions before you depart.

After you pass through Almont, follow the signs to **Tincup,** a sleepy little town that has one cafe, one general store, and a handful of residents. **Frenchy's Cafe** doesn't have an exact address, but you won't have trouble finding it. Pies here are especially good, and menu items are named after mining terms and local places. You'll find Miner's Muck (biscuits with sausage gravy) and Minnie Hall (a burger with cheese and bacon).

Stories vary about the source of Tincup's name, but some say that a local entrepreneur sold whiskey by the tin cup to miners in the late 1800s. Another version states that one of the early settlers searched the streams for gold with a tin cup.

On the edge of town is the **Tincup Cemetery,** which may be unlike any graveyard you have ever seen. For starters *cemetery* is misspelled, which makes the location all the more endearing. Graves are separated by religion, and you'll see signs that say Jᴇᴡɪꜱʜ Kɴᴏʟʟ, Cᴀᴛʜᴏʟɪᴄ Kɴᴏʟʟ, Pʀᴏᴛᴇꜱᴛᴀɴᴛ Kɴᴏʟʟ, ᴀɴᴅ Bᴏᴏᴛ Hɪʟʟ.

As you proceed up Cumberland Pass Road, you'll climb above treeline to the 12,015-foot summit of **Cumberland Pass.** The road is narrow and the air thin, but the rewards are awesome views, glorious wildflowers, and, on most days, blue skies. As you descend, keep your eyes peeled for deer and elk along the road.

LUNCH: Your next stop is **Pitkin,** where there's a picnic site with several tables located just behind the Pitkin Historical Society Museum on Main Street. Pitkin is twice the size of Tincup. Ask a local what the population is and you may get a one-minute narration about how much the town has grown. The answer? "About eighty-five persons, give or take a baby or two."

Afternoon

Tour the small but interesting **Pitkin Historical Society Museum**—sorry, it doesn't have a phone—and visit with local volunteers. The museum is open from 11:00 ᴀ.ᴍ. to 3:00 ᴘ.ᴍ. daily during summer. Donations are welcome. For more information write Pitkin Historical Society, P.O. Box 218, Pitkin, CO 81241.

If you need a fishing license, gas, snacks, nightcrawlers, or an "I Lᴏᴠᴇ Pɪᴛᴋɪɴ" bumpersticker, stop at **Silver Plume General Store** (204 Ninth Street, Pitkin; 970–641–3866). It also sells arts and crafts.

On the north edge of Pitkin is the **Kid's Fishing Pond.** This crystal-clear lagoon is reserved for youngsters, as you'll learn when you read the nearby sign, which says, Nᴏ ᴀᴅᴜʟᴛꜱ, ᴘʟᴇᴀꜱᴇ.

An optional side trip, in which getting there truly is half the fun, is a visit to the **Alpine Tunnel,** constructed by the Denver South Park and Pacific Railroad in 1882. An engineering feat, the tunnel cut through the Continental Divide and, at an elevation of 11,523 feet, was the highest railroad station in the United States. The tunnel was abandoned in 1910, but today you'll see remains of original buildings. A knowledgeable volunteer is on-site to answer questions and give a history lesson for as long as you're willing to listen. Admission is free. Follow the marked road 3 miles beyond Pitkin and continue on a narrow dirt path for 10 miles to the tunnel. Once you're on the dirt road, there's virtually no place to turn around. It takes about thirty minutes to motor the 10 miles of rough road, but the scenery is fantastic and the drive will keep you on the edge of your seat.

Continue on the circle trip through **Ohio City,** which is not a city but a small burg, until the road intersects with Highway 50 west into Gunnison.

DINNER: As the name implies, **The Trough** (located a mile west of Gunnison on Highway 50; 970–641–3724) emphasizes hearty portions. The Trough is a longtime favorite in these parts, and the bounteous meals include blackened prime rib, pork chops, and fresh seafood. The selection varies, and on occasion there are some exotic additions, such as ostrich, kangaroo, and caribou. The menu lightheartedly lists prices for knives, forks, spoons, salt and pepper shakers, and mugs, and the dessert selection reads, "Sorry, cow pie is only available during stock drives!"

LODGING: The Mary Lawrence Inn.

DAY 3

Morning

BREAKFAST: The Mary Lawrence Inn.
Return to Denver via U.S. Highways 50 and 285.

LUNCH: Go a few miles out of your way after you reach Bailey, to **Buck Snort Saloon** (15921 Elk Creek Road, Pine, CO; 303–838–0284). This legendary mountain bar-restaurant has a reputation for Buckburgers, renegade regulars, and a great deck that overlooks the river. The Buck Snort is open from noon until midnight on weekends; it opens at 4:00 P.M. Wednesday through Friday and closes Monday and Tuesday. Travel south at Pine Junction (Route 126) for 6 miles to Pine. Signs will direct you to the Buck Snort.

THERE'S MORE

Morrow Point boat tour. You'll see towering canyon walls and possibly an eagle or two as you travel for ninety minutes in a forty-two-seat covered pontoon boat through Morrow Point Reservoir. To get to the departure point, there is a 232-step hike down (and back up after the boat trip) and 0.25 mile of flat walking. During summer, trips depart twice a day, at 10:00 A.M. and 12:30 P.M. Contact Elk Creek Marina (970–641–0707) for reservations and information.

Blue Mesa Reservoir. This lake in Curecanti National Recreation Area is the largest body of water in Colorado. Because of its easy access, the lake is popular with windsurfers, boaters, and anglers. Blue Mesa Reservoir is 15 scenic miles west of Gunnison on Highway 50.

Four-wheel-drive tours. Alpine Express (970–641–5074) will take you on a guided tour of the considerable four-wheel-drive trails in the area.

SPECIAL EVENTS

May. Blue Mesa Fishing Tournament awards cash prizes for the biggest fish caught in this annual competition.

June. Rage in the Sage Race is a mountain-bike race event that takes place on the sagebrush plains near Gunnison.

July. Cattlemen's Days is a several-day festival that includes a parade, a carnival, barbecues, a rodeo, a dance, and more. The celebration was originated by a group of ranchers and businessmen in the 1930s and since then has been an annual happening. For more information call the Chamber of Commerce at (970) 641–1501.

August. The Classic Car Show is a weekend event in which owners gather with their vintage automobiles at Jorgensen Park.

Fall. Hunter Hospitality Days is sponsored by the Gunnison Chamber of Commerce. Hunters are invited to stop in for information on big-game hunting, maps, and coffee and doughnuts.

OTHER RECOMMENDED RESTAURANTS AND LODGINGS

Gunnison

Mario's Pizza (213 West Tomichi; 970–641–1374) serves munchies such as oven-baked chicken wings and Italian foccacia bread. Entrees include vegetarian lasagne, ravioli, and barbecue pizza.

Mochas! (901 North Main Street; 970–641–2006) is a drive-thru coffeehouse where you can get your daily shot of espresso in a hurry.

Sidewalk Cafe (113 West Tomichi Avenue; 970–641–4130) serves plate-size pancakes at a reasonable price.

Columbine Victorian Hotel (134 West Tomichi Avenue, Gunnison, CO 81230; 970–641–6834 or 888–970–1880) began operation as a hotel in 1880 and, with its recent restoration, has become a popular accommodation. Rooms have high ceilings, clawfoot tubs, down comforters, and Victorian furnishings.

Almont

Harmel's Ranch Resort (P.O. Box 399, Almont, CO 81210; 970–641–1740) offers vacation packages that include lodging, meals, and activities such as horseback riding, river rafting, fishing, square dancing, and trapshooting. This family mountain guest ranch sits at the confluence of Spring Creek and the Taylor River and is surrounded by the Gunnison National Forest.

FOR MORE INFORMATION

Gunnison Chamber of Commerce and Visitor Center, 500 East Tomichi Avenue, P.O. Box 36, Gunnison, CO 81230; (970) 641–1501 or (800) 274–7580.

Curecanti National Recreation Area, National Park Service, 102 Elk Creek, Gunnison, CO 81230; (970) 641–2337.

Crested Butte
and Mt. Crested Butte
MEET ME AT PARADISE
2 NIGHTS

Walking tour of historic town • Mountain golf course
• Wildflower Festival • Mountain-biking mecca •
Extreme skiing • Ski-free program

Referred to by locals as "the last great Colorado ski town," Crested Butte greets you with glorious alpine basins, dynamic terrain, and down-home friendliness.

The ski area of Mt. Crested Butte and the town of Crested Butte are located a comfortable 3 miles apart from each other. The two areas blend trendiness with a sense of community. Bronzed cyclists cruise through town on mountain bikes as horses graze nonchalantly in the pasture across from the elementary school. Spend a little time on Elk Avenue and you'll notice that locals not only greet each other but will ask a stranger how his or her day is going.

Crested Butte traces its roots to the 1800s mining boom and is listed as a National Historic District. Today you'll find art galleries, shops, and restaurants serving cuisine that ranges from sushi to fried chicken.

When someone says, "Meet me at Paradise," the person is speaking of Paradise Warming House, midway up Crested Butte Mountain. In winter the mountain has gentle slopes for beginners and enough extreme terrain to thrill the gnarliest of dudes.

As a summer destination Crested Butte's attractions are unequaled. Wildflowers flourish in lush meadows, the countryside basks in mild mountain weather, bicycling is bliss, and the living is easy.

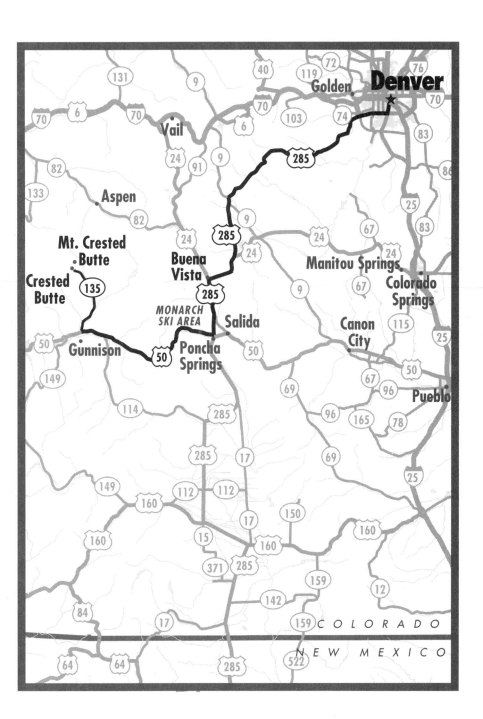

DAY 1

Morning

To get to Crested Butte, take U.S. 285 southwest from Denver to Poncha Springs. Continue west on U.S. 50 to Gunnison and travel north on Highway 135 for 30 miles to Crested Butte.

LUNCH: After three and a half hours on the road, you'll be ready for lunch about the time you arrive in Gunnison. For traditional favorites such as prime rib, barbecued ribs, and chicken with all the fixin's, eat at **Cattlemen Inn** (301 West Tomichi, Gunnison; 970–641–1061).

Afternoon

Your first stop in Crested Butte is the **Chamber of Commerce and Visitor Center** (601 Elk Avenue, at the four-way stop; 970–349–6438). It has a wealth of valuable information. Familiarize yourself with Crested Butte on a **self-guided walking tour;** a map is available at the visitor center. Be sure to check out the defunct **two-story outhouse,** located in the alley behind the Company Store, at Elk Avenue and Third Street. One explanation for the two levels is that both could be used simultaneously, and another is that during winter, the first level became inaccessible because of snow.

If you need up-to-date news on area fly fishing, stop at **Dragonfly Anglers** (307 Elk Avenue; 970–349–1228 or 800–491–3079), where the latest fishing information is written on a chalkboard. The staff will arrange guided overnight or day trips to the Gold Medal Black Canyon of the Gunnison River or custom trips to a remote Gunnison County lodge. You can also buy a rod, flies, and a fishing license.

Rendezvous Gallery & Framing (418 Elk Avenue; 970–349–6804) has a selection of work by local artist Sean Guerrierio. You'll see his characteristic benches along Elk Avenue.

DINNER: Soupçon Restaurant is a real find, literally. Located in the alley behind the Forest Queen Hotel and Restaurant (129 Elk Avenue), Soupçon serves phenomenal French food in an intimate European atmosphere. The cafe is housed in a modest log cabin, and the small dining area makes for a romantic dinner. Tables are close together but not disturbingly so. Start with baked polenta or escargot, then move on to an entree such as roast duck or elk tenderloin. For reservations call Soupçon Restaurant at (970) 349–5448.

LODGING: Formerly the Grande Butte Hotel, the **Crested Butte Marriott Resort** (500 Gothic Road, Mt. Crested Butte, CO 81225; 800–544–8448) is an amenity-conscious lodge. The hotel is ideally situated at the base of the Silver Queen and Keystone Quad Lifts. With its multimillion-dollar makeover, Crested Butte Marriott Resort offers private balconies, whirlpool tubs, and a complete exercise room.

DAY 2

Morning

BREAKFAST: The **Antlers Restaurant and Bar,** at Crested Butte Marriott Resort (970–349–4042) offers custom-made omelets, a cappuccino bar, and a selection of pastries and muffins. Best of all, the outside deck looks onto the ski slopes. The restaurant is open daily for breakfast, lunch, and dinner.

Steps away from the patio of the Antlers is the **Silver Queen Quad Lift,** which offers a breathtaking ride to the top of Crested Butte Mountain. You'll get glorious views of the town of Crested Butte below and the surrounding snow-covered peaks. During summer, hike the trails. As the sign at the top of the mountain says, GET ACQUAINTED WITH THE LOCALS, which include yellow-bellied marmots, blue grouse, and red-tailed hawks. If you have energy to burn, walk back down to the base of the ski area.

During winter, skiers will want to be on the slopes the moment the lifts open. Beware the double-black-diamond runs with names like Total Recall, Rambo, and Toilet Bowl. Beginners will want to learn on wide, gentle, slopes such as Little Lizzie and Houston.

Nonskiers can return to downtown Crested Butte to visit the **Mountain Bike Hall of Fame & Museum** (120 Sopris Avenue; 970–349–1880). Founded in 1988, the museum traces the brief but interesting history of the sport. Vintage bikes, photos, and highlights from important races will interest mountain-bike buffs.

LUNCH: The food at **Idlespur,** home of Crested Butte Brewery & Pub (226 Elk Avenue, Crested Butte; 970–349–5026), is exactly what you'd imagine from a brewpub—and much more. Appetizers include Cajun-style popcorn shrimp and game sausage. For an entree select from items such as elk steak, filet mignon, and jumbo Gulf prawns. The Rodeo Stout and India Pale Ale are two of the excellent beers brewed on-site. Brewery tours are available.

Afternoon

During summer you can enjoy a leisurely lunch and still make it for a 1:00
P.M. tee time at **Crested Butte Country Club** (385 Country Club Drive,
Crested Butte, CO 81224; 970–349–6127). At 9,000 feet above sea level, this
mountain course, designed by Robert Trent Jones II, is one of the most
beautiful in the state. LPGA golf pro Sharon Moran instructs first-time and
advanced golfers on putting and driving. The course is open to the public,
and reservations are recommended. During winter the course is transformed
into a superb **cross-country ski track.** Ask about Crested Butte Country
Club's sleigh-ride dinners.

DINNER: Sometimes you just want to overdo it with skillet-fried chicken,
mashed potatoes and gravy, powder biscuits with homemade preserves, and
sweet corn in cream sauce. Luckily, **Slogar Bar & Restaurant** (Second Street
and Whiterock Avenue, Crested Butte; 970–349–5765) will satisfy the craving.
Meals are served family-style in the Victorian setting of this antique-filled
restaurant. Steak dinners are also available. Reservations are recommended.

LODGING: Crested Butte Marriott Resort.

DAY 3

Morning

BREAKFAST: Coffee is the first order of the day, and you'll find a variety at
the **Bakery Cafe** (Fourth Street and Elk Avenue, downtown Crested Butte;
970–349–7280). When you hear locals mention "the bakery," this is the one.
The raspberry croissants are divine. The Bakery Cafe is open from 7:00 A.M.
to 9:00 P.M. daily, year-round.

   If weather permits, drive to Gunnison via **Ohio Pass.** You'll travel on a
dirt road that twists and turns through lush forests, wild meadows, and spectacular mountain scenery. During summer, you'll see brilliant wildflowers,
and in fall, golden aspen. The elevation is about 10,000 feet above sea level.
Follow County Road 12 from the west end of Crested Butte. Driving time
to Gunnison is about one hour.

   At Gunnison take U.S. Highway 50 east to Poncha Springs and then U.S.
Highway 285 to Denver.

THERE'S MORE

Ski free. That's right. Free lift tickets are offered certain times of the year (late November through mid-December, and most of April) at Crested Butte Mountain Resort. Call (800) SKI–FREE for details.

Ski mountaineering. For guided expeditions of the backcountry, contact Adventures to the Edge, Ltd. (P.O. Box 91, Crested Butte, CO 81224; 800–349–5219). The company offers several options, including a hut-to-hut ski trek, as well as classes in avalanche awareness, winter mountaineering, and ice climbing. For the less daring there's snowshoeing.

Sleigh-ride dinner. Technically you'll arrive via Sno-Cat, rather than sleigh, at Bubba's on the Mountain, a restaurant located at Paradise Warming House, halfway up Crested Butte Mountain. Entree choices include prime rib, shrimp scampi, and Colorado lamb. For details call (970) 349–2211.

Mountain biking. As a mountain-biking haven, Crested Butte has an abundance of backcountry trails, single-track paths, and four-wheel-drive roads to indulge bikers.

Rocky Mountain Biological Laboratory (P.O. Box 519, Crested Butte, CO 81224; 970–394–7231) is a nonprofit corporation that facilitates research for scientists and promotes environmental education. Wildflower tours are available Wednesday afternoons the months of June, July, and August.

SPECIAL EVENTS

February. With its radical terrain Mt. Crested Butte is ideal for daredevils. Skiers and snowboarders gather here for the U.S. Extreme Free Skiing Championships and the U.S. No Limits Extreme Snowboarding Championships. Spectators are welcome.

June. Fat Tire Bike Festival, Crested Butte, attracts mountain-bike zealots from around the world for a week of clinics, rides, races, and more.

July. Wildflower Festival. Alpine hikes, garden tours, and butterfly walks are a few of the events that happen during this celebration of summer, when the area becomes a dazzling display of bluebells, columbines, and a host of other flowers.

August. Crested Butte Chamber Music Festival. Concerts featuring renowned musicians are performed in informal settings.

December. Rocky Mountain Holidays. Celebrate the holidays mountain-style in the historic town of Crested Butte. Enter one of several contests that include gingerbread-house making, wreath decorating, and snowman building.

OTHER RECOMMENDED RESTAURANTS AND LODGINGS

Mt. Crested Butte

The Avalanche, a bar-restaurant located next to the Marriott (970–349–7195), serves breakfast from 7:30 to 11:00 A.M.; lunch and dinner from 11:30 A.M. to 9:00 P.M.

Crested Butte

Lil's Land & Sea (321 Elk Avenue; 970–349–5457) has a sushi bar and an extensive menu that includes pastas and seafood.

Cristiana Guesthaus Bed and Breakfast, 621 Maroon Avenue, P.O. Box 427, Crested Butte, CO 81224; (800) 824–7899. This European-style lodge is ideally located several blocks from the shops and restaurants on Elk Avenue and near the free shuttle to the ski area. Each of the twenty-one rooms has a private bath. After a day of skiing or exploring, you'll appreciate the outdoor hot tub and the warm lobby with its stone fireplace. Breakfast includes homemade muesli, granola, and pastries. Hosts Martin and Rosemary Catmur are avid outdoorspeople and will suggest a hiking or cross-country ski trail.

FOR MORE INFORMATION

Crested Butte/Mt. Crested Butte Chamber of Commerce, 601 Elk Avenue, P.O. Box 1288, Crested Butte, CO 81224; (970) 349–6438 or (800) 545–4505.

Crested Butte Reservations and Lodging Information, 500 Gothic Road, P.O. Box A, Dept. 81, Mt. Crested Butte, CO 81225; (800) 215–2226 or (800) 544–8448.

Durango

ONE OF AMERICA'S BEST SMALL TOWNS

3 NIGHTS

*San Juan Skyway • Hot springs • Shopping • Durango
& Silverton Narrow Gauge Railroad*

Durango offers numerous attractions, not the least of which is the beauty of its setting. Tucked between the spectacular San Juan Mountains and the Animas River Valley, this scenic town captures the hearts of visitors.

Named by *Outside* magazine as one of the most desirable small cities in the country, Durango is a mecca for sports enthusiasts. Durango is also the home station for the popular Durango & Silverton Narrow Gauge Railroad. You'll hear the whistle blast and see the yellow cars behind the steam locomotive as it arrives and departs on daily runs. The town also boasts several delightful B & Bs, a couple of microbreweries, and a string of shops and art galleries.

The San Juan Skyway, a 236-mile route designated as one of six "All American" roads by the U.S. Department of Transportation, loops through alpine forests, rolling hills, and towering mountains. The skyway connects several towns, including Durango, Telluride, Ridgway, Ouray, and Silverton. You can drive the entire route in six hours or take days to soak in the incredible scenery and recreation the area offers.

Spend some time in Ridgway, population 820, located at the northern entrance to the San Juan Skyway, 81 miles north of Durango. Nearby Ridgway State Park has more than 1,000 acres of water for boating, fishing, and swimming. There are easy trails that can be hiked even in winter. You'll have plenty of elbow room here.

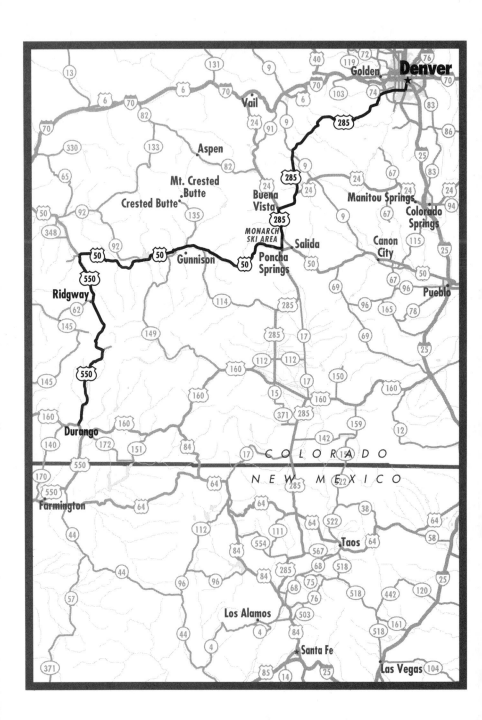

DAY 1

Morning

To get to Durango, take Highway 285 south from Denver past Buena Vista. At Poncha Springs take Highway 50 west through Gunnison to Montrose and connect with Highway 550 south to Durango. From Ridgway to Durango you'll be on a section of the San Juan Skyway, with three mountain passes topping 10,000 feet.

LUNCH: Casa del Sol (303 North Highway 24, Buena Vista, CO 81211; 719–395–8810) serves excellent Mexican food. House favorites are the chicken enchilada, shrimp quesadilla, and chile relleno. The cafe serves lunch daily (except for Tuesday, when it closes) from 11:30 A.M. to 2:30 P.M. (summer hours are extended) and dinner from 4:30 to 8:30 P.M.

Afternoon

Downtown Durango is a **National Historic District.** Main Avenue dates back to the late 1800s, and the Durango & Silverton Narrow Gauge Railroad goes back to the days when the town served as a transportation center for the region's booming silver and gold mines. Today you'll find a mix of galleries, tourist shops, museums, and restaurants. The **Visitors Center,** at 111 South Camino del Rio (970–247–0312), has a comprehensive guide to the town's galleries, as well as other valuable information on the area. The Visitors Center is open seven days a week from 8:00 A.M. to 5:00 P.M. (8:00 A.M. to 7:00 P.M. May through September).

Shopping in Durango is a good choice for the afternoon. You'll find plenty of outdoor clothing, recreational equipment, and western wear in the shops on Maine Avenue. **Appaloosa Trading Company** (501 Main Avenue; 970–259–1994) sells Stetsons, cowboy boots, custom-made leather goods, and more at its three downtown locations.

DINNER: Steamworks Brewing Company (801 East Second Avenue, Durango; 970–259–9200) is such a good restaurant that you'll want to dine here more than once. Hardwood floors, exposed brick, an ebullient staff, and superb food and beer provide an unbeatable combination. Try the Lizard Head Red, an excellent amber ale, or the Steam-Engine Steam. The Southwest Chicken Pizza is a savory selection from the wood-fired pizza choices. Other menu items include Jamaican Style Buffalo Wings and Colorado Trail

The San Juan Skyway *is a 236-mile route that winds through stunning scenery.*
(photo by Tom Maxwell).

Steak, a charbroiled, eighteen-ounce ribeye bone-in cut served with sautéed mushrooms, au gratin potatoes, and vegetables. Brewery tours are available. Steamworks Brewing Company is open daily from 11:00 A.M. until last call.

LODGING: Request the suite where Louis L'Amour stayed at the **Strater Hotel** (699 Main Avenue, Durango, CO 81301; 800–247–4431 or 970–247–4431). This more-than-a-century old, red brick hotel is located in the middle of the Main Avenue Historical District, 2 blocks from the Durango & Silverton Narrow Gauge depot. Priceless artifacts, such as a Stradivarius violin and a gold-plated Winchester, fill display cases throughout the Strater. Crystal lamps, lace curtains, period wallpaper, marble-topped dressers, and Victorian antiques decorate the ninety-three rooms.

The hotel's bar, the **Diamond Belle Saloon,** features an imposing wooden bar and a ragtime pianist who plays honky-tonk on the Steinway. For melodrama and vaudeville comedy in a turn-of-the-century theater, visit the Strater's **Diamond Circle Theatre.** For information call the Strater

Hotel at (800) 247–4431 or (970) 247–4431.

DAY 2

Morning

BREAKFAST: Get an early start before you catch the train, at the **Durango Coffee Company** (730 Main Avenue, Durango, CO 81301; 970–259–2059). This shop serves every kind of coffee from New Guinea to Royal Hawaiian Kona, and the pastries are delicious. Durango Coffee Company opens at 7:30 A.M. Monday through Saturday and at 8:00 A.M. Sunday.

This morning, ride on Colorado's most famous train, the **Durango & Silverton Narrow Gauge.** You'll travel through the San Juan National Forest wilderness on the coal-fired steam locomotive to the old mining town of Silverton.

A round-trip ride on the Durango & Silverton Narrow Gauge takes eight and a half hours: three and a quarter hours each way and a two-hour stop in Silverton. The Durango & Silverton Narrow Gauge runs from the end of April through the last Sunday in October. July through mid-August, trains depart weekdays at 7:30, 8:15, 9:00 and 9:45 A.M., and on weekends the 7:30 departure is omitted. The Winter Holiday Train runs from late November through the first of April and travels to Cascade Canyon. Refreshments and snacks are available on the train. Reservations are essential. Contact Durango & Silverton Narrow Gauge, 479 Main Avenue, Durango, CO 81302; (970) 247–2733. The round-trip fare for adults is $49.10; for children ages five to eleven, $24.65.

LUNCH: The **Pickle Barrel,** 1304 Greene Street, Silverton, CO; (970) 387–5713. House specials change daily, but you might find selections such as a green chile Cheddar burger or filet of chicken sandwich. Regular menu items include a hot pastrami sandwich, burgers, and soup. The Pickle Barrel is located in a historic brick building and serves lunch daily from 11:30 A.M. to 3:00 P.M. Memorial Day through September.

Afternoon

At an altitude of 9,318 feet above sea level, the old mining town of **Silverton** was home to gambling halls and saloons in the late 1800s when miners removed "silver by the ton" from the region. Today you'll find tourist shops, restaurants, and Victorian architecture here. The **San Juan County Histori-cal Museum** (1567 Greene Street; 970–387–5838), located in the old San Juan County Jail, displays mining artifacts. The museum is open daily from 9:00 A.M. to 5:00 P.M. June 1 to mid-September and from 10:00 A.M. to 3:00 P.M. until mid-October.

DINNER: Cyprus Cafe, 725 East Second Avenue, Durango; (970) 385–6884. The Cypress specializes in Mediterranean cuisine within a sleek urban set-ting. The menu offers appetizers such as spanakopitta (a spinach and feta cheese mixture in phyllo dough) and baba ganoush. Lunch entrees include souvlakia, the Cyprus burger, and falafel. The dinner menu features Tunisian prawns, rainbow springs trout, and Cyprus pasta.

LODGING: Strater Hotel.

DAY 3

Morning

BREAKFAST: Le Rendezvous Swiss Bakery (750 Main Avenue; 970–385–5685) is more than a bakery. The cafe serves a Swiss breakfast that consists of cheese, a roll, and an apple and also offers stuffed croissants, break-fast burritos, and *huevos rancheros*. Le Rendezvous serves breakfast from 7:00 A.M. to noon on weekends and from 7:00 to 11:30 A.M. weekdays. Closed Monday.

Drive a portion of the spectacular **San Juan Skyway** on Highway 550 from Durango to Ridgway. You'll parallel the Durango & Silverton Narrow Gauge Railroad for several miles as you pass through the Animas Valley and will then climb to 10,000 feet over Coal Bank and Molas Passes. Shortly after you cross Red Mountain Pass at the impressive elevation of 11,075 feet above sea level, you'll reach the pretty little Victorian town of **Ouray,** which calls itself the Little Switzerland of America. From Ouray continue north on Highway 550 to Ridgway.

Stop at the **Ridgway Information Center** (150 Racecourse Road, at the fairgrounds on Route 62 just off Highway 550; 970–626–5181 or 800–220–4959) for maps and information on the area.

LUNCH: True Grit Cafe (123 North Lena, P.O. Box 2003, Ridgway, CO 81432; 970–626–5739) is named for *True Grit,* which was filmed in Ridgway and the surrounding area. The cafe has old pictures of the film's star, John

Wayne, displayed everywhere. The menu features daily specials such as chicken-fried steak and regular items of burgers, soup, salads, and sandwiches. True Grit is open daily from 11:00 A.M. to 9:30 P.M.

Afternoon

Ridgway State Park and Reservoir, located 3.5 miles north of Ridgway on Highway 550, offers fishing, swimming, boating, hiking, and camping. With views of the San Juan Mountains and Sneffels Range, this 1,000-acre reservoir is one of the area's main attractions. Stop at the visitor center, located just past the entrance, for maps and information. Contact Ridgway State Park, 28555 Highway 550, Ridgway, CO 81432; (970) 626–5822.

DINNER: The Adobe Inn and Restaurant, P.O. Box 470, Ridgway, CO 81432; (970) 626–5939. This restaurant alone is worthy of your drive across the state. You'll be greeted with Southwestern adobe decor, excellent margaritas, and superb cuisine. Begin with homemade chips and the best salsa this side of the border. Move on to a house specialty such as Chimichanga de Carne or the Burrito Grande. Owners Joyce and Terre Bucknam use the freshest ingredients available and original recipes. Enjoy your drink on the courtyard patio before dinner. The bar opens at 5:00 P.M., and dinner is served from 5:30 to 9:30 P.M. daily, year-round. Lodging is also available year-round at The Adobe Inn. To get to the restaurant, turn south from Sherman Street, which is Highway 62, onto Liddell Drive for 1 block.

LODGING: Chipeta Sun Lodge Bed & Breakfast, 304 South Lena, P.O. Box 2013, Ridgway, CO 81432; (970) 626–3737 or (800) 633–5868. This solar adobe, Santa Fe–style inn is peaceful and quiet and offers dramatic views of the San Juan Mountain peaks. The stone fireplace dominates the "great room," where guests visit, read, or listen to music. Guest rooms have rustic log furniture, goose-down comforters, and Mexican tile in the private bath. The Sneffels Room has its own spa tub. A favorite with guests is the hot tub in the third floor turret, with views of Sneffels Range. If you prefer, ask for a suite, complete with a gas-log fireplace and two-person hot tub. Rates at Chipeta Sun Lodge range from $65 to $125, depending on the room and the season. A two-bedroom suite is $155. Half-price ski vouchers to Telluride (37 miles west) and hot springs discounts are included.

DAY 4

Morning

BREAKFAST: Chipeta Sun Lodge Bed & Breakfast. Help yourself to homemade granola, yogurt, and an entree such as banana pancakes, French toast, or an omelet, with tea or coffee from the Steaming Bean Coffee Company in Telluride. Visit with other guests in the airy, sun-drenched 2-story solarium, or chat with owners Lyle and Shari Braund about the seemingly endless recreational opportunities in the area. The Braunds are avid outdoor enthusiasts and can recommend an area for hiking, mountain biking, cross-country skiing, or snowshoeing.

THERE'S MORE

San Juan Skyway. You could spend a day or a week on this 236-mile drive through valleys, canyons, historic mining towns, and incredible mountain terrain. For more information on the San Juan Skyway, call (970) 247–0312 or (800) 525–8855.

Mesa Verde National Park. Anasazi cliff dwellings fascinate visitors at this incredible site. The park is located an hour from Durango on Highway 160 west. The park is open 365 days a year. Admission is $10 per vehicle. For more information contact Mesa Verde National Park, CO 81330; (970) 529–4465 or (970) 529–4475.

Purgatory Resort. Located 26 miles north of Durango on Highway 550, Purgatory offers an average annual snowfall of 300 inches for some excellent downhill skiing. During summer, rent a mountain bicycle at the base of the ski area, take it on the chairlift, then ride down one of the well-marked trails. For information contact Purgatory Resort, 1 Skier Place, Durango, CO 81302; (970) 247–9000.

Trimble Hot Springs, 6475 County Road 203, Durango, CO 81301; (970) 247–0111. Take a soak in the Olympic-size natural hot springs pool or schedule a massage. The facility is open daily during summer from 7:00 A.M. to 11:00 P.M. and during winter from 8:00 A.M. to 10:00 P.M. Admission is $7.00 for adults and $5.00 for children twelve and under. Trimble Hot Springs is located 6 miles north of Durango on U.S. Highway 550.

SPECIAL EVENTS

May. On Memorial Day weekend the Iron Horse Bicycle Classic pits elite cyclists in a punishing road race against the Durango & Silverton Narrow Gauge train. For information call (970) 259–4621.

June. Animas River Days, Durango. Billed as Colorado's premier whitewater festival, this event attracts whitewater fanatics from around the United States. Spectators watch as contestants guide their craft through the whitewater course. For details contact Animas River Race Association, P.O. Box 3626, Durango, CO 81302; (970) 259–3893.

June–August. Sherbino Theater, 604 West Clinton Street, Ridgway; (970) 626–4414. The Ouray County Performing Arts Foundation sponsors summer performances by the Ridgway Repertory Theater Company in a renovated historic theater.

Mid-September to mid-October. Colorfest. When spectacular fall colors arrive, the entire area celebrates. Days are usually sunny and warm and nights crisp for the events, which include a vintage car show, fishing contests, art shows, and more. For information call (970) 247–0312.

OTHER RECOMMENDED RESTAURANTS AND LODGINGS

Durango

The Ore House, 147 East College Drive; (970) 247–5707. Steak lovers will be satisfied at this restaurant, which serves beef that is aged on the premises. Seafood is also available. The Ore House is open from 5:30 to 11:00 P.M. daily.

The New Rochester Hotel, 726 East Second Avenue, Durango, CO 81301; (970) 385–1920 or (800) 664–1920. This well-appointed B&B is located in a 2-story brick building that dates back to the late 1800s. The common area, guest rooms, and dining area are enhanced with western-movie decor. Suites are available at Leland House, located across the street. Leland House is run by the same management. Call (970) 385–1920 or (800) 664–1920.

General Palmer Hotel, 567 Main Avenue, Durango, CO 81301; (970) 247–4747. Named for the gentleman who brought the Denver & Rio Grande Western Railroad to Durango, this lovely Victorian hotel offers an elegant lobby, fresh cookies in the afternoon, and a location in the heart of downtown Durango.

Ridgway

The Big Barn, Box 257, Ridgway, CO 81432; (970) 626–3600. Run by
Dennis Weaver, this restaurant and pool hall offers dining, cowboy poetry
gatherings, and dance lessons. Open during the summer months.

FOR MORE INFORMATION

Durango Area Chamber Resort Association, P.O. Box 287, 111 South
Camino del Rio, Durango, CO 81302; (970) 247–0312 or (800)
525–8855.

Durango Central Reservations, 945 Main Avenue, Durango, CO 81301;
(800) 525–0892.

Ridgway Information Center, 150 Racecourse Road, Ridgway, CO 81432;
(970) 626–5181 or (800) 220–4959.

Silverton Chamber of Commerce, P.O. Box 565, Silverton, CO 81433; (800)
752–4494 or (970) 387–5654.

Inns of the San Juan Skyway, P.O. Box 307, Ridgway, CO 81432; (800)
962–2493.

Taos and Santa Fe, New Mexico

THE SOUTHWEST EXPERIENCE

3 NIGHTS

Art • Fine dining • Downhill skiing •
Summer hiking • Outdoor opera • Galleries •
Kit Carson Home and Museum

Taos brims with color, character, and charm. This cultural mecca, located just 40 miles south of the Colorado border, carries traditions that began when the Spanish first visited the area.

In the early 1800s Taos was the headquarters for fur trappers who traded pelts for supplies and services. Kit Carson, the legendary figure of the Old West, made his home here from 1826 to 1868. Today you'll discover a town rich in history and an area abundant with recreational possibilities. Explore the museums, old pueblos, and more than eighty art galleries. Dine on traditional northern New Mexico cuisine, which can include red or green chile, posole, tamales, and bread baked in an outside adobe oven.

Venture into the rugged backcountry adjacent to millions of acres of pristine wilderness on a summer day-hike or a winter cross-county ski outing and enjoy the extensive trails, fabulous sunsets, and powerful panoramas.

Seventy scenic miles south of Taos lies the town of Santa Fe, one of the oldest cities in the United States. The allure of this picturesque city lies in its gallery-lined streets, superb restaurants, and gorgeous setting. Visit the museums, browse the boutiques, and attend the renowned Santa Fe Opera. You'll delight in the authentic Southwestern ambience of this gracious town.

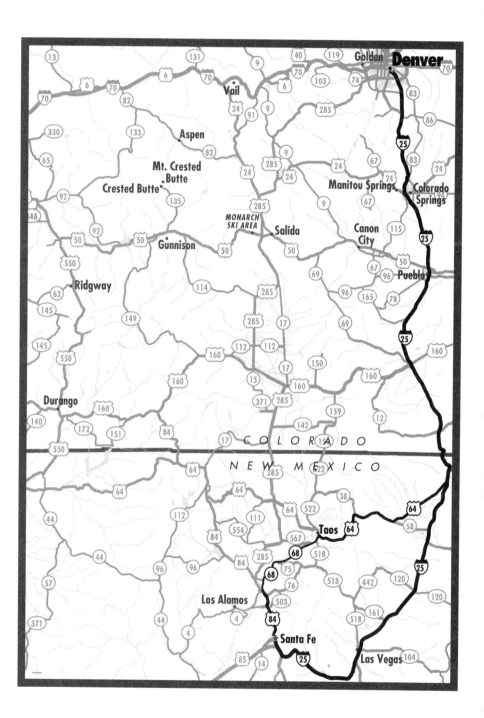

SOUTHERN

DAY 1

Morning

To get to Taos (about 300 miles from Denver), travel south on I–25. At the Colorado–New Mexico border, you'll cross Raton Pass, at an elevation of 7,834 feet.

LUNCH: El Matador (1012 South Second Street, Raton, New Mexico; 505–445–9575) serves dynamite Mexican food. Take the first exit (the business loop) into the town of Raton, shortly after you cross into New Mexico. Follow South Second Street through town to get to the restaurant. El Matador is nothing fancy, but prices are affordable and the food authentic. Don't leave without trying the green chile. The restaurant serves breakfast, lunch, and dinner and is open daily (except for Tuesday, when it closes) from 7:00 A.M. to 8:30 P.M.

Afternoon

After lunch in Raton, follow the business loop through town and connect with I–25. Continue south until you reach the turnoff for Highway 64 to Taos.

Get a feel for the town at **Taos Plaza,** located in the center of the city. Browse the many galleries and shops for Southwestern souvenirs and art, or sit a spell on one of the decorative benches under the shade of a tree in the historic Plaza.

DINNER: Eske's Brew Pub (106 Des Georges Lane, located ½ block off Taos Plaza; 505–758–1517) serves fresh beer on tap and great pub grub. Try the Taos Green Chile Beer, or order a taster tray for a sampling of the brewed-on-site beers. Bangers and mash, also known as bratwurst cooked in beer served with mashed potatoes, is an excellent selection. The pub has daily specials, including sushi on Tuesday nights. Weather permitting, you'll want to sit outside at the picnic tables or on the back patio.

LODGING: Touchstone Bed and Breakfast Inn (110 Mabel Dodge Lane, P.O. Box 2896, Taos, NM 87571; 505–758–0192) is a luxury historic adobe hacienda that lies on two acres of land on the northern edge of Taos. Owner-artist Bren Price has decorated this lovely inn with her exquisite watercolor paintings. Several of the eight rooms have Jacuzzi tubs, and seven have wood-burning kiva fireplaces. The decor is time-honored Southwestern refinement blended with a touch of whimsy. Your room may be adorned

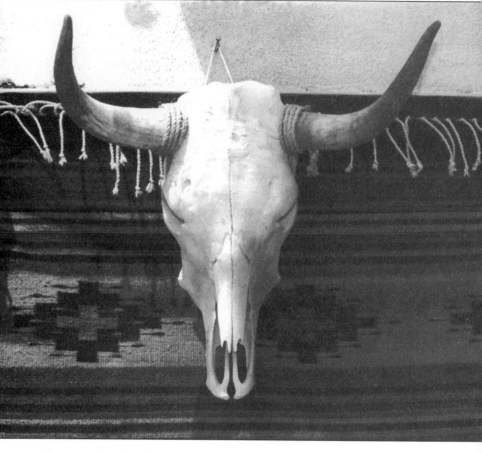

A familiar scene *in the southwest*

(photo by Sherry Spitsnaugle).

with a lariat on the wall, a saddle, or cowhide. Oriental rugs and antiques add to the charm of this sophisticated B&B.

Guests can lounge in the hammock or outdoor hot tub, surrounded by towering cottonwood trees, willows, and pines. Stroll through the wildflower garden, relax by the fireplace as the aroma of burning cedar logs drifts through the common room, or play a few notes on the baby grand piano. You will be within walking distance of town but feel as if you're miles away on a secluded country estate. Rooms at Touchstone range from $85 to $150, and a two-night-minimum stay is requested. Ask about off-season specials.

DAY 2

Morning

BREAKFAST: Touchstone Inn. Gourmet breakfast is served on white lace tablecloths in the airy, art-filled dining room. Enjoy coffee or tea in a cobalt blue cup and savor the chef's selection of the day, which may be waffles with fresh strawberries or herbal quiche. Classical music plays in the background.

There are seven museums in the area, and if you plan to visit several or all, purchase a museum combination ticket for $20. The ticket is honored for up to a year from date of purchase, is transferable, and can be bought at any of the seven museums.

The **Kit Carson Home and Museum** (on Kit Carson Road, east of the Plaza; 505–758–4741), illustrates the life of Kit Carson, one of the Old West's most famous figures. Here you'll learn about Carson's remarkable life as a fur trapper, mountain man, explorer, and military officer. Exhibits portray the various phases of Carson's life, and several rooms are furnished as they would have been in the Carson era. The Kit Carson Museum is open daily from 9:00 A.M. to 5:00 P.M. in winter and from 8:00 A.M. to 6:00 P.M. in summer.

The combination ticket also includes the **Ernest L. Blumenschein Home and Museum** (222 Ledoux Street; 505–758–0505), filled with European antiques; the **Harwood Museum** (238 Ledoux Street; 505–758–9826), featuring nineteenth-century art; and **Hacienda Martinez** 2 miles south of the Plaza; 505–758–0505), a Spanish Colonial hacienda. You can also visit the **Fechin Institute,** (227 Paseo del Pueblo Norte; 505–758–1710), former home of Russian artist Nicolai Fechin; the **Millicent Rogers Museum** (on Museum Road, 4 miles north of the Plaza; 505–758–2462), exhibiting northern New Mexico art; and the **Van Vechten Lineberry Museum** (501 Paseo del Pueblo Norte; 505–578–2690), showcasing the work of local artists.

LUNCH: The **Alley Cantina** (121 Teresina Lane; 505–758–2121), located just off the Plaza, has a sign out front that says it is the oldest building in Taos. The restaurant serves a great chicken enchilada, pizzas, burgers, a gourmet version of macaroni and cheese, and other selections. From mid-May through October, the Catina is open daily from 11:00 A.M. to 2:00 P.M. Hours for the remainder of the year are Monday through Friday from 5:00 P.M. to 2:00 A.M.; Saturday from 11:00 A.M. to 2:00 P.M.; and Sunday from noon to midnight.

Afternoon

Taos Pueblo, located approximately 3 miles northeast of the town of Taos, is a community inhabited by members of the Taos Pueblo Tribe. The pueblo is made up of ancient adobe structures, many of which are built one on top of another, connected by ladders. Visitors are welcome in designated areas, and many of the private homes are open as small curio or art shops. Tribe members sell homemade fry bread. Taos Pueblo is open to the public except during certain religious ceremonies; the pueblo closes late February through early April. Admission fees are $5.00 per vehicle, plus $2.00 per person, and there is an additional charge if you take photographs.

DINNER: Apple Tree Restaurant (123 Bent Street; 505–758–1900) serves gourmet meals in its Southwestern-decorated adobe rooms. Dine indoors by candlelight or outside on the patio beneath the apple tree. Choose fresh rainbow trout served with a different sauce each night—for example, lemon basil nut. Other choices include mango carnitas enchiladas and filet mignon with shiitake mushroom brandy sauce. Reservations are recommended. The restaurant serves lunch Monday through Saturday from 11:30 A.M. to 3:00 P.M., dinner daily from 5:30 to 9:00 P.M., and brunch Sunday from 10:00 A.M. to 3:00 P.M.

LODGING: Touchstone Bed and Breakfast.

DAY 3

Morning

BREAKFAST: Touchstone Bed and Breakfast.

Drive to **Santa Fe** (about 70 miles south of Taos) and take in the art, museums, fine restaurants, and charisma of this cultivated city.

Sign up for a walking tour of downtown and Canyon Road, at the **Palace of the Governors,** North Plaza, or browse the area on your own. You could spend days exploring the several blocks around the Plaza in the center of town. You will see Native American artists, some in colorful dress, sitting in front of the Palace of the Governors, displaying and selling jewelry, pottery, and handcrafts.

LUNCH: Blue Corn Cafe (133 Water Street, Santa Fe; 505–984–1800) advertises "Tortillas y Tequila" on its business card, and the restaurant delivers. The menu has a seemingly endless list of tequilas and margaritas, including

Herradura Gold Tequila, and a Tequila Diablo Margarita, but you can't go wrong ordering the house margarita. The cafe's signature red, green, yellow, and blue stripes are sure to catch your attention. Salsa and chips are superb, and the enchilada plate is a winner. The restaurant is open from 11:00 A.M. to 11:00 P.M. daily and has live entertainment on weekends.

Afternoon

Visit the **Museum of Fine Arts** (107 East Palace Avenue; 505–827–4455), which features art by Georgia O'Keeffe, John Sloan, and Gerald Cassidy, as well as a permanent collection of work by other artists. Admission is $5.00 for adults; free to persons age sixteen and under. The museum is open from 10:00 A.M. to 5:00 P.M. daily and closes Monday.

Ask about the three-day pass to four museums. The pass includes entrance to the **Museum of Fine Arts;** the **Palace of the Governors** (505–827–6483); the **Museum of Indian Arts and Culture** (710 Camino Lejo; 505–827–6344); and the **Museum of International Folk Art** (706 Camino Lejo; 505–827–6350). The pass can be purchased for $10 at any of the museums listed above.

DINNER: Coyote Cafe (132 West Water Street, Santa Fe; 505–983–1615) is classy, cosmopolitan, and very "Santa Fe." Owner Mark Miller and executive chef Mark Kiffin have created a deliciously chic restaurant. Set on the second floor of a downtown building, the cafe has high ceilings and tall windows, and the decor includes colorful folk-art animal sculptures. The open kitchen is visible to diners, yet does not distract.

The menu changes with the seasons, but you'll almost always find appetizers such as Crispy Fried Soft Shell Crab and Spring Asparagus Soup. An entree may be Pan Roasted Atlantic Salmon or Pan Fried Quail tossed with Arugula and Bing Cherry Salsa on a Toasted Pistachio Waffle. Order the Roasted Garlic Mashed Potatoes as a side dish. For dessert try the Roasted Banana Flan or Coyote's Box of Chocolates, a small box filled with truffles and chocolate-covered roasted almonds. Be sure to order a cocktail, just to get the green rattlesnake swizzle stick, and try to leave with a bright yellow "to-go" bag, which carries the restaurant's theme, "Coyote Cocina . . . Foods that'll make you howl!"

LODGING: Homewoods Suites (400 Griffin Street, Santa Fe, NM 87501; 505–988–3000 or 800–225–5466) is located 5 blocks from the Plaza and offers spacious, immaculate accommodations. Perfect for an extended stay, each suite has a bedroom separate from the living and kitchen area. You'll find an outdoor pool, two outdoor hot tubs, and a well-equipped Executive Center here. The Southwestern decor of the lobby is especially inviting, and the patio is a great place to enjoy morning coffee or late-afternoon refreshment. A suite during high season begins at $150; ask about the extended-stay discount.

DAY 4

Morning

BREAKFAST: Included in the price of your room at **Homewoods Suites** is a continental breakfast.

Return to Denver via I–25 north.

THERE'S MORE

Taos Ski Valley. Ski light, dry powder during the winter months and hike the rolling, forested trails when summer arrives. Taos Ski Valley has more than a dozen lodges and condominium complexes for overnight accommodations, as well as stays in private homes. To make a reservation, call Taos Valley Resort Association at (800) 776–1111. For information about skiing or hiking, call Taos Ski Valley at (505) 776–2291. To get to Taos Ski Valley, take Highway 150 east from Taos for about 15 miles; Highway 150 dead-ends at the ski area.

Santa Fe Opera. Noted for its classic performances and spectacular setting, the open-air opera is a must if you're in Santa Fe during opera season, which runs from late June through late August. Contact the Santa Fe Opera, P.O. Box 2408, Santa Fe, NM 87504; (505) 986–5900 or (800) 280–4654.

SPECIAL EVENTS

Mid-June–Labor Day. The Downs at Santa Fe features thoroughbred horse racing. For more information about the races, call (505) 471–3311.

Early July–late August. The Santa Fe Chamber Music Festival features chamber music, jazz, and preconcert lectures in the beautiful setting of the St. Francis Auditorium. Call the box office at (505) 983–2075 for information and tickets.

Mid-September–early October. Taos Arts Festival features art exhibits, crafts fairs, and receptions at local galleries. In addition, you'll see the brilliant colors of autumn. The festival is sponsored by Taos County Chamber of Commerce; (800) 732–8267.

October. Taos Mountain Balloon Rally, held late in the month, is a hot-air balloon lover's paradise. Observers can sign up to take a balloon ride or to work with a chase crew. Taste of Taos takes place the same weekend, so you can sample cuisine from some of Taos's finest restaurants.

OTHER RECOMMENDED RESTAURANTS AND LODGINGS

Taos

Lambert's of Taos (309 Paseo del Pueblo Sur; 505–758–1009) serves contemporary American cuisine. The menu changes daily, but you'll find grilled yellowfin tuna, as well as other good selections.

The Historic Taos Inn (125 Paseo del Pueblo Norte, Taos, NM 87572; 505–758–2233 or 800–826–7466) is listed on both the State and the National Register of Historic Places. The 2-story lobby of this inn is decorated with Southwestern art and handwoven rugs. Rooms, depending on size and the season, begin at $85 and go up to $225 for a suite.

Tesuque

El Nido (505–988–4340), a restaurant located on Highway 285 north in the historic town of Tesuque (pronounced Teh-SU-kay), several miles north of Santa Fe, offers daily specials such as grilled skinless duck breast and an exquisite rack of lamb. El Nido is also known for its excellent steaks and fresh seafood. Try the Mild Jalapeño Shiitake Mushroom Butter as a topping on your filet. To get to the restaurant, follow Highway 285 north to Tesuque. El Nido is open for dinner only, Tuesdays through Sundays. Reservations are recommended.

Santa Fe

Inn of the Anasazi (113 Washington Avenue, Santa Fe, NM 87501; 505–988–3030 or 800–688–8100) is located minutes from the Plaza. Prices range from $199 to $395, depending on the size of the room and the season.

FOR MORE INFORMATION

Taos County Chamber of Commerce, P.O. Drawer I, Taos, NM 87571; (800)
732–8267 or (505) 758–3873.

Santa Fe Visitors and Convention Bureau, 201 March Street, P.O. Box 909,
Santa Fe, NM 87504; (505) 984–6760 or (800) 777–CITY.

INDEX

A

Academy Riding Stables, 168
Adobe Creek Golf Course, 163
Adobe Inn and Restaurant, The, 207
Alaskan Shop, 133
Alley Cantina, 215
Alpenglow Stube, 126
Alpine Hideaway, 119
Alpine Tunnel, 190
Always CHRISTmas, 102
Anheuser-Busch Brewery, 36
Antlers Restaurant and Bar, 197
Appaloosa Trading Company, 203
Apple Tree Restaurant, 216
Arapahoe Basin, 125
Arkansas River, 181
Arkansas Valley Expeditions, 180
Art on the Corner, 159
Ashcroft, 153
Aspen, 148
Aspen Art Museum, 150
Aspen Chamber Resort Association, 150
Aspen Historical Society, 151
Aspen Skiing Company, 151
Aspen Square Condominium Hotel, 151
Austin's American Grill, 36
Avalanche Niteclub, 57
Avery House, 40

B

Back at the Ranch, 187
Bakery Cafe, 198
Bandana's Cafe, 91
Baron's Mesquite Grille, 48
Barry Goldwater Air Force Academy Visitor Center, 174
Beano's Cabin, 136
Bear Lake, 15
Beaver Creek, 131

Beaver Creek Resort Golf Club, 135
Bertie's, 21
Betty Ford Alpine Gardens, 136
Bicycling Adventures, 15
Bikesmith, The, 7
Bistro Adde Brewster, 64
Black American West Museum & Heritage Center, 78
Black Forest Inn, 30
Black Hawk, 27
Blazing Adventures, 153
Blue Corn Cafe, 216
Blue Iguana, 187
Blue Mesa Reservoir, 192
Blue Moon Bar, 133
Boaters Choice, 22
Boettcher Concert Hall, 66
Boeve's Coins and Antiques, 101
Boogie's Diner, 150
Boulder, 2
Boulder Creek Path, 7
Boulder Museum of Contemporary Art, 9
Boulder's Leanin' Tree Museum of Western Art, 9
Breckenridge Ski Area, 125
Bridgestone Winter Driving School, 56
Broadmoor, The, 168, 170
Broadmoor's Golden Bee, 173
Broadmoor's Spa and Fitness Center, 173
Brown Palace Hotel, 75
Browner's Guide Service, 181
Brown's Canyon, 180
Bryers-Evans House, 73
Buck Snort Saloon, 191
Buckhorn Llama Company, 40
Butterfly Pavilion and Insect Center, 68

C

Cache la Poudre River, 40

ABOUT THE AUTHOR

SHERRY SPITSNAUGLE has lived in Denver since 1980 and has spent years exploring the main attractions of Colorado, as well as those out-of-the-way places known only to locals.

After earning a degree in journalism and mass communications from Kansas State University in 1976, Sherry began her career as a reporter and photographer at the *Great Bend Tribune* in western Kansas. She has covered destinations in Colorado and around the world and has been published in *The Denver Post* and the *Rocky Mountain News,* as well as other national and foreign publications. She is a member of the Colorado Authors' League and the Denver Woman's Press Club.